THE ATLAS OF THE ISLAND OF IRELAND

Mapping Social and Economic Change

JUSTIN GLEESON, ROB KITCHIN, BRENDAN BARTLEY, JOHN DRISCOLL, RONAN FOLEY,
STEWART FOTHERINGHAM AND CHRIS LLOYD

First published 2008
by All-Island Research Observatory (AIRO) and International
Centre of Local and Regional Development (ICLRD)

AIRO, National University of Ireland Maynooth,
County Kildare, Ireland
ICLRD, c/o Centre for Cross Border Studies,
39 Abbey Street, Armagh, BT61 7EB, Northern Ireland

ISBN 978-0-9015-1991-7

Photographs are reproduced with kind permission of NIRSA
and Eamon Sinnott & Partners.

Designed and produced by Eamon Sinnott & Partners, Naas.
Printed by Colourworld.

CENSUS DATA

All census data for the Republic of Ireland in 1991
and 2002 have been made available through the
CSO Small Area Population Statistics.
Source: Central Statistics Office, website: www.cso.ie

All census data for Northern Ireland in 1991 and
2001 have been made available through NISRA.
Source: Northern Ireland Statistics, website:
www.nisra.gov.uk
Crown copyright material is reproduced with the
permission of the Controller of HMSO.

MAPPING AND BOUNDARY DATA

All Republic of Ireland boundary data have been
made available through the Ordnance Survey
Ireland.
© Ordnance Survey Ireland/Government of Ireland
Copyright Permit No. MP 007407

All Northern Ireland boundary data have been
made available through the Ordnance Survey of
Northern Ireland.
© Crown Copyright 2007
Ordnance Survey of Northern Ireland
Permit No. 70189

The Transportation Network displayed in Map 4
has been made available through MAPFLOW
and NAVTEC
© NAVTEC 2007

ACKNOWLEDGEMENTS

The Atlas of the Island of Ireland principally maps census data available in both the Republic of Ireland and Northern Ireland. Two main organisations are responsible for gathering and disseminating this key demographic, social and economic information. The Central Statistics Office (CSO) in the Republic of Ireland are responsible for the development of the Small Area Population Statistics (SAPS), that are released through the Irish Social Science Data Archive (ISSDA). We are particularly grateful to Aidan Punch and the staff at the CSO for assisting us on this project and for developing additional tables that were not available through SAPS. The Northern Ireland Statistics and Research Agency (NISRA) have provided all the required statistical information for Northern Ireland. We are very grateful to the staff at NISRA especially Carrie Doole, Richard Elliott and Jonathan Alexander for their continued and dedicated assistance.

The transfer from raw census data to maps required the use of a variety of geographical boundaries files. We are most grateful to Daniel O'Connell from the Ordnance Survey Ireland and John Sharkey from the Ordnance Survey of Northern Ireland who assisted in administering the relevant copyright licences.

The linking of census data to the relevant geographical boundaries within the Republic of Ireland for 1991 and 2002 has been helped considerably by the previous work of Mary O'Brien and Paul Lewis at NIRSA/NCG. The required methodology for the development of cartograms for 1991 and 2001/02 was greatly assisted by the input of Martin Charlton at NCG. We would like to acknowledge the efforts of Greg White for his continued assistance in the development of census datasets and the production of many of the maps within this Atlas.

The advice of Niall Cussen, Dave Walsh and John Martin at the Department of Environment, Heritage & Local Government in the Republic of Ireland and Mike Thompson and Jim Hetherington at the Department of Regional Development in Northern Ireland was much appreciated.

The design and layout of the Atlas have been undertaken by Eamon Sinnott and Partners. The photos were taken from the NIRSA Photoarchive – http://www.photoarchive.ie

Parts of Chapters 2 and 6 are based on Kitchin, R., Bartley, B., Gleeson, J., Cowman, M., Fotheringham, S. and Lloyd, C. (2007) Joined-up thinking across the Irish Border: Making the data more compatible. *Journal of Cross Border Studies* 2: 22-33.

JOINT FOREWORD BY:

MINISTER JOHN GORMLEY T.D. & MINISTER CONOR MURPHY M.P. M.L.A

The island of Ireland is changing at a pace never experienced before. The population is increasing, more houses than ever are being built, more journeys are being made and the islands infrastructure is fast improving. The island's cities are expanding, the roles of urban and rural areas are becoming less distinct and there are new challenges to be faced in protecting and enhancing the quality of our environment.

New policies have been formulated to deal with our island's new-found success and economic strength, to maintain progress in a sustainable way. The island of Ireland has two Spatial Strategies: the National Spatial Strategy in the South of Ireland and the Regional Development Strategy in the North of Ireland. Both these strategies deal with real and practical issues, where people live and work and how good planning can create better places.

The successful implementation of these and other policies depends on access to good information, taking account of the latest trends and anticipating the new challenges. However, while there have been good datasets in both North and South of Ireland on a vast range of topics, information on a combined island of Ireland basis has been much more limited. For example, where people live and work on this island, how and where they travel as they move about the island are amongst many topics about which there has traditionally been limited information.

This atlas has been assembled by experts in the analysis of spatial databases built upon the foundation of the census of population taken regularly both North and South of Ireland. This atlas, for the first time, shines a light on many fascinating similarities and contrasts between North and South. We share similar challenges in addressing the disparities between eastern and western parts and there are fascinating contrasts in our social and spatial structure.

The atlas also presents fascinating insights into the island of Ireland in recent times and will provide an exceptional source of information for planning at different levels. However, this Atlas does not represent the finished article, further analyses will be required. We are determined that such analyses and the information that will flow from them, are facilitated through better harmonisation of information sets North and South so that we can plan better for an even more prosperous and sustainable future on our remarkable island.

Comhréamhrá:

An tAire John Gormley T.D. & An tAire Conor Murphy M.P. M.L.A.

Tá oileán na hÉireann ag athrú i bhfad níos gaiste ná riamh. Tá an daonra ag méadú, tá níos mó tithe ná riamh á dtógáil, tá níos mó turas á ndéanamh agus tá infreastruchtúr an oileáin ag feabhsú go gasta. Tá cathracha an oileáin ag éirí níos mó, níl rólanna na limistéar uirbeach agus na limistéar tuaithe chomh soiléir agus a bhíodh agus tá dúshláin nua le sárú i dtaca le caighdeán ár dtimpeallachta a chaomhnú agus a fheabhsú.

Ceapadh polasaithe nua chun déileáil leis an rath agus leis an neart eacnamaíoch nua atá bainte amach ag oileán s'againne, ionas gur féidir dul chun cinn a choinneáil ar bhealach inmharthana. Tá dhá Straitéis Spásúla ag oileán na hÉireann: an Stráitéis Náisiúnta Spásúlachta i nDeisceart na hÉireann agus an Straitéis Forbartha Réigiúnaí i dTuaisceart na hÉireann. Déileálann an dá straitéis sin le saincheisteanna praiticiúla: áiteanna cónaithe agus ionaid oibre na ndaoine, agus an dóigh ar féidir áiteanna níos fearr a chruthú ach pleanáil mhaith a dhéanamh.

Tá cur i bhfeidhm rathúil na bpolasaithe seo agus polasaithe eile nach iad ag brath ar eolas maith bheith ar fáil, na treochtaí is déanaí á gcur san áireamh agus dúshláin nua a réamh-mheas. Mar sin féin, fad is go raibh tacair mhaithe sonraí ar fáil i dTuaisceart agus i nDeisceart na hÉireann araon ar réimse leathan ábhar, bhí eolas ar bhonn uile-Éireann i bhfad ní ba theoranta. Mar shampla, ní raibh ach eolas teoranta le fáil go traidisiúnta faoi ábhair ar nós: áiteanna cónaithe agus ionaid oibre na ndaoine ar an oileán seo, an dóigh a mbíonn siad ag taisteal agus na háiteanna a dtéann siad chucu agus iad ag bogadh thart ar an oileán.

Daoine a bhfuil saineolas acu ar anailís a dhéanamh ar bhunachair shonraí spásúla a chuir an t-atlas seo le chéile; tá na bunachair shonraí sin bunaithe ar na daonáirimh a eagraítear go rialta i dTuaisceart agus i nDeisceart na hÉireann araon. Den chéad uair, léiríonn an t-atlas seo cuid mhaith de na cosúlachtaí agus na contrárthachtaí suntasacha idir an Tuaisceart agus an Deisceart. Tá na dúshláin chéanna le sárú againn ó thaobh aghaidh a thabhairt ar na héagothroimeachtaí idir ceantair in oirther agus in iarthar na tíre agus tá contrárthachtaí suntasacha ann inár struchtúr sóisialta agus spásúil.

Tugann an t-atlas seo leiriú íontach ar oileán na hÉireann le déanaí agus cuireann sé eolas ar fáil do phleanáil ag leibhéil áirithe. Ach, níl an obair críochnaithe fós toisc go mbeidh anailís nios doimhne ag teastaíl. Is é ár n-aidhm go mbeidh feabhas ar an anailís sa todhchaí mar thoradh ar cheangal níos fearr idir eolas faoi thuaisceart agus desiceart na hÉireann, ionas gur féidir linn cursai pleanála níos cruinne a chur i bhfeidhm ar an oileán.

SUPPORT

A generous subvention towards the cost of producing The Atlas of The Island of Ireland was provided by the Department of Environment, Heritage and Local Government. We are very grateful for their financial support.

The All-Island Research Observatory (AIRO) has received funding from Interreg 3A administered by the Special EU Programmes Body (SEUPB) and through the Programme for Research in Third Level Institutions (PRTLI) administered by the Higher Education Authority (HEA).

The International Centre for Local and Regional Development (ICLRD) is funded by the International Fund for Ireland and the Irish government.

The National Institute for Regional and Spatial Analysis is funded by the Programme for Research in Third Level Institutions (PRLTI), Cycles 2 and 4, administered by the Higher Education Authority (HEA).

The National Centre for Geocomputation is funded by Science Foundation Ireland.

AUTHORS

Justin Gleeson is Project Manager of the All-Island Research Observatory (AIRO) and is based in the National University of Ireland, Maynooth

Prof. Rob Kitchin is Director of the National Institute for Regional and Spatial Analysis (NIRSA) at the National University of Ireland, Maynooth. He is a member of ICLRD and AIRO, and Chair of the Irish Social Sciences Platform (ISSP).

Brendan Bartley is a member of NIRSA, the ICLRD Project Coordinator in the National University of Ireland, Maynooth and a member of AIRO.

John Driscoll is the Director of the International Centre for Local and Regional Development (ICLRD), a member of the International Institute of Urban Development and the Centre for Joint Housing Studies at Harvard University.

Dr. Ronan Foley is a Lecturer in Geography at the National University of Ireland, Maynooth and a member of NIRSA, NCG and AIRO.

Prof. Stewart Fotheringham is a SFI Research Professor, Director of the National Centre for Geocomputation at the National University of Ireland, Maynooth, and a member of AIRO.

Dr. Chris Lloyd is a Lecturer in Geography at Queen's University Belfast and a member of AIRO.

CONTENTS

Contents

Chapter 1: Introduction

Chapter 1: Introduction

We live in a time of ever-increasing cooperation between the administrations and peoples of the Republic of Ireland and Northern Ireland. Since the ceasefires of the early 1990s, numerous cross-border initiatives, costing millions of euro/pounds, have been enacted aimed at fostering peace and reconciliation, increasing trade, sharing resources, and producing meaningful collaboration on issues of shared benefit. Significant progress has been made to date, despite the fact that there is a dearth of data that might have informed key decision making in such initiatives.

The lack of comparable, cross-border data seems surprising in today's modern world and yet, at present, it is extremely difficult to create the all-island data sets that might underpin evidence-informed, cross-border planning. This is not to say that detailed information does not exist for, or that detailed analysis has not taken place within, both jurisdictions. This is clearly the case. The problem, as we discuss in detail in Chapter 6, is marrying data sets that have often been collected using different questions, at different time intervals, and aggregated into different spatial units. As this book demonstrates, this problem is not insurmountable, but it is nevertheless a significant challenge.

This aim of this book is straightforward. It is to present a set of data relating to the whole island of Ireland to provide a basic evidence base for thinking about the social and economic questions affecting both jurisdictions. It is not the first all-island atlas of publicly available data. We are aware of at least one other: Horner, Walsh and Harrington (1987) produced an all-island population atlas using 1971 and 1981 census data for Ireland and Northern Ireland, and also 1986 census data for Ireland. It is, however, the first detailed, full colour atlas with data displayed in units below counties and districts and which tackles issues of data compatibility and scalar effects. It also the first to undertake novel kinds of analysis such as all-island continuous cartograms and journey to work patterns.

The Atlas is a collaborative venture between the All-Island Research Observatory (AIRO) and the International Centre for Local and Regional Development (ICLRD). In short, AIRO, a collaborative venture between NIRSA (National Institute for Regional and Spatial Analysis) and NCG (National Centre for Geocomputation) at the National University of Ireland, Maynooth, Dundalk Institute of Technology, and Queen's University Belfast, produced comparable datasets and the maps and cartograms. ICLRD, a collaborative venture between NIRSA, the University of Ulster, the International Institute for Urban Development in Cambridge, Massachusetts, the Centre for Cross-Border Studies in Armagh, and Athlone Institute of Technology, along with Queen's University Belfast, produced the accompanying text.

To provide a meaningful structure, the Atlas is divided into three sections: Demographics; Housing, Travel and Transport; and the Economy. Within each section we focus on a number of important issues using maps and cartograms of census data generated in Northern Ireland and Ireland to detail patterns of stasis and change across the whole island between 1991 and 2001/02. Each issue is generally explored across a double page spread. On the left hand page are maps of the relevant variable in 1991 and 2001(NI)/02 (ROI) along with a cartogram of overall rates in 2001/02. On the right hand page are a map and cartogram of change between 1991 and 2001/02 calculated as a percentage change from the 1991 rate. We have limited the textual description, instead letting the maps largely speak for themselves.

Our belief is that the maps and cartograms we present provide a fascinating insight into demographic, social and economic issues, and provide a platform for evidence-informed analysis of the processes and trends operating across the island. Our hope is that they will stimulate wider discussion about particular policy issues, especially those of a cross-border nature, but also about the collection and analysis of data itself. Looking to the future, it is clear to us that interoperable, all-island data sets will be of significant benefit to government and business, both North and South, and that their creation should be given high priority.

Chapter 2: Interpreting the Maps and Cartograms

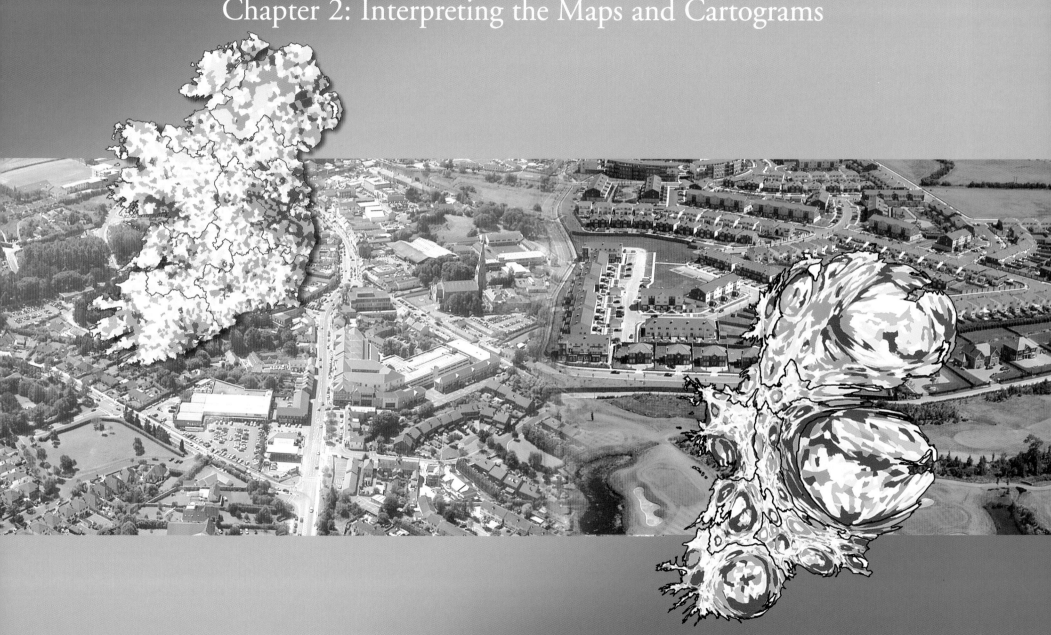

Chapter 2: Interpreting the Maps and Cartograms

Each map and cartogram uses a thematic choropleth scheme to display the data – that is, the data are divided and displayed in classes shaded in proportion to the measurement of the variable being represented on the map (in this case with low values shaded light yellow and high values dark brown). To ensure that the data are comparable between 1991 and 2001, the 1991 data are used as a benchmark with each variable for that year being divided into 6 class intervals based on natural breaks within the data distribution. This classification is generated using an automated algorithm within GIS software; in this case, MapInfo Professional. MapInfo bases its natural break algorithm on a procedure described by Jenks and Caspall (1971). Their natural breaks procedure analyses the spread of the data for peaks (or clusters of similar data) and troughs across the full range of data, with a natural break said to occur at the nadir of a trough. In this way, natural groupings of data are placed within the same choropleth category. This technique has been used in the development of many previous atlases such as *People and Place* (Walsh, 2007) and *Mapping Census 2000: The Geography of US* (Suchan and Brewer, 2002).

CALCULATING AND REPRESENTING CHANGE

With respect to calculating and representing change between 1991-2001/02 we have used percentages rather than raw counts because the underlying population base varied widely across the spatial units. In the majority of maps we report relative change. However, in a few limited cases, where we feel it is of benefit, we have displayed both absolute and relative percentage change.

Absolute change measures the absolute difference between two variables – for example, if the percentage of the population declaring themselves Catholic in an area in 1991 was 68% and increased to 71% in 2001/02 then the absolute change would be reported at increase of 3%. Relative change on the other hand looks at the specific variable itself and how much the Catholic stock has increased or decreased from its 1991 value to 2001/02. Using this method, the relative change figure would be an increase of 4.41% [e.g., ((2001-1991)*100/1991]. This approach allows the 1991 stock figure to be used as a baseline index that would make comparative review easier in the future.

The 1991 to 2001/02 change maps are represented using two color schemes – red indicates an increase and blue indicates a decrease. Each parent classification (increase and decrease) is then broken into three bands – Minor In/Decrease, Medium In/Decrease and Major In/Decrease. Minor In/Decrease represents the wards/DEDs in the first 40% of the parent class, Medium represents the wards/DEDs in the second 40% of the parent class, and finally Major represents the wards/DEDs in the top 20% of the parent class. One additional point to note here is that in some wards/DEDs there was no baseline figure for 1991 so that relative change could not be calculated. These wards/DEDs are highlighted as "Increase, no 1991 Value" on the change maps and shaded green.

CARTOGRAMS

Cartograms are a useful representation to complement the traditional maps for two reasons. First, using cartograms partially addresses the significant technical issues created by producing a single map where a variable is outputted at different unit scales in different parts of the map (in this case Northern Ireland and the Republic of Ireland) as the size of the unit displayed is calibrated by a variable, in our case raw population counts (as a result it is sometimes referred to as an isodemographic map). Second, by scaling each output area in proportion to the population living there cartograms reveal a 'truer' picture of the relative importance/influence of that variable at a location. In the case of Ireland, this often has the effect of revealing the importance of change/stasis in urban areas which otherwise look small and insignificant on the traditional map.

There is a wide variation within both the physical size of DEDs in Ireland and Wards in Northern Ireland. DEDs range from 0.05 km2 (Shortcourse DED, Waterford County Borough) to 119 km2 (Oughterard DED, Galway) and yet the smallest areas often contain the highest populations. For instance the DED with the smallest population in 2002 was Branchfield in Sligo with a population count of 55 and a geographical area of 15.56 km2. In contrast, Blanchardstown-Blakestown DED in Dublin had a population count of 24,404 in 2002 and an area of 7.84 km2. Yet visually, Branchfield appears the more significant DED (see Figure 1 which shows the DEDs of Branchfield and Blanchardstown-Blakestown using the normal map projection and the transformed cartogram). From this it

is clear that the population count within Blanchardstown-Blakestown is more significant on the cartogram than the normal projection). By proportioning the size of the output area to population such visual bias and masking is removed.

In order to make the cartogram as meaningful as possible an attempt is made to retain the shape and relative location of each output area as possible (we have used the Gastner and Newman 2004, algorithm). Regardless, a large amount of distortion results, with large urban areas such as Dublin, Belfast, Cork, Limerick and Derry becoming dominant in the representation.

Figure 1: Comparing the normal projection with a cartogram

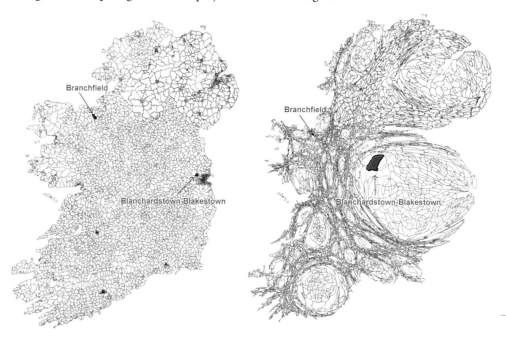

We have used two different cartogram bases to display the data. The first cartogram has been generated using the 2001/02 population distribution and also uses the same natural breaks as the 2001/02 map. The second cartogram has used the 1991 population distribution to provide a base for displaying change between 1991 and 2001/02. There are some minor differences between the internal dynamics of the two cartograms developed for 1991 and 2001/02. Figure 2 highlights some of the differences that are evident as a result of a changing population distribution across the island. First, the 2001/02 cartogram is a little larger given the overall growth in population. Second, the population has grown most substantially in the principal cities. For example, Galway County Borough had a 29% increase in population between 1991 to 2001. Figure 2 also highlights the increased significance of the Mid East Region of Ireland, particularly the northern part of the region that has experienced quite high growth since 1991 in areas such as Asbourne, Navan, Trim and Kells.

To provide some context for interpreting the maps and cartograms, at the end of this chapter we provide five contextual maps: Counties and Districts of the island of Ireland; Regional Cartograms of the Island of Ireland; Urban Centres; the Road Network; and the Rail Network.

Figure 2: Cartogram 1991 and 2001/02
Cartogram 1991

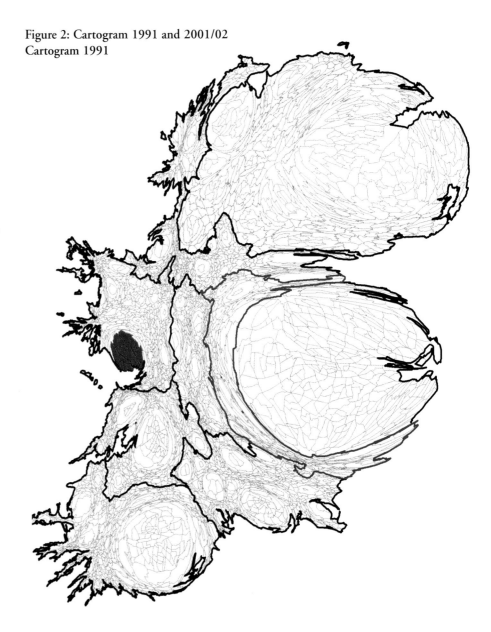

**Cartogram
2001/02**

IN SUMMARY

For the reasons discussed in Chapter 6, interpreting the maps and cartograms in this Atlas is not always straightforward despite our attempts to address the pertinent issues. Indeed, *all* of our maps come with a 'health warning' given how we have had to clean and manipulate the data to create best-fit, comparable datasets. That is not to say that the maps lack value, but to acknowledge that they need to be interpreted with care and not simply read at face value. Where appropriate we have acknowledged any significant manipulation undertaken in the Appendix.

It should also be remembered that the interpretation given to data needs to consider the context in which the data were generated. Different policies and economies operate across the two jurisdictions meaning that the issues the data purport to measure are shaped in different ways. For example, 'take home' or disposable income varies as a function of the tax regime not simply the level of earnings, and the number of people living in local authority housing is dependent on housing policy and public sector provision. In these cases, a straight interpretation of the data that fails to take account of policy or regime will lead to erroneous conclusions.

Despite these 'health warnings', we believe that the Atlas has significant merit and will be of use to a wide range of policy makers and organizations interested in cross-border and all–island issues, revealing patterns of progress through a critical period of development in the North (the peace process) and South (the Celtic Tiger boom).

Map 1: Counties and Districts of Ireland

- Ireland NUTS Regions
- RoI County Boundaries
- NI District Boundaries

Map 2: Regional Cartograms of the Island of Ireland

- Ireland Regional Boundaries
- Irish County/District Boundaries

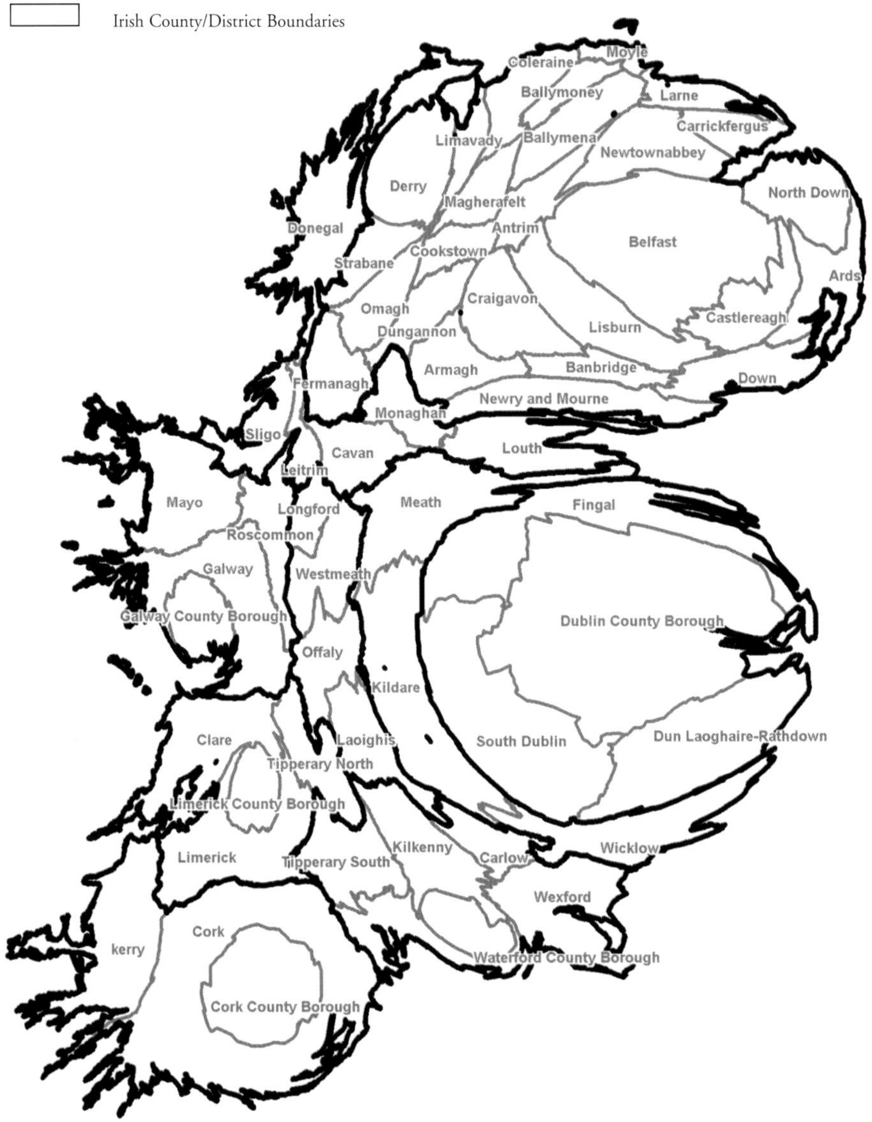

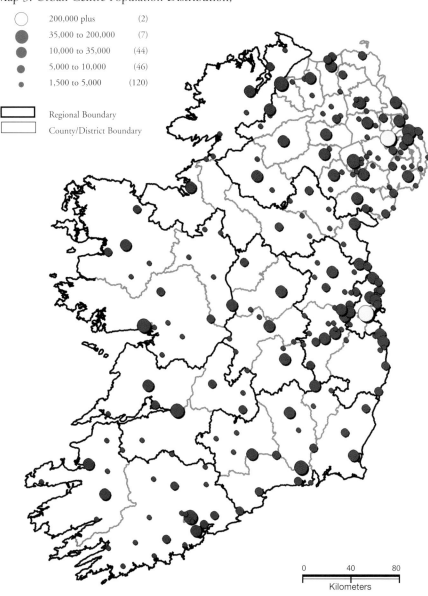

Map 3: Urban Centre Population Distribution,

○	200,000 plus	(2)
●	35,000 to 200,000	(7)
●	10,000 to 35,000	(44)
●	5,000 to 10,000	(46)
•	1,500 to 5,000	(120)

Regional Boundary

County/District Boundary

0   40   80
Kilometers

Map 4: Road Network and Principal Towns

Motorway
National Primary Road
National Secondary Road
Regional Roads
Regional Boundaries

Derry/Londonderry
Belfast
Sligo
Dundalk
Athlone
Galway
Dublin
Limerick
Cork

0   40   80
Kilometers

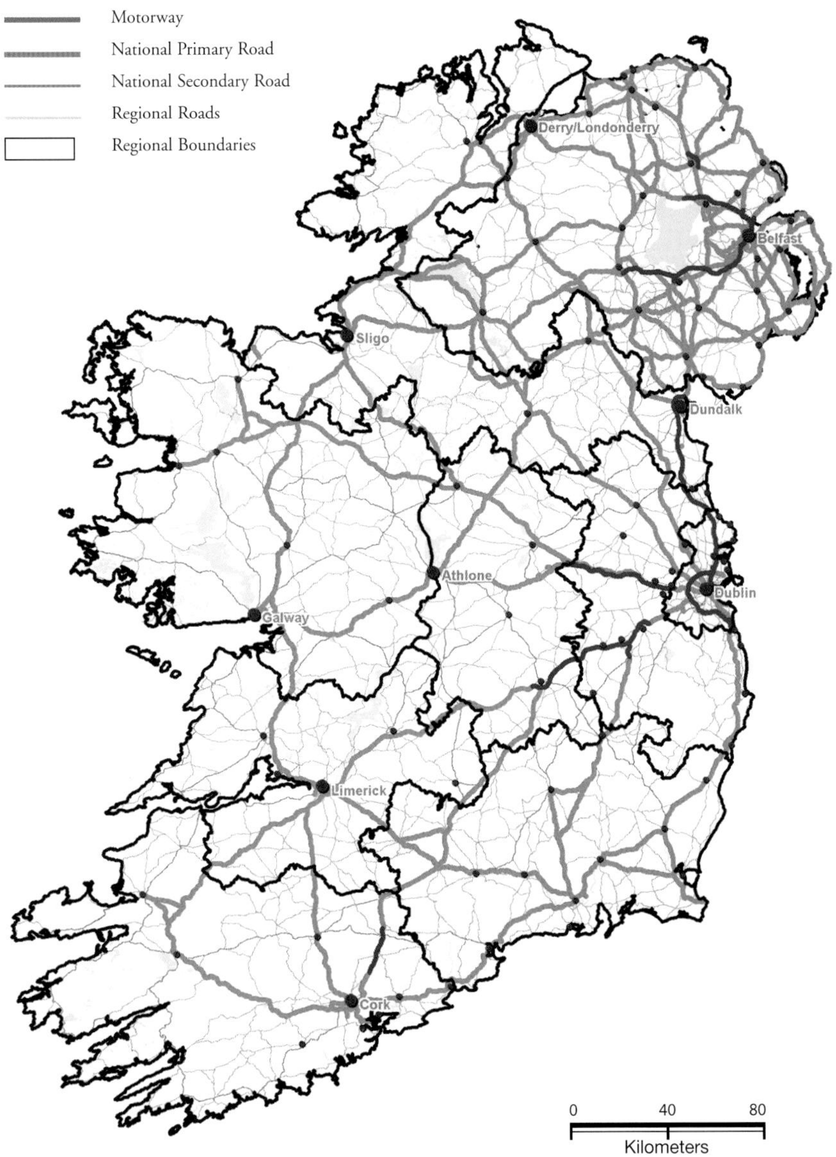

Map 5: All Ireland Rail Network and Principal Towns

Rail Network
Regional Boundaries

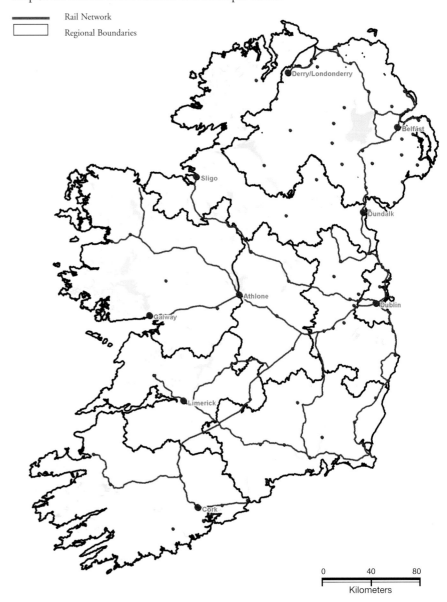

Derry/Londonderry
Belfast
Sligo
Dundalk
Athlone
Galway
Dublin
Limerick
Cork

0   40   80
Kilometers

Chapter 3: Demographics

POPULATION DENSITY: PERSONS PER km²

Map 6.1: Population Density 1991

Map 6.2: Population Density 2001/02

Map 6.3: Population Density 2001/02 Cartogram

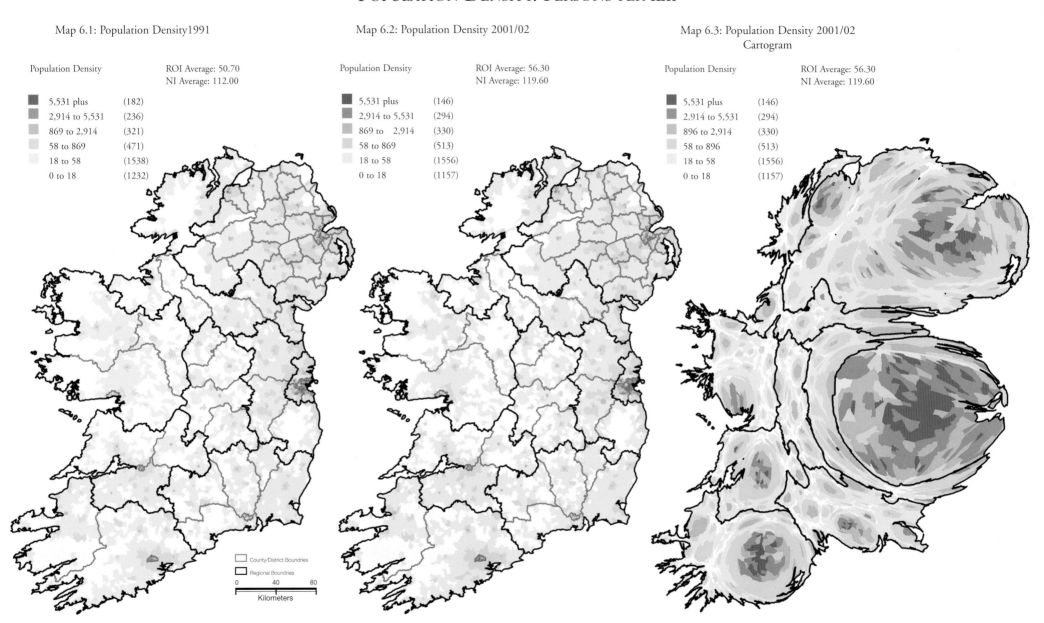

Population Density

ROI Average: 50.70
NI Average: 112.00

■	5,531 plus	(182)
■	2,914 to 5,531	(236)
■	869 to 2,914	(321)
■	58 to 869	(471)
■	18 to 58	(1538)
■	0 to 18	(1232)

Population Density

ROI Average: 56.30
NI Average: 119.60

■	5,531 plus	(146)
■	2,914 to 5,531	(294)
■	869 to 2,914	(330)
■	58 to 869	(513)
■	18 to 58	(1556)
■	0 to 18	(1157)

Population Density

ROI Average: 56.30
NI Average: 119.60

■	5,531 plus	(146)
■	2,914 to 5,531	(294)
■	896 to 2,914	(330)
■	58 to 896	(513)
■	18 to 58	(1556)
■	0 to 18	(1157)

County/District Boundries

Regional Boundries

0   40   80

Kilometers

Maps 6.1 and 6.2 reveal that large parts of the island have low population densities. Unsurprisingly, as the cartogram of population density (Map 6.3) makes clear, the highest concentrations of people are living in the cities, with significant proportions of Dublin, Belfast and Cork in particular having over 3000 per head of population per km2. This pattern is relatively stable, although there are distinct patterns of increasing and declining population. Between 1991-2001/02 there was significant change in the absolute number of people living across the whole island. Despite the gradual growth in population in the North and the rapid growth in the South, many areas continued to experience population decline, mainly through out-migration. These areas included a large swathe of

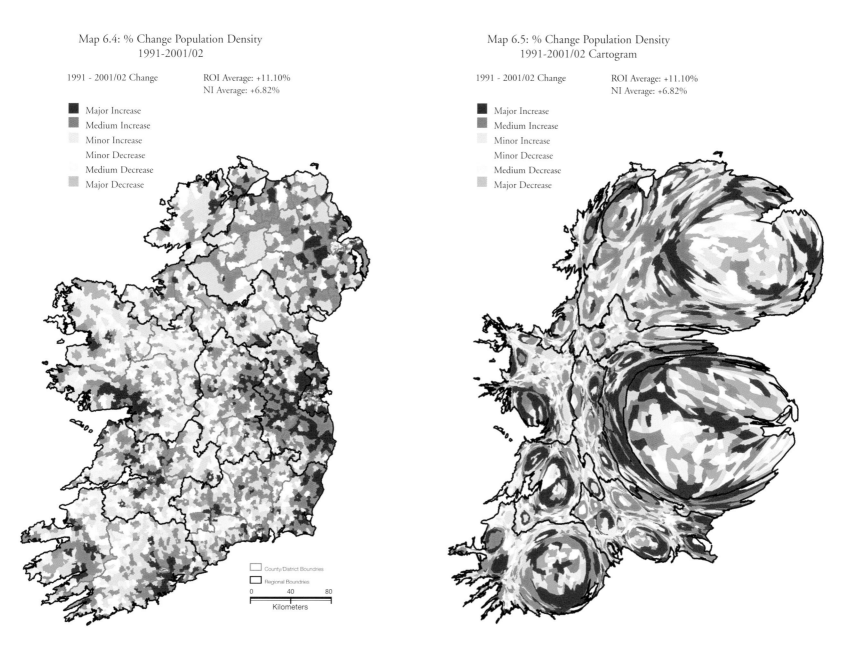

Map 6.4: % Change Population Density
1991-2001/02

1991 - 2001/02 Change   ROI Average: +11.10%
                             NI Average: +6.82%

■ Major Increase
▨ Medium Increase
░ Minor Increase
  Minor Decrease
  Medium Decrease
▨ Major Decrease

Map 6.5: % Change Population Density
1991-2001/02 Cartogram

1991 - 2001/02 Change   ROI Average: +11.10%
                             NI Average: +6.82%

■ Major Increase
▨ Medium Increase
░ Minor Increase
  Minor Decrease
  Medium Decrease
▨ Major Decrease

□ County/District Boundries
■ Regional Boundries

0   40   80
╟─────────┼─────────╢
    Kilometers

the western seaboard including south Donegal, western Mayo and north Cork, portions of the midlands (see Map 6.4) and, as revealed by the change cartogram (Map 6.5), the inner suburbs of the major cities including Belfast, Dublin, Cork, Limerick and Waterford, though largely excluding Galway. The cartogram also reveals that while rural depopulation is, and continues to be, a cause of concern, as a proportion population decline is most significant in the cities. In terms of rising population density this has been most significant in inner city cores in the South (though not in the North), the outer suburbs, and commuter areas surrounding the major towns and cities.

15

MALES AS A PERCENTAGE OF THE POPULATION

Map 7.1: % Male 1991

Map 7.2: % Male 2001/02

Map 7.3: % Male 2001/02 Cartogram

% Population Male

ROI Average: 49.70%
NI Average: 48.70%

■	56 plus	(219)
■	54 to 56	(361)
■	52 to 54	(845)
■	50 to 52	(1139)
■	48 to 50	(880)
■	33 to 48	(536)

% Population Male

ROI Average: 49.68%
NI Average: 48.74%

■	56 plus	(142)
■	54 to 56	(326)
■	52 to 54	(787)
■	50 to 52	(1219)
■	48 to 50	(989)
■	33 to 48	(533)

% Population Male

ROI Average: 49.68%
NI Average: 48.74%

■	56 plus	(142)
■	54 to 56	(326)
■	52 to 54	(787)
■	50 to 52	(1219)
■	48 to 50	(989)
■	33 to 48	(533)

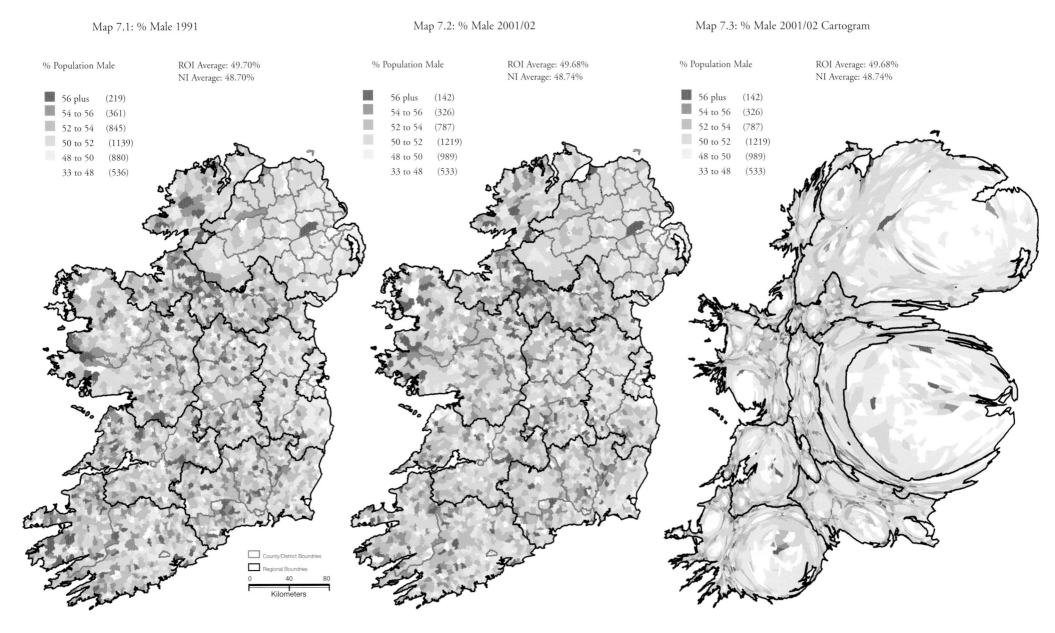

☐ County/District Boundries

☐ Regional Boundries

0   40   80
Kilometers

The percentage of the population who are male is remarkably consistent across the island between 1991 and 2001/02. In the Republic, the percentage rate is 49.70% in 1991 and 49.68% in 2002 (see Maps 7.1 and 7.2). In the North, the percentage rate is slightly lower than the South at 48.70% in 1991 and 48.74% in 2001. Interestingly there is a slightly variable geography to the percentage of males in an area. The maps and the cartogram of percentage male in 2001/02 highlight that there is a rural/urban effect in operation with low rates of males in all of the urban centres.
In contrast there are a number of rural DEDs and wards, especially in the border counties of Cavan, Leitrim and Donegal, along with West Mayo, where the percentage male is above the average.

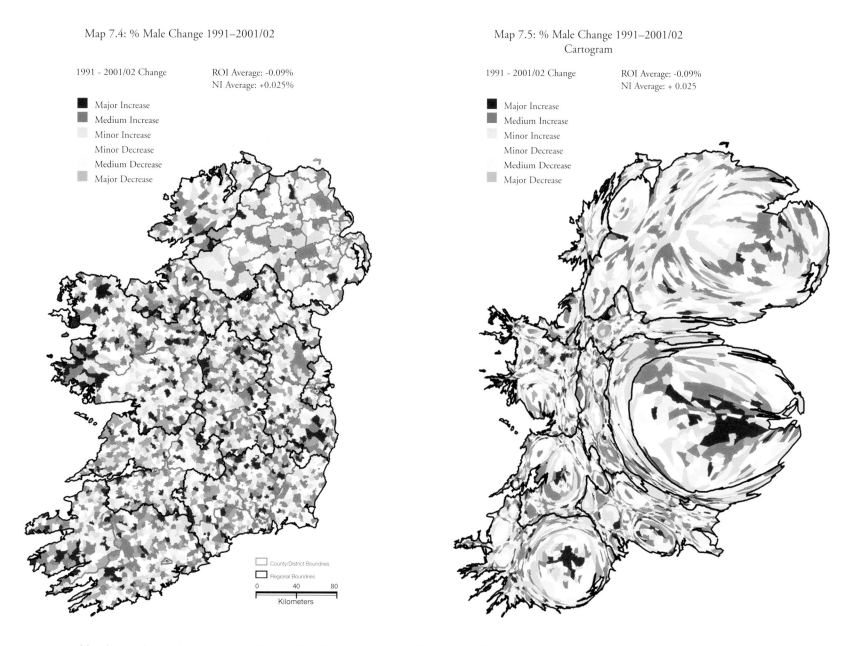

Map 7.4: % Male Change 1991–2001/02

1991 - 2001/02 Change

ROI Average: -0.09%
NI Average: +0.025%

Major Increase
Medium Increase
Minor Increase
Minor Decrease
Medium Decrease
Major Decrease

Map 7.5: % Male Change 1991–2001/02
Cartogram

1991 - 2001/02 Change

ROI Average: -0.09%
NI Average: + 0.025

Major Increase
Medium Increase
Minor Increase
Minor Decrease
Medium Decrease
Major Decrease

County/District Boundries
Regional Boundries
0   40   80
Kilometers

Given that women in general live longer than males, so one would expect females to outnumber males across the island, this suggests that women have left these areas for education and work in greater numbers than males. The map and cartogram of change between 1991 and 2001/02 show a variable rate of change across the island, with significant increases in the city centres of Dublin and Cork in particular (see Map 7.4 and 7.5). These areas have seen significant gentrification and development attracting new urban living which proportionally has seemingly appealed to slightly more men than women.

FEMALES AS A PERCENTAGE OF THE POPULATION

Map 8.1: % Female 1991

Map 8.2: % Female 2001/02

Map 8.3: % Female 2001/01
Cartogram

% Population Female

ROI Average: 50.30%
NI Average: 51.30%

■	53 plus	(298)
■	51 to 53	(635)
■	50 to 51	(539)
□	48 to 50	(1087)
□	45 to 48	(1075)
□	29 to 45	(346)

% Population Female

ROI Average: 50.32%
NI Average: 51.26%

■	53 plus	(285)
■	51 to 53	(679)
■	50 to 51	(609)
□	48 to 50	(1169)
□	45 to 48	(996)
□	29 to 45	(258)

% Population Female

ROI Average: 50.32%
NI Average: 51.26%

■	53 plus	(285)
■	51 to 53	(679)
■	50 to 51	(609)
□	48 to 50	(1169)
□	45 to 48	(996)
□	29 to 45	(258)

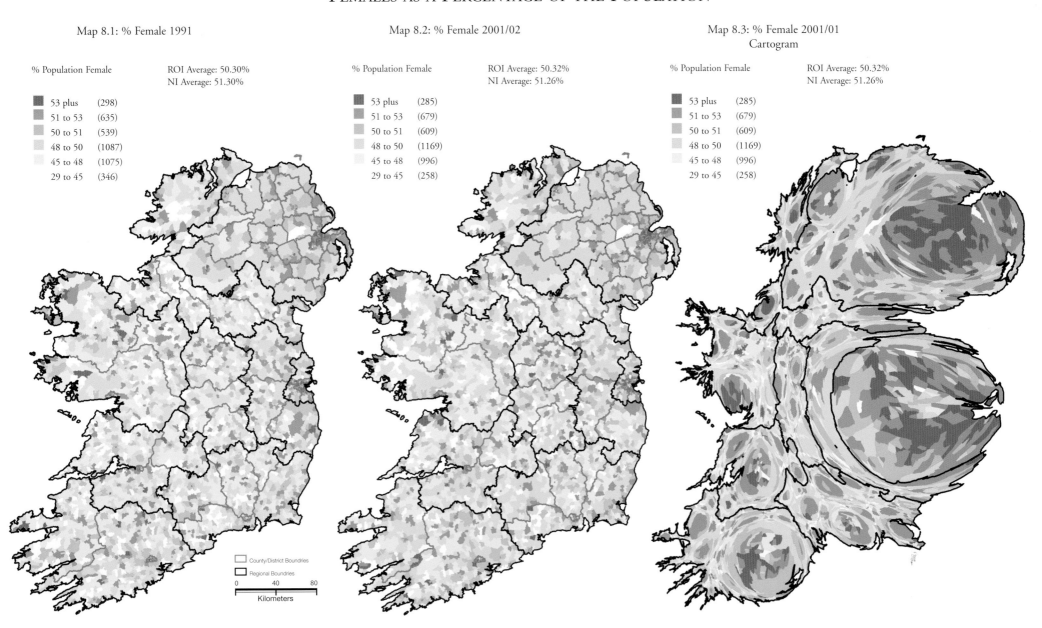

County/District Boundries
Regional Boundries

0   40   80
Kilometers

As one would expect, the pattern of females mirrors that of males. Given, on average, slightly better longevity the percentage number of females is slightly above average for both the Republic (50.32% in 1991, 50.3% in 2002) and the North (51.3% in 1991, 51.26% in 2001) (Map 8.1 and 8.2). The cartogram of percentage female in 2001/02 strikingly reveals the urban centres, with females being a larger proportion of the population in all of the major towns and cities across the island (Map 8.4). In many cases, large portions of these urban areas have above 53 percent female residents. The map and cartogram of change show a mixed pattern across the island, but in general the proportion of women has gone up in suburban areas and fallen at the cores of urban areas, particularly in Dublin

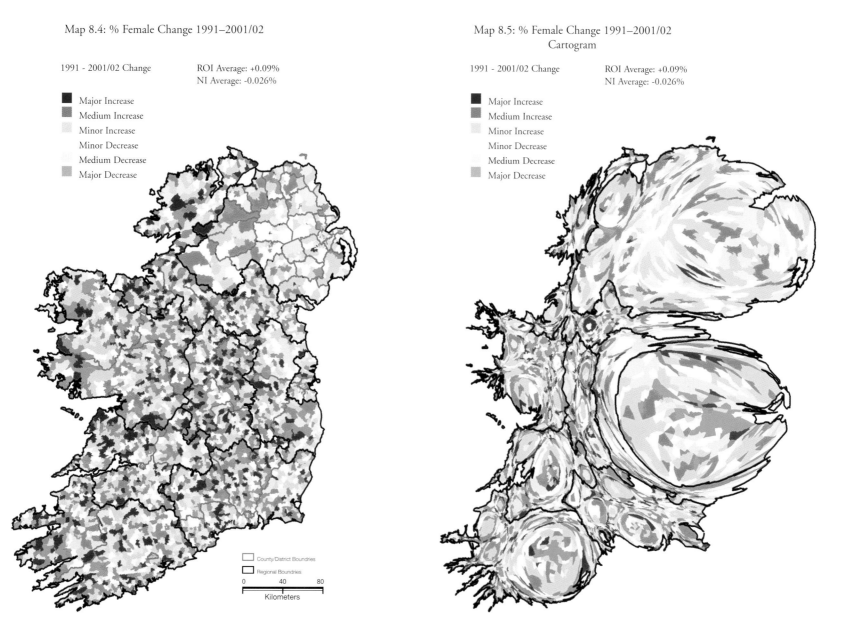

Map 8.4: % Female Change 1991–2001/02

1991 - 2001/02 Change

ROI Average: +0.09%
NI Average: -0.026%

■ Major Increase
▨ Medium Increase
░ Minor Increase
  Minor Decrease
  Medium Decrease
▨ Major Decrease

County/District Boundries
Regional Boundries

0   40   80
Kilometers

Map 8.5: % Female Change 1991–2001/02
Cartogram

1991 - 2001/02 Change

ROI Average: +0.09%
NI Average: -0.026%

■ Major Increase
▨ Medium Increase
░ Minor Increase
  Minor Decrease
  Medium Decrease
▨ Major Decrease

and Cork. Interestingly, there are some significant outliers caused by small DED size and specific circumstances. In 1991 only 29 percent of the population in Mountheaton in Offaly was female (there was a very high number of boys aged 15-19 skewing the figures); in 2001/02 the lowest ratio had passed to Cushkillary in west Galway again with only 29 percent of the population female (again skewed by a large number of boys present on census night at an activity centre).

SEX RATIO: FEMALES PER 1000 MALES

Map 9.1: Sex Ratio 1991

Map 9.2: Sex Ratio 2001/02

Map 9.3: Sex Ratio 2001/02 Cartogram

Females per 1000 Males

ROI Average: 1010
NI Average: 1052

■	1,155 plus	(203)
■	1,040 to 1,155	(742)
	967 to 1,040	(974)
	900 to 967	(968)
	818 to 900	(747)
	422 to 818	(346)

Females per 1000 Males

ROI Average: 1012
NI Average: 1051

■	1,155 plus	(181)
■	1,040 to 1,155	(797)
	967 to 967	(1097)
	900 to 967	(985)
	818 to 900	(678)
	424 to 818	(258)

Females per 1000 Males

ROI Average: 1012
NI Average: 1051

■	1,155 plus	(181)
■	1,040 to 1,155	(797)
	967 to 967	(1097)
	900 to 967	(985)
	818 to 900	(678)
	424 to 818	(258)

County/District Boundries
Regional Boundries

0   40   80
Kilometers

These set of maps show the ratio of women to men across the island. Unsurprisingly the ratio of women to men follows the pattern of male and female distribution as shown in the previous maps. In general terms, women outnumber men in the urban areas with the exception of some inner city cores such as Dublin, Cork and Londonderry. In contrast men outnumber women in a number of rural areas, particularly in the South, with some very low ratios in the border counties of Cavan and Leitrim, west Galway and central Waterford. In these cases, and in rural areas in general, the low

Map 9.4: % Sex Ratio Change 1991–2001/02

Map 9.5: % Sex Ratio Change 1991–2001/02
Cartogram

1991 - 2001/02 Change

ROI Average: + 0.19%
NI Average: -0.05%

1991 - 2001/02 Change

ROI Average: + 0.19%
NI Average: -0.05%

Major Increase
Medium Increase
Minor Increase
Minor Decrease
Medium Decrease
Major Decrease

Major Increase
Medium Increase
Minor Increase
Minor Decrease
Medium Decrease
Major Decrease

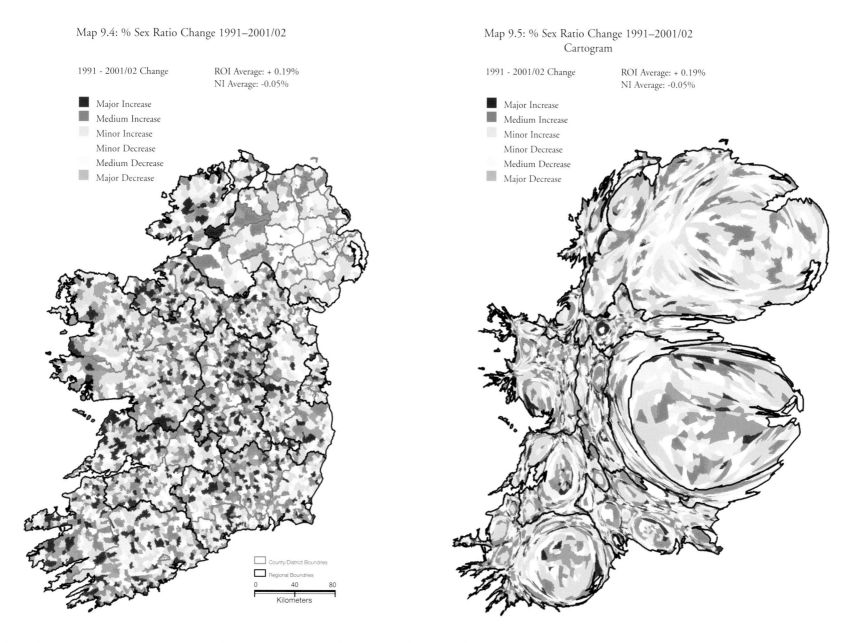

County/District Boundries
Regional Boundries

0   40   80
Kilometers

ratio is probably the outcome of out-migration to the urban centres across several generations. This effect is less pronounced in the North, with most areas across the province having approximately equal ratios or slightly more females to males. This differential pattern between the two jurisdictions is likely the result of long term economic and social processes, with several decades of generally poor economic performance in the South shaping migration patterns that seemingly affected women more than men.

PERSONS AGED 0 - 14 YEARS AS A PERCENTAGE OF TOTAL POPULATION

Map 10.1: % Age Band 0 - 14 1991

Map 10.2: % Age Band 0 - 14 2001/02

Map 10.3: % Age Band 0 - 14 2001/02
Cartogram

% Population Aged 0 -14   ROI Average: 26.70%
                                 NI Average: 24.40%

32 plus	(424)
29 to 32	(818)
27 to 29	(739)
24 to 27	(888)
19 to 24	(742)
3 to 19	(369)

% Population Aged 0 - 14   ROI Average: 21.10%
                                  NI Average: 23.60%

32 plus	(30)
29 to 32	(102)
27 to 29	(234)
24 to 27	(857)
19 to 24	(1900)
0,7 to 19	(873)

% Population Aged 0 -14   ROI Average: 21.10%
                                 NI Average: 23.60%

32 plus	(30)
29 to 32	(102)
27 to 29	(234)
24 to 27	(857)
19 to 24	(1900)
0 to 19	(873)

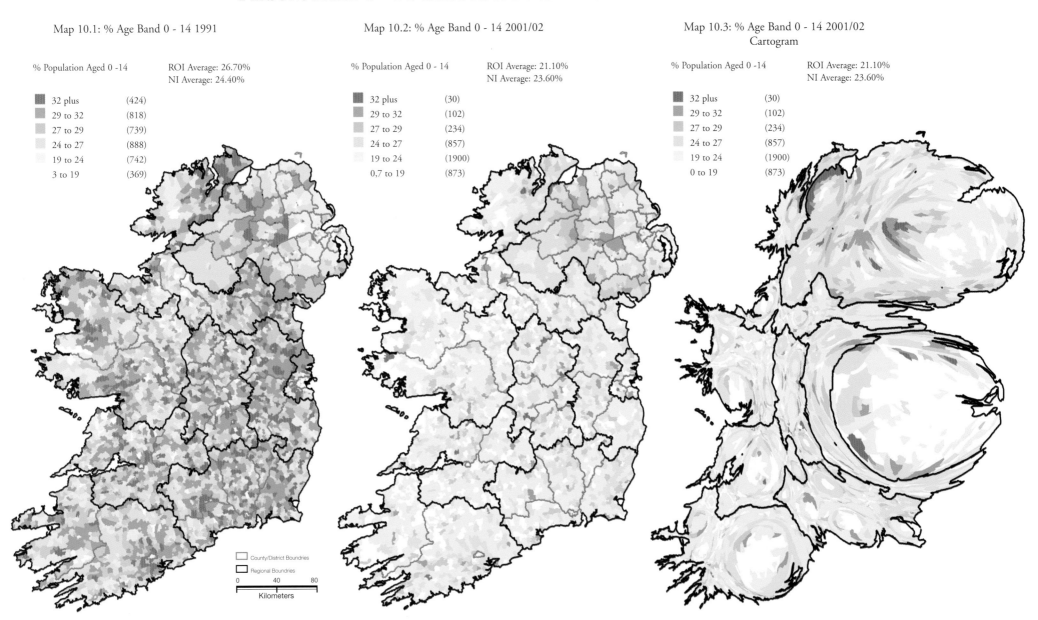

County/District Boundries

Regional Boundries

0   40   80
Kilometers

In 2001/02 the overall percentage of the population aged 0-14 (children) was 21.1% in the Republic and 23.6% in Northern Ireland. However, the Republic figure had dropped from 26.7% in 1991 (a relative decrease of -20.8%) whereas the figure in the North remained relatively stable, down from 24.4% (a relative decrease of only 3.3%). This stark contrast is shown clearly on the two change maps (Maps 10.4 and 10.5) where most of the Republic's DEDs suffered major decreases whereas the wards in Northern Ireland tended to suffer only minor decreases in the percentage of children or experienced medium increases. The reasons for this are possibly the increased use of birth control in the Republic as the influence of the Catholic church waned combined with increased immigration of

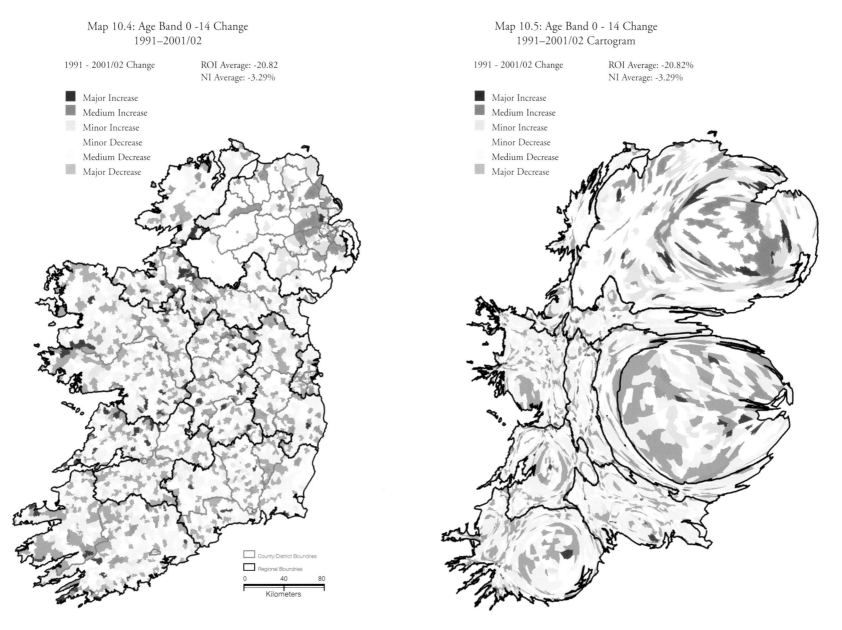

Map 10.4: Age Band 0 -14 Change
1991–2001/02

1991 - 2001/02 Change   ROI Average: -20.82
                               NI Average: -3.29%

■ Major Increase
▨ Medium Increase
  Minor Increase
  Minor Decrease
  Medium Decrease
▨ Major Decrease

□ County/District Boundries
□ Regional Boundries

0   40   80
Kilometers

Map 10.5: Age Band 0 - 14 Change
1991–2001/02 Cartogram

1991 - 2001/02 Change   ROI Average: -20.82%
                               NI Average: -3.29%

■ Major Increase
▨ Medium Increase
  Minor Increase
  Minor Decrease
  Medium Decrease
▨ Major Decrease

largely young adults which has reduced the proportion of children in the population in many areas. The contrast between Dublin and Belfast is noticeable in Map 10.5 with Dublin's DEDs mainly experiencing a large decline in the proportion of the population aged 0-14 and Belfast's wards mainly experiencing moderate increases. Again, this is probably linked to changes in the young adult population (see subsequent maps) with Dublin experiencing large increases of young adults and Belfast experiencing relatively large losses.

PERSONS AGED 15 - 24 YEARS AS A PERCENTAGE OF THE POPULATION

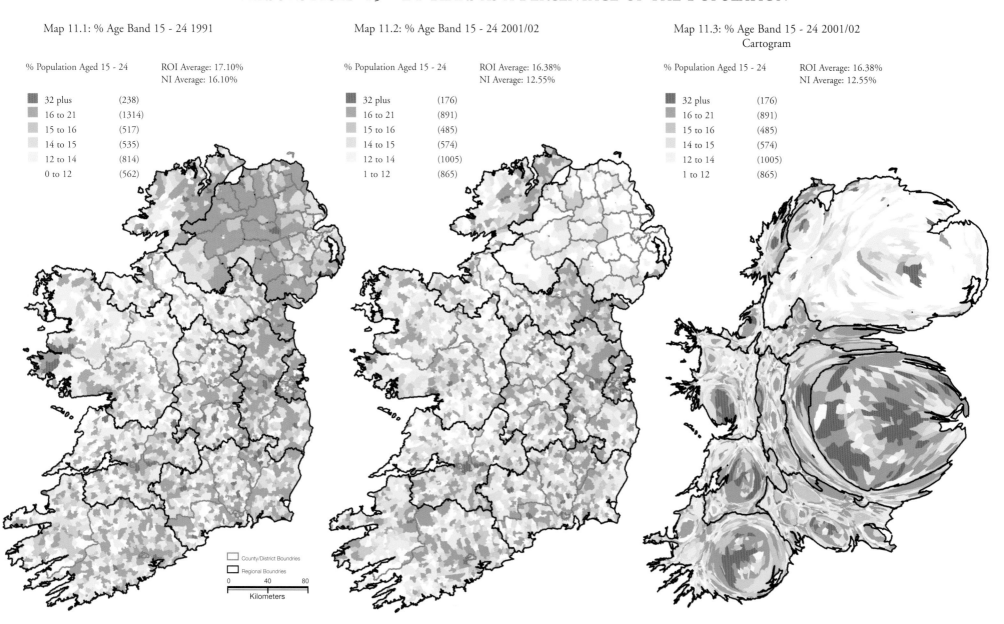

Map 11.1: % Age Band 15 - 24 1991

% Population Aged 15 - 24

ROI Average: 17.10%
NI Average: 16.10%

▪	32 plus	(238)
▪	16 to 21	(1314)
▪	15 to 16	(517)
▪	14 to 15	(535)
▪	12 to 14	(814)
▪	0 to 12	(562)

Map 11.2: % Age Band 15 - 24 2001/02

% Population Aged 15 - 24

ROI Average: 16.38%
NI Average: 12.55%

▪	32 plus	(176)
▪	16 to 21	(891)
▪	15 to 16	(485)
▪	14 to 15	(574)
▪	12 to 14	(1005)
▪	1 to 12	(865)

Map 11.3: % Age Band 15 - 24 2001/02
Cartogram

% Population Aged 15 - 24

ROI Average: 16.38%
NI Average: 12.55%

▪	32 plus	(176)
▪	16 to 21	(891)
▪	15 to 16	(485)
▪	14 to 15	(574)
▪	12 to 14	(1005)
▪	1 to 12	(865)

County/District Boundries
Regional Boundries

0   40   80
Kilometers

In 2001/02 the overall percentage of the population aged 15-24 (young adults) was 16.4% in the Republic but only 12.6% in Northern Ireland. Whereas the Republic figure had dropped only marginally from 17.1% in 1991 (a relative decrease of 4.2%), the NI figure had dropped substantially from 16.1% (a relative decrease of 22%). This stark contrast is shown clearly on the two change maps (Maps 11.4 and 11.5) where most of the Northern Ireland wards suffered major decreases in young adults in contrast to the Republic where many of the DEDs experienced moderate or large increases in the proportion of young adults. Map 11.4 shows the effect of the border on the rates of change of young adults quite clearly. The cartogram (Map 11.5) also shows this but indicates that

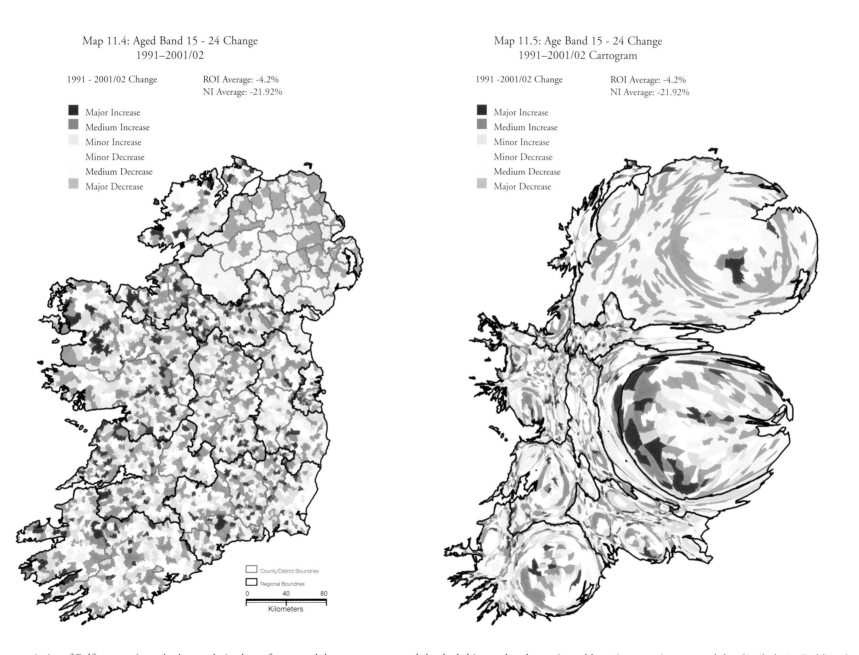

Map 11.4: Aged Band 15 - 24 Change
1991–2001/02

1991 - 2001/02 Change

ROI Average: -4.2%
NI Average: -21.92%

■ Major Increase
▨ Medium Increase
░ Minor Increase
  Minor Decrease
  Medium Decrease
▨ Major Decrease

Map 11.5: Age Band 15 - 24 Change
1991–2001/02 Cartogram

1991 -2001/02 Change

ROI Average: -4.2%
NI Average: -21.92%

■ Major Increase
▨ Medium Increase
░ Minor Increase
  Minor Decrease
  Medium Decrease
▨ Major Decrease

▢ County/District Boundries
▢ Regional Boundries

0   40   80
Kilometers

although the vast majority of Belfast experienced a large relative loss of young adults, one or two wards bucked this trend and experienced large increases in young adults. Similarly, in Dublin, the change in the proportion of young adults was not constant throughout the metropolitan area with west Dublin and parts of the central area experiencing large increases in the proportion of young adults and the north and south suburbs experiencing large relative losses. The reasons for these trends are likely to be related to migration with a general net out-migration of young adults from Northern Ireland and a stable base of young adults in to the Republic.

Persons Aged 25 - 44 1991

Map 12.1: % Age Band 25 - 44, 1991

Map 12.2: % Age Band 25 - 44, 2001/02

Map 12.3: % Aged Band 25 - 44, 2001/02
Cartogram

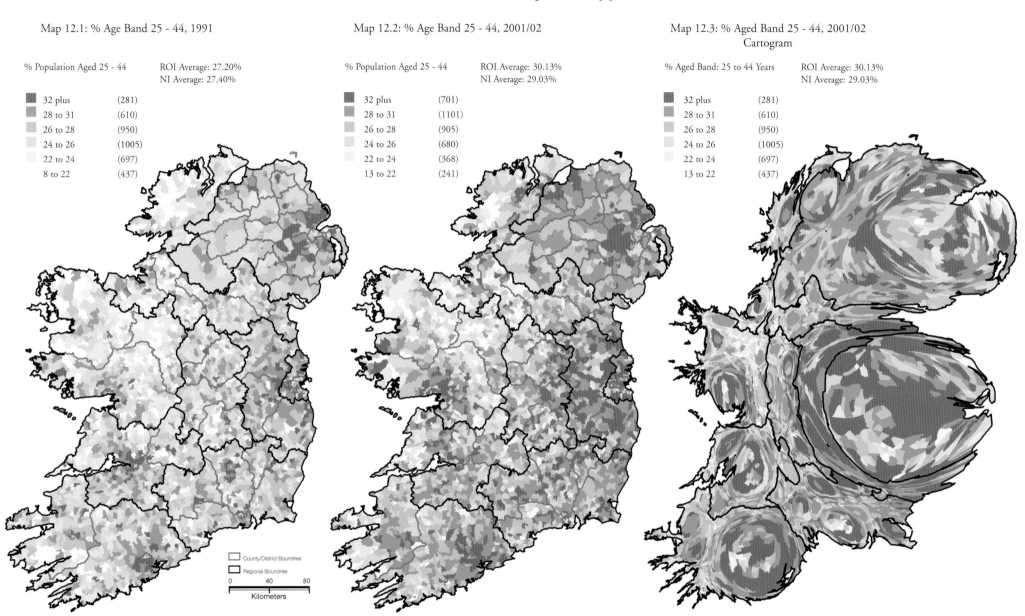

% Population Aged 25 - 44

ROI Average: 27.20%
NI Average: 27.40%

32 plus	(281)
28 to 31	(610)
26 to 28	(950)
24 to 26	(1005)
22 to 24	(697)
8 to 22	(437)

% Population Aged 25 - 44

ROI Average: 30.13%
NI Average: 29.03%

32 plus	(701)
28 to 31	(1101)
26 to 28	(905)
24 to 26	(680)
22 to 24	(368)
13 to 22	(241)

% Aged Band: 25 to 44 Years

ROI Average: 30.13%
NI Average: 29.03%

32 plus	(281)
28 to 31	(610)
26 to 28	(950)
24 to 26	(1005)
22 to 24	(697)
13 to 22	(437)

County/District Boundries
Regional Boundries

0   40   80
Kilometers

In 2001/02 the overall percentage of the population aged 25-44 (mature adults) was 30.1% in the Republic and 29.0% in Northern Ireland and this demographic group accounted for the largest proportion of the population in both jurisdictions. In both the North and South there was a slight increase in this percentage over the decade from 1991 and the geographic distribution of this increase was fairly even (see maps 12.4 and 12.5). Dublin, Cork and Limerick showed the greatest local variation in the change in the percentage of mature adults with the rest of the country and most of Northern Ireland experiencing relatively little change. Map 12.3 shows that the largest concentrations of mature adults are unsurprisingly found in the suburbs of the major cities.

Map 12.4: Age Band 25 - 44, Change
1991–2001/02

1991 - 2001/02 Change   ROI Average: +10.77%
                             NI Average: +5.76%

- Major Increase
- Medium Increase
- Minor Increase
- Minor Decrease
- Medium Decrease
- Major Decrease

County/District Boundries
Regional Boundries

0   40   80
Kilometers

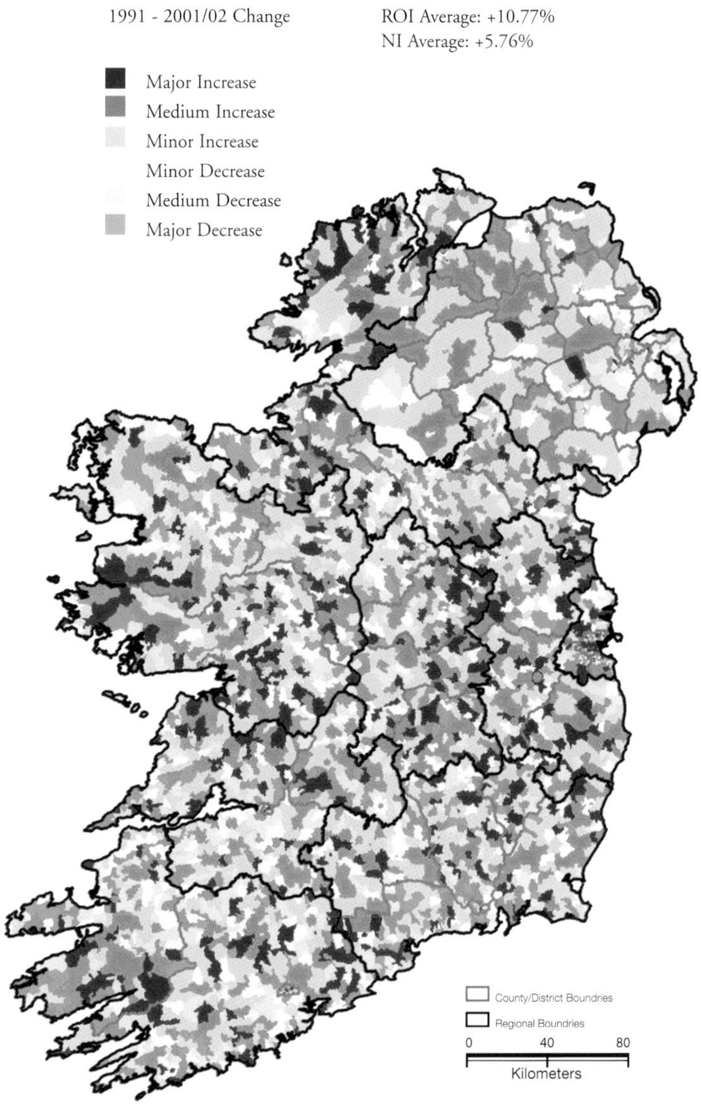

Map 12.5: Age Band 25 - 44 Change
1991–2001/02 Cartogram

1991 - 2001/02 Change   ROI Average: +10.77%
                             NI Average: +5.76%

- Major Increase
- Medium Increase
- Minor Increase
- Minor Decrease
- Medium Decrease
- Major Decrease

PERSONS AGED 45 - 64 YEARS AS A PERCENTAGE OF TOTAL POPULATION

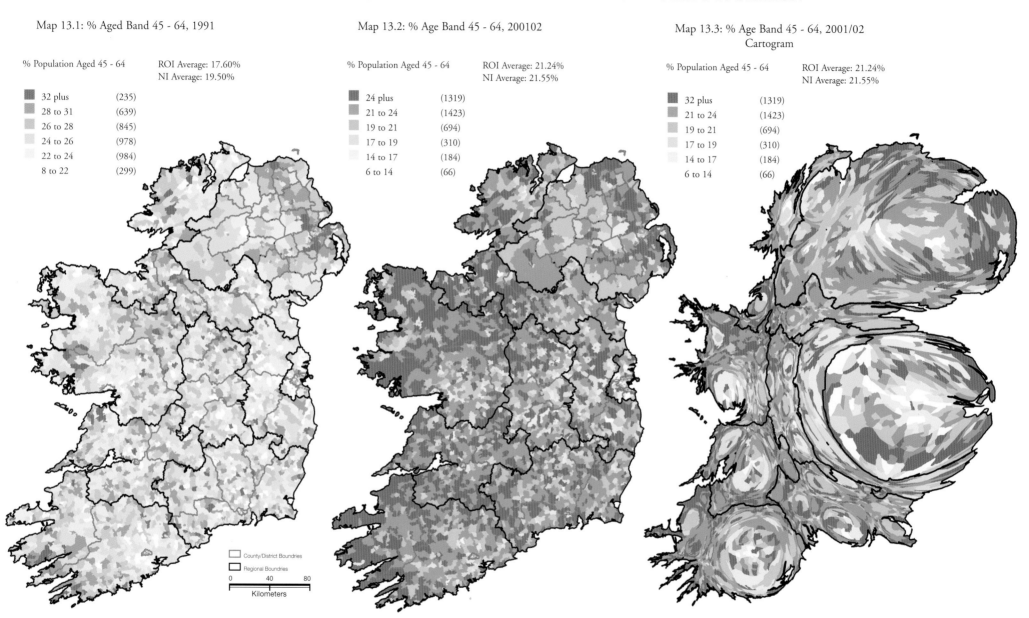

Map 13.1: % Aged Band 45 - 64, 1991

% Population Aged 45 - 64   ROI Average: 17.60%
                            NI Average: 19.50%

■	32 plus	(235)
■	28 to 31	(639)
■	26 to 28	(845)
■	24 to 26	(978)
□	22 to 24	(984)
□	8 to 22	(299)

Map 13.2: % Age Band 45 - 64, 200102

% Population Aged 45 - 64   ROI Average: 21.24%
                            NI Average: 21.55%

■	24 plus	(1319)
■	21 to 24	(1423)
■	19 to 21	(694)
■	17 to 19	(310)
□	14 to 17	(184)
□	6 to 14	(66)

Map 13.3: % Age Band 45 - 64, 2001/02
Cartogram

% Population Aged 45 - 64   ROI Average: 21.24%
                            NI Average: 21.55%

■	32 plus	(1319)
■	21 to 24	(1423)
■	19 to 21	(694)
■	17 to 19	(310)
□	14 to 17	(184)
□	6 to 14	(66)

□ County/District Boundries
■ Regional Boundries

0   40   80
Kilometers

In 2001/02 the overall percentage of the population aged 45-64 (middle-aged adults) was 21.2% in the Republic and 21.6% in Northern Ireland. In both places the percentage had increased slightly over the decade since 1991. The maps of geographic distribution in 2001/02 (Map 13.2 and 13.3) show the highest concentrations of middle-aged adults on the periphery of cities with city centres tending to have relatively lower proportions of middle-aged adults. The maps of change over the decade (Maps 13.4 and 13.5) show that most of the major increases in the percentage of middle-aged

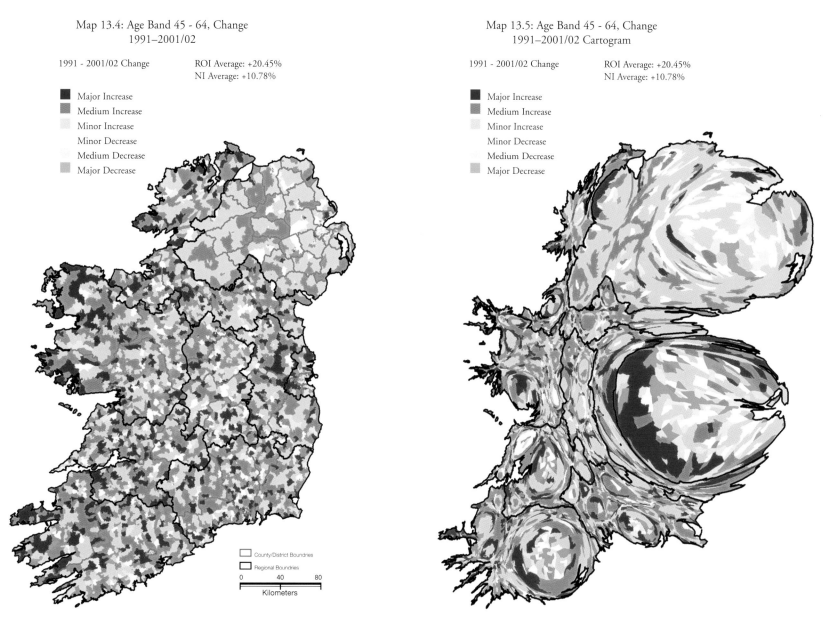

Map 13.4: Age Band 45 - 64, Change
1991–2001/02

1991 - 2001/02 Change   ROI Average: +20.45%
                          NI Average: +10.78%

■ Major Increase
▨ Medium Increase
░ Minor Increase
  Minor Decrease
  Medium Decrease
▨ Major Decrease

Map 13.5: Age Band 45 - 64, Change
1991–2001/02 Cartogram

1991 - 2001/02 Change   ROI Average: +20.45%
                          NI Average: +10.78%

■ Major Increase
▨ Medium Increase
░ Minor Increase
  Minor Decrease
  Medium Decrease
▨ Major Decrease

☐ County/District Boundries
☐ Regional Boundries

0   40   80
Kilometers

adults were in the peripheries of the larger cities and in the more rural areas of the Republic. The figures in Northern Ireland were relatively stable. Increases in this age group tend to reflect the general ageing of the population as birth rates drop and locally large increases may also reflect the out-migration of younger age groups.

PERSONS AGED 65+ YEARS AS A PERCENTAGE OF TOTAL POPULATION

Map 14.1: % Age Band 65+ 1991

% Population Aged 65+   ROI Average: 11.40%
                        NI Average: 12.60%

▉	19 plus	(529)
▉	14 to 19	(1281)
▩	12 to 14	(730)
▨	10 to 12	(638)
░	6 to 10	(603)
░	0 to 6	(199)

Map 14.2: % Age Band 65+ 2001/02

65+ Population Aged 65+   ROI Average: 11.13%
                          NI Average: 13.25%

▉	19 plus	(373)
▉	14 to 19	(1193)
▩	12 to 14	(815)
▨	10 to 12	(723)
░	6 to 10	(726)
░	0 to 6	(166)

Map 14.3: % Age Band 65+ 2001/02
Cartogram

% Population Aged 65+   ROI Average: 11.13%
                        NI Average: 13.25%

▉	19 plus	(373)
▉	14 to 19	(1193)
▩	12 to 14	(815)
▨	10 to 12	(723)
░	6 to 10	(726)
░	0 to 6	(166)

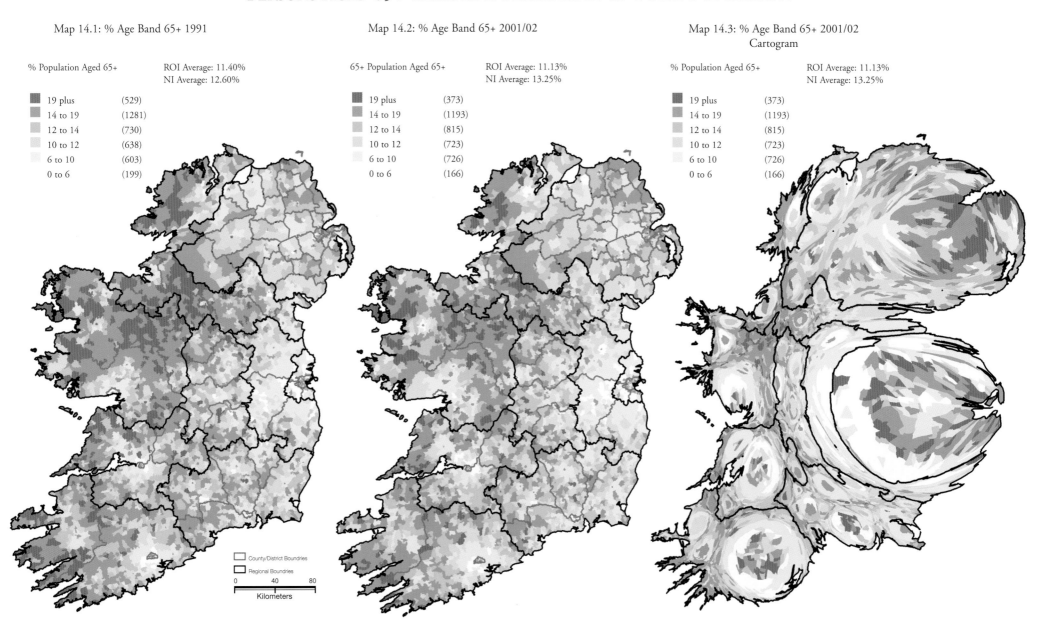

County/District Boundries
Regional Boundries

0   40   80
Kilometers

In 2001/02 the overall percentage of the population aged 65+ (elderly) was 11.1% in the Republic and 13.3% in Northern Ireland. The Republic figure had dropped slightly from 11.4% in 1991 whereas the elderly population in the North had increased slightly from 12.6%. The geographic distribution of the elderly in 2001/02 largely mirrors that of 1991 with highest concentrations being in the more rural areas in both jurisdictions. The major cities tend to have relatively low percentages of elderly population. That is not to say that there are not as many older people living in urban areas,

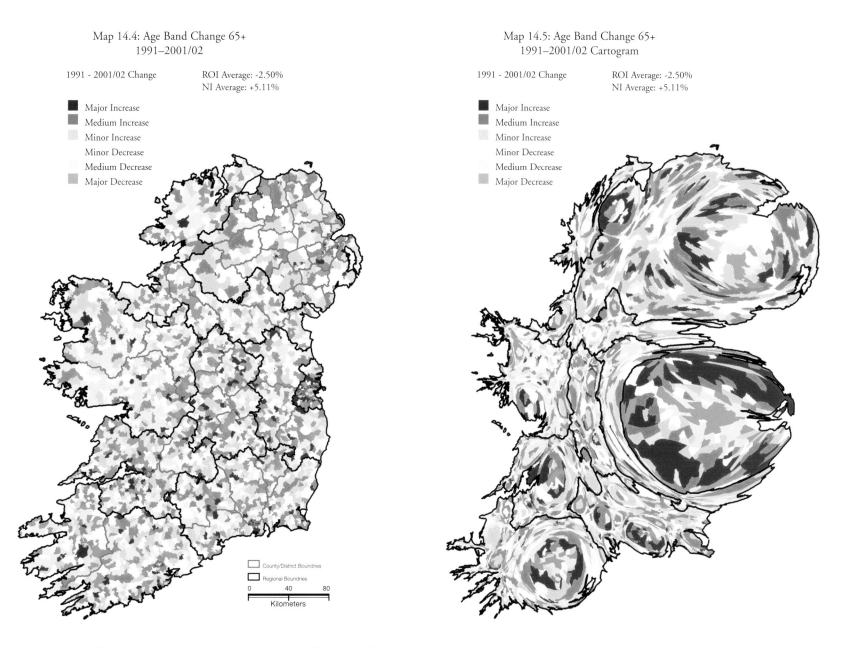

Map 14.4: Age Band Change 65+
1991–2001/02

1991 - 2001/02 Change ROI Average: -2.50%
NI Average: +5.11%

Major Increase
Medium Increase
Minor Increase
Minor Decrease
Medium Decrease
Major Decrease

County/District Boundries
Regional Boundries

0   40   80
Kilometers

Map 14.5: Age Band Change 65+
1991–2001/02 Cartogram

1991 - 2001/02 Change ROI Average: -2.50%
NI Average: +5.11%

Major Increase
Medium Increase
Minor Increase
Minor Decrease
Medium Decrease
Major Decrease

but rather that they form a smaller relative proportion of overall population. The maps of change over the decade since 1991 (Maps 14.4 and 14.5) indicate that the areas experiencing major declines in the proportions of elderly population were the rural areas and the city centres. Areas experiencing major increases tended to be the suburban areas of the larger cities. This is very clearly depicted, for example, for the Dublin region on Map 14.5.

DEMOGRAPHIC VITALITY RATIO

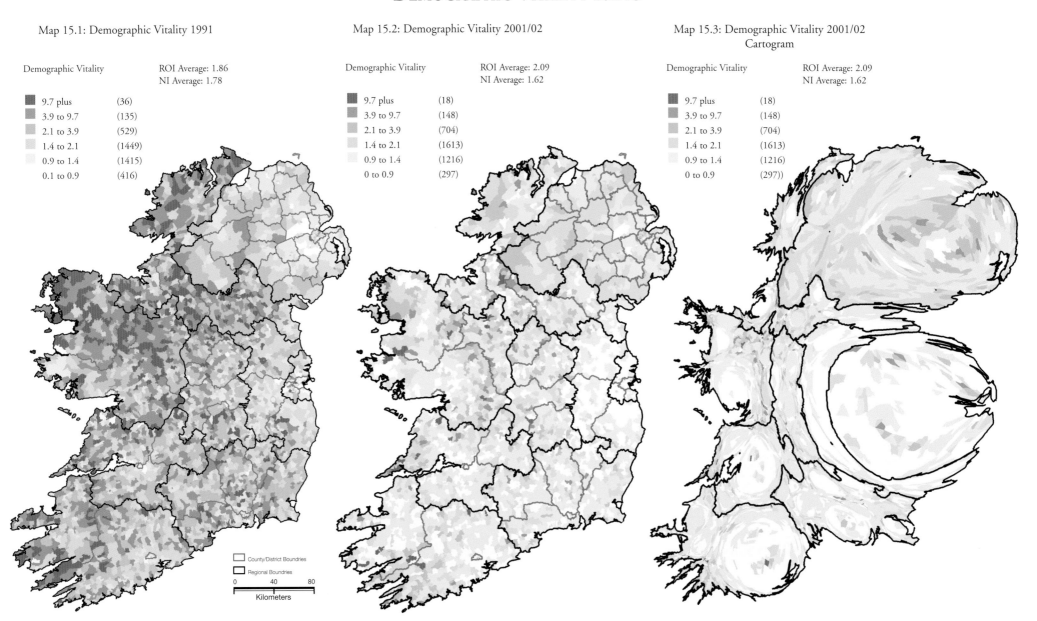

Map 15.1: Demographic Vitality 1991

Demographic Vitality

ROI Average: 1.86
NI Average: 1.78

■	9.7 plus	(36)
■	3.9 to 9.7	(135)
■	2.1 to 3.9	(529)
■	1.4 to 2.1	(1449)
■	0.9 to 1.4	(1415)
■	0.1 to 0.9	(416)

Map 15.2: Demographic Vitality 2001/02

Demographic Vitality

ROI Average: 2.09
NI Average: 1.62

■	9.7 plus	(18)
■	3.9 to 9.7	(148)
■	2.1 to 3.9	(704)
■	1.4 to 2.1	(1613)
■	0.9 to 1.4	(1216)
■	0 to 0.9	(297)

Map 15.3: Demographic Vitality 2001/02
Cartogram

Demographic Vitality

ROI Average: 2.09
NI Average: 1.62

■	9.7 plus	(18)
■	3.9 to 9.7	(148)
■	2.1 to 3.9	(704)
■	1.4 to 2.1	(1613)
■	0.9 to 1.4	(1216)
■	0 to 0.9	(297))

County/District Boundries

Regional Boundries

0   40   80
Kilometers

The Demographic Vitality Ratio (DVR) is the ratio of the percentage of the most active age groups (20-39) to the percentage of population aged 60 years or over. High values therefore depict areas with a young, economically active population whereas areas with low values have an older, less economically active, population. The cartogram (Map 15.3) unsurprisingly shows that the areas of highest DVR tend to be associated with the major cities. However, Belfast has very few areas of high DVR and these are in the centre of the city whereas Dublin, Cork, Limerick and Galway all have substantial areas of high DVR on their peripheries as well as some high values in the city centres. The change map in 15.5 shows clearly that this pattern is being reinforced over time with the greatest increases in DVR

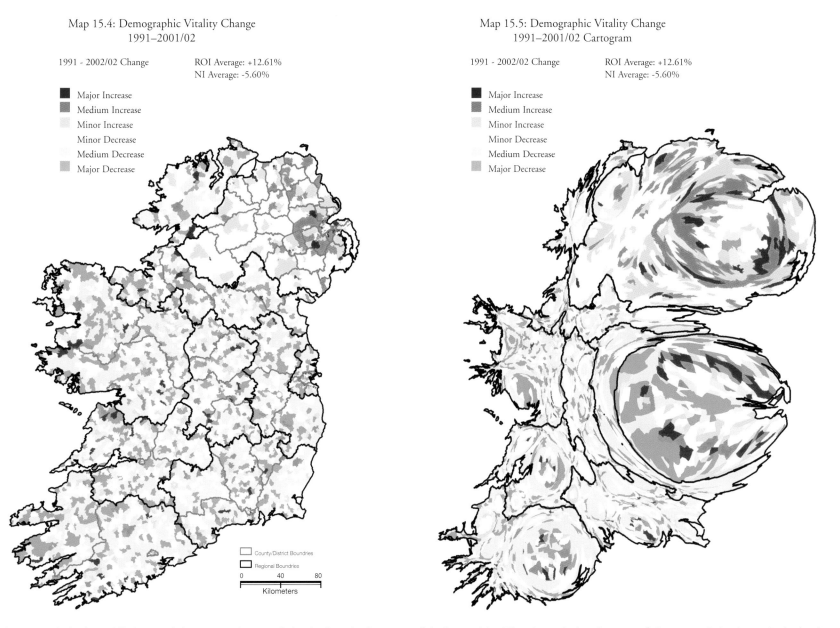

Map 15.4: Demographic Vitality Change
1991–2001/02

1991 - 2002/02 Change   ROI Average: +12.61%
                             NI Average: -5.60%

■ Major Increase
▨ Medium Increase
▦ Minor Increase
  Minor Decrease
  Medium Decrease
▨ Major Decrease

Map 15.5: Demographic Vitality Change
1991–2001/02 Cartogram

1991 - 2002/02 Change   ROI Average: +12.61%
                             NI Average: -5.60%

■ Major Increase
▨ Medium Increase
▦ Minor Increase
  Minor Decrease
  Medium Decrease
▨ Major Decrease

▭ County/District Boundries
▭ Regional Boundries

0   40   80
Kilometers

being in the city centres in both jursidictions and the greatest decreases being in the suburban areas of the larger cities. The picture is therefore one of city centres being increasingly dominated by young adults and the surrounding suburban areas being increasingly the domain of the more elderly.

DEPENDENCY RATE

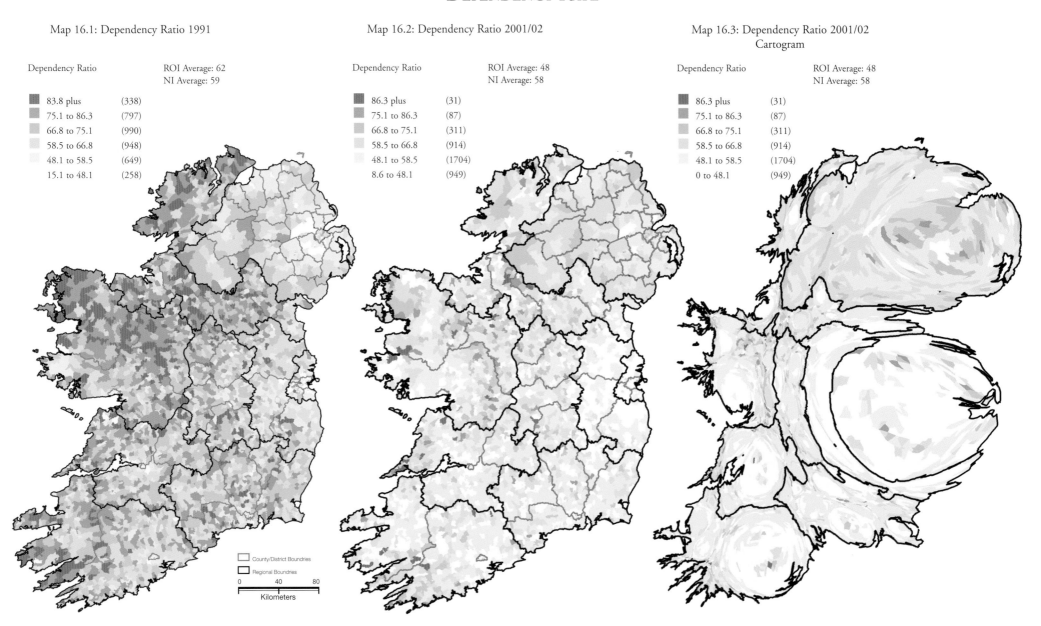

Map 16.1: Dependency Ratio 1991

Dependency Ratio   ROI Average: 62
    NI Average: 59

■	83.8 plus	(338)
■	75.1 to 86.3	(797)
■	66.8 to 75.1	(990)
■	58.5 to 66.8	(948)
■	48.1 to 58.5	(649)
■	15.1 to 48.1	(258)

Map 16.2: Dependency Ratio 2001/02

Dependency Ratio   ROI Average: 48
    NI Average: 58

■	86.3 plus	(31)
■	75.1 to 86.3	(87)
■	66.8 to 75.1	(311)
■	58.5 to 66.8	(914)
■	48.1 to 58.5	(1704)
■	8.6 to 48.1	(949)

Map 16.3: Dependency Ratio 2001/02
Cartogram

Dependency Ratio   ROI Average: 48
    NI Average: 58

■	86.3 plus	(31)
■	75.1 to 86.3	(87)
■	66.8 to 75.1	(311)
■	58.5 to 66.8	(914)
■	48.1 to 58.5	(1704)
■	0 to 48.1	(949)

□ County/District Boundries
□ Regional Boundries

0   40   80
Kilometers

The dependency ratio is the population aged 65+ (primarily retired population) and the population aged 0-14 (children) expressed as a percentage of the population aged 15-64 (the most economically active age groups). High values indicate areas of relatively high percentages of less economically active population. Overall, the Republic value was 48% in 2001/02 compared with 58% in the North showing a potentially more economically active population in the South. The maps of the geographic distribution of the dependency ratio in 2001/02 (16.2 and 16.3) appear to be relatively uninteresting with lower values being found in the inner city areas of the South although there are some large differences between individual values across the island. The change maps however, present

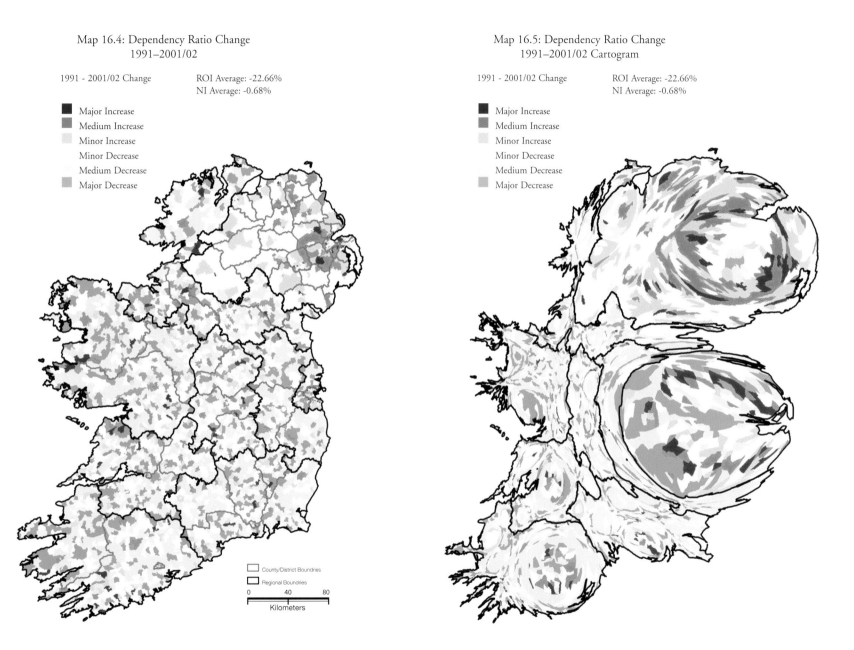

Map 16.4: Dependency Ratio Change
1991–2001/02

1991 - 2001/02 Change   ROI Average: -22.66%
                         NI Average: -0.68%

■ Major Increase
■ Medium Increase
□ Minor Increase
  Minor Decrease
  Medium Decrease
■ Major Decrease

Map 16.5: Dependency Ratio Change
1991–2001/02 Cartogram

1991 - 2001/02 Change   ROI Average: -22.66%
                         NI Average: -0.68%

■ Major Increase
■ Medium Increase
□ Minor Increase
  Minor Decrease
  Medium Decrease
■ Major Decrease

County/District Boundries
Regional Boundries

0   40   80
Kilometers

a very different picture with a large difference between Northern Ireland and the Republic. Generally, many areas in the North are experiencing medium to major increases in the dependency ratio whereas many areas in the South are experiencing medium to major decreases. The overall change in the North is a slight decrease of 0.7% whereas the overall change in the Republic is a major decrease of almost 23%.

YOUTH DEPENDENCY RATE

Map 17.1: Young Dependency Ratio 1991

Young Dependency Ratio   ROI Average: 43
                                      NI Average: 39

■	58.1 plus	(338)
■	50 to 58.1	(909)
■	44 to 50	(987)
■	37.4 to 44	(836)
■	28.2 to 37.4	(6.3)
	3.9 to 28.2	(307)

Map 17.2: Young Dependency Ratio 2001/02

Young Dependency Ratio   ROI Average: 31
                                      NI Average: 37

■	58.1 plus	(20)
■	50 to 58.1	(58)
■	44 to 50	(273)
■	37.4 to 44	(914)
■	28.2 to 37.4	(1930)
	0 to 28.2	(801)

Map 17.3: Young Dependency Ratio 2001/02
Cartogram

Young Dependency Ratio   ROI Average: 31
                                      NI Average: 37

■	58.1 plus	(20)
■	50 to 58.1	(58)
■	44 to 50	(273)
■	37.4 to 44	(914)
■	28.2 to 37.4	(1930)
	0 to 28.2	(801)

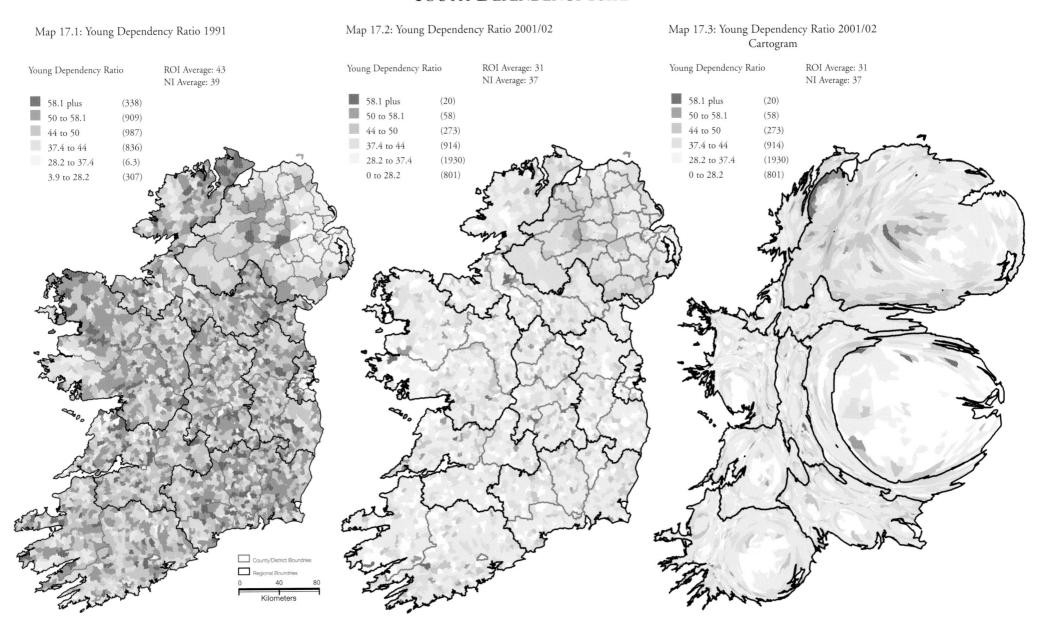

County/District Boundries

Regional Boundries

0   40   80

Kilometers

The youth dependency ratio is the population aged 0-14 (children) expressed as a percentage of the population aged 15-64 (the most economically active age groups). High values indicate areas of relatively high percentages of children compared to those in the workforce. Overall, the Republic value was 31% in 2001/02 compared with 37% in Northern Ireland showing a generally greater ratio of children to economically active age groups in the North compared to the South. The maps of the geographic distribution of this variable in 2001/02 (17.2 and 17.3) indicate that there is little

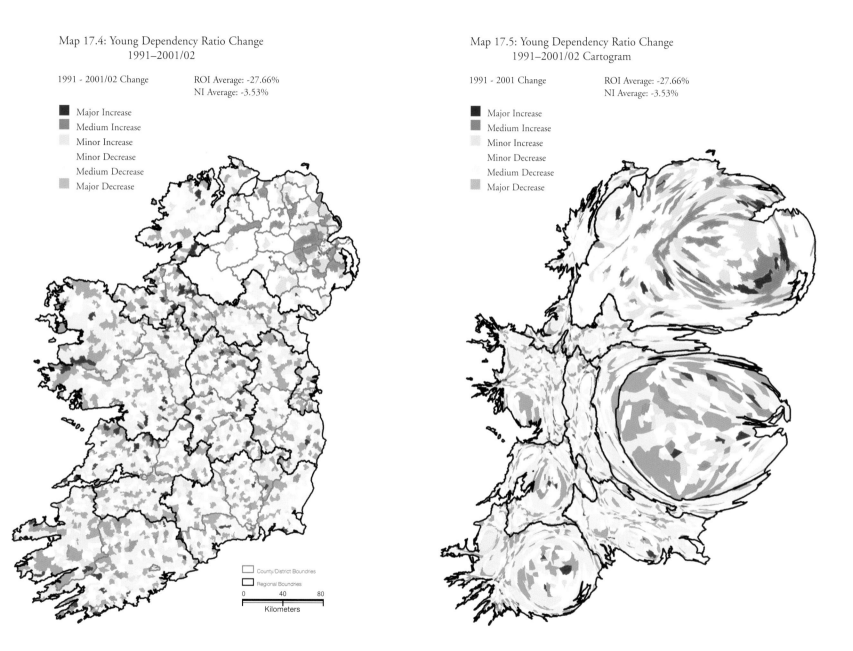

Map 17.4: Young Dependency Ratio Change
1991–2001/02

1991 - 2001/02 Change

ROI Average: -27.66%
NI Average: -3.53%

- ■ Major Increase
- ■ Medium Increase
- ☐ Minor Increase
- Minor Decrease
- Medium Decrease
- ■ Major Decrease

County/District Boundries

Regional Boundries

0   40   80

Kilometers

Map 17.5: Young Dependency Ratio Change
1991–2001/02 Cartogram

1991 - 2001 Change

ROI Average: -27.66%
NI Average: -3.53%

- ■ Major Increase
- ■ Medium Increase
- ☐ Minor Increase
- Minor Decrease
- Medium Decrease
- ■ Major Decrease

geographic variability in this ratio although slightly lower values tend to be found in the inner city areas of the Republic. The change maps in 17.4 and 17.5, however, show a marked difference between the North and South with many areas in Northern Ireland experiencing medium or major increases in this ratio and the Republic generally experiencing decreases. The average change in the North was -3.6% but in the South it was -28%.

OLD DEPENDENCY RATE

Map 18.1: Old Dependency Ratio 1991

Old Dependency Ratio

ROI Average: 18
NI Average: 20

■	38.6 plus	(249)
■	29.5 to 38.6	(644)
▨	23.8 to 29.5	(871)
▨	18.6 to 23.8	(992)
▨	12.6 to 18.6	(829)
▨	0.6 to 12.6	(395)

Map 18.2: Old Dependency Ratio 2001/02

Old Dependency Ratio

ROI Average: 16
NI Average: 21

■	38.6 plus	(101)
■	29.5 to 38.6	(367)
▨	23.8 to 29.5	(713)
▨	18.6 to 23.8	(1138)
▨	12.6 to 18.6	(1174)
▨	0 to 12.6	(503)

Map 18.3: Old Dependency Ratio 2001/02
Cartogram

Old Dependency Ratio

ROI Average: 16
NI Average: 21

■	38.6 plus	(101)
■	29.5 to 38.6	(367)
▨	23.8 to 29.5	(713)
▨	18.6 to 23.8	(1138)
▨	12.6 to 18.6	(1174)
▨	0 to 12.6	(503)

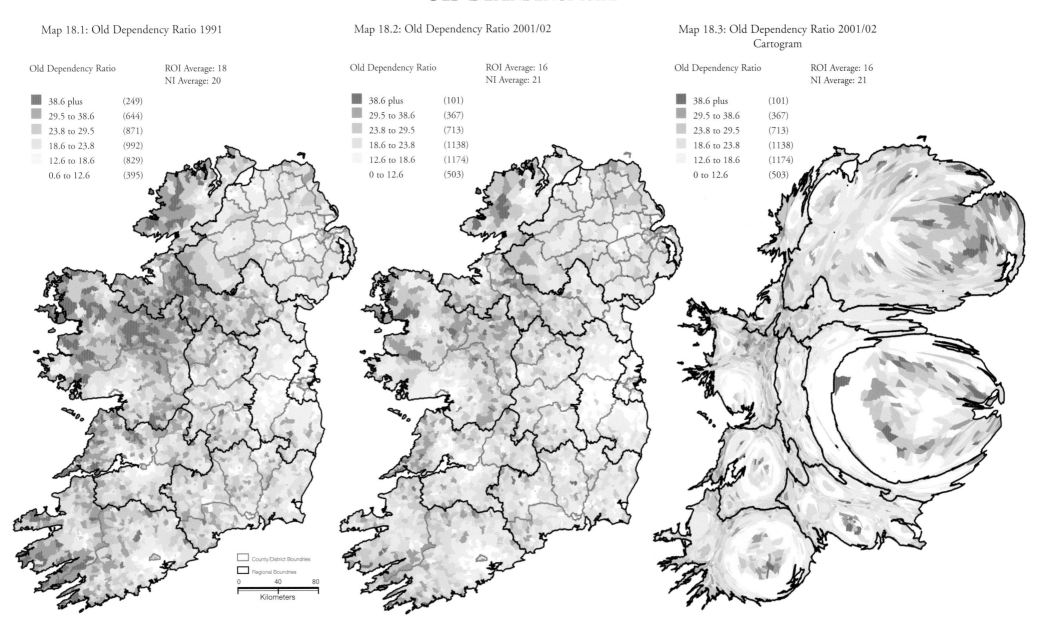

County/District Boundries
Regional Boundries

0   40   80
Kilometers

The old dependency ratio is the population aged 65+ (primarily retired population) expressed as a percentage of the population aged 15-64 (the most economically active age groups). High values indicate areas of relatively high percentages of older, less economically active population. Overall, the Republic value was 16% in 2001/02 compared with 21% in Northern Ireland showing a generally greater ratio of elderly to economically active people in the North than South. The maps of the geographic distribution of this variable in 2001/02 (18.2 and 18.3) are interesting as the traditional land-based map (Map 18.2) depicts high values being associated with more rural areas but the cartogram (Map 18.3) demonstrates that the highest values are found in the inner suburbs of the major cities;

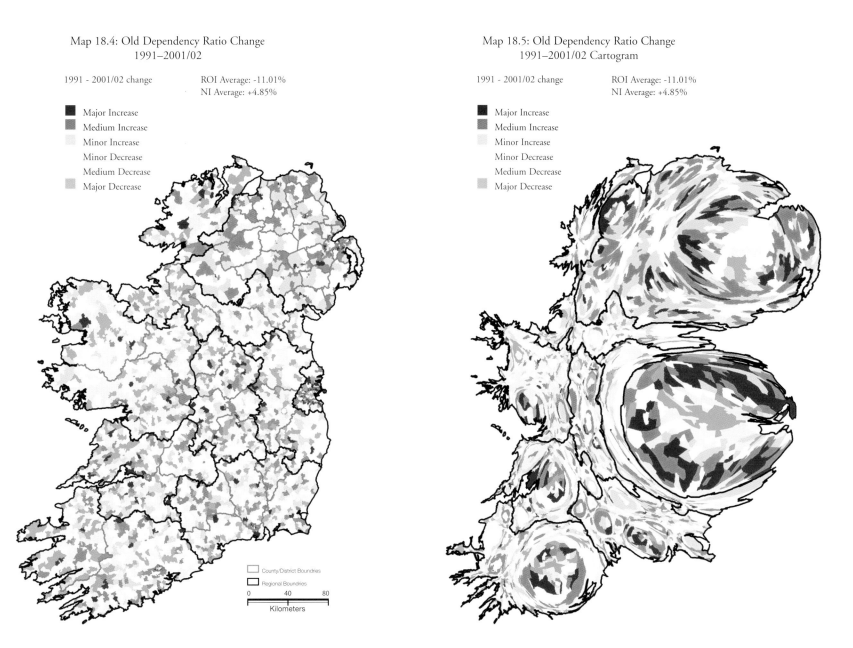

Map 18.4: Old Dependency Ratio Change
1991–2001/02

1991 - 2001/02 change ROI Average: -11.01%
NI Average: +4.85%

■ Major Increase
▨ Medium Increase
▨ Minor Increase
Minor Decrease
Medium Decrease
▨ Major Decrease

Map 18.5: Old Dependency Ratio Change
1991–2001/02 Cartogram

1991 - 2001/02 change ROI Average: -11.01%
NI Average: +4.85%

■ Major Increase
▨ Medium Increase
Minor Increase
Minor Decrease
Medium Decrease
Major Decrease

☐ County/District Boundries
☐ Regional Boundries

0   40   80
Kilometers

this detail being lost in the land-based map. The change maps (Maps 18.4 and 18.5 show that the old dependency ratios in Northern Ireland tend to be increasing whereas they tend to be decreasing in the Republic. The exception to this is in the outer suburban areas of the major cities in the South where there are major increases in the old dependency ratio. Overall, the Republic experienced an 11% drop in this ratio whereas Northern Ireland experienced a 4.9% increase.

FERTILLITY RATE

Map 19.1: Fertility Rate Ratio 1991

Fertility Ratio

ROI Average: 352
NI Average: 374

■	555 plus	(325)
■	453 to 555	(750)
■	384 to 453	(974)
■	320 to 384	(941)
□	237 to 320	(692)
□	0 to 237	(298)

Map 19.2: Fertility Rate Ratio 2001/02

Fertility Ratio

ROI Average: 305
NI Average: 325

■	555 plus	(92)
■	453 to 555	(297)
■	384 to 453	(753)
■	320 to 384	(1189)
□	237 to 320	(1138)
□	0 to 237	(527)

Map 19.3: Fertility Rate Ratio 2001/02
Cartogram

Fertility Ratio

ROI Average: 305
NI Average: 325

■	555 plus	(92)
■	453 to 555	(297)
■	384 to 453	(753)
■	320 to 384	(1189)
□	237 to 320	(1138)
□	0 to 237	(527)

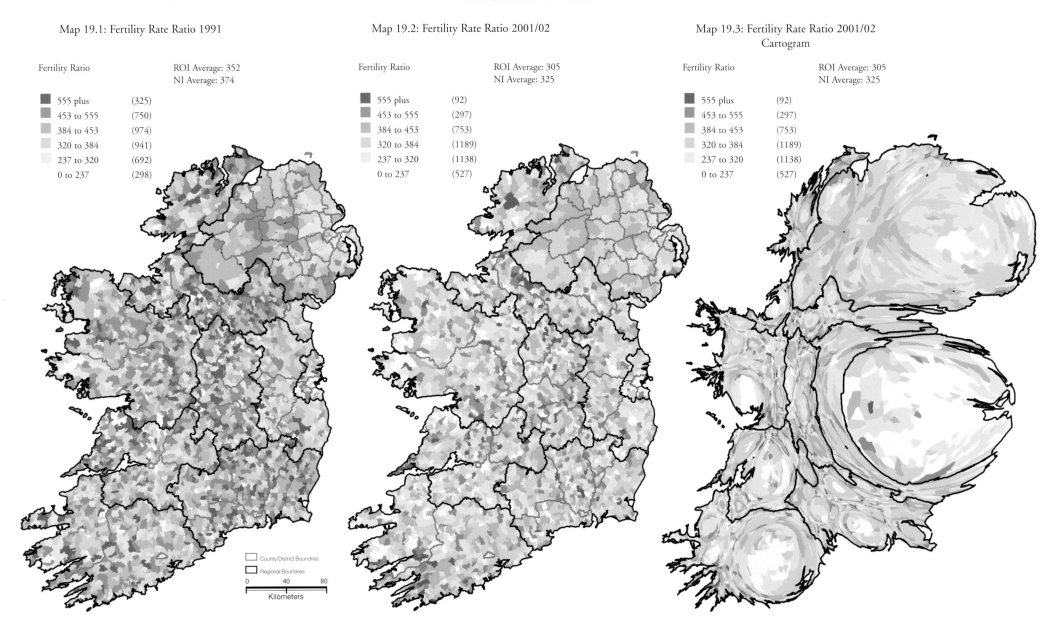

County/District Boundries
Regional Boundries

0   40   80
Kilometers

The overall fertility ratio is calculated as the number of children aged 0 to 4 per 1,000 females between the ages of 15 and 44. The overall ratio for the South in 1991 (352) was slightly lower than the North (374) (Map 19.1). By 2001/02 the fertility ratio had declined in both jurisdictions (South 305, North 325) though the relative difference between North and South remained constant (Map 19.2). This decline reflects a general reduction in overall fertility as more couples decided not to have children and those that did had less. The rate of decline at a little over 13% was almost identical in both North and South (Map 19.4) though this rate was variable across the island. Spatially the ratios were generally higher in rural areas and lower in urban settings while the overall decline was

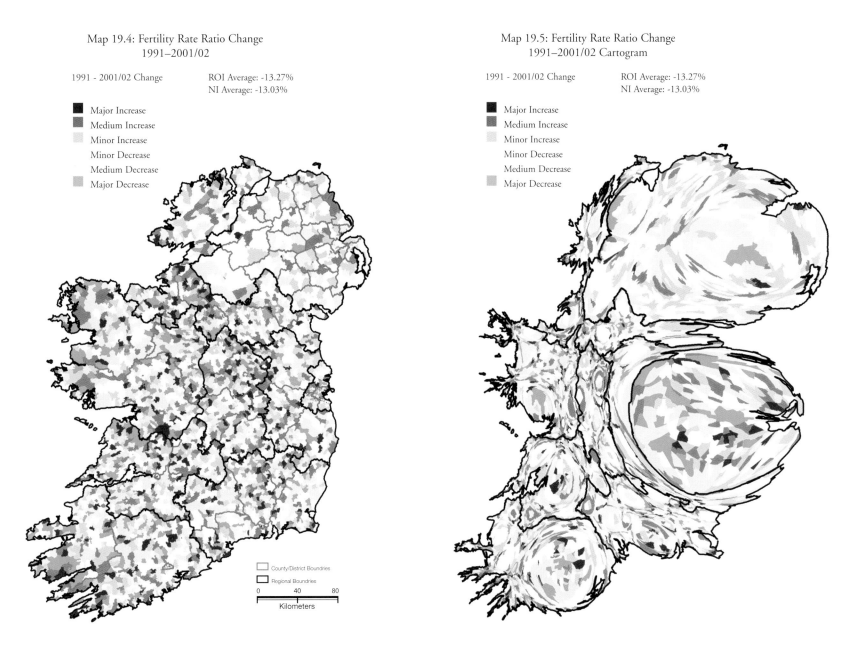

Map 19.4: Fertility Rate Ratio Change
1991–2001/02

1991 - 2001/02 Change   ROI Average: -13.27%
                          NI Average: -13.03%

■ Major Increase
■ Medium Increase
  Minor Increase
  Minor Decrease
  Medium Decrease
  Major Decrease

Map 19.5: Fertility Rate Ratio Change
1991–2001/02 Cartogram

1991 - 2001/02 Change   ROI Average: -13.27%
                          NI Average: -13.03%

■ Major Increase
■ Medium Increase
  Minor Increase
  Minor Decrease
  Medium Decrease
  Major Decrease

County/District Boundries
Regional Boundries

0   40   80
Kilometers

reflected in the much smaller numbers of DEDs/wards with rates over 453 (declining from 1075 in 1991 to 389 in 2001/02). Despite the overall pattern of decline between 1991 and 2001/02, there were also a number of areas which recorded significant increases. The cartogram (Map 19.5) suggests that this pattern is quite mixed, although a weak pattern of increase is visible around the periphery of urban centres.

MARRIED FERTILITY RATE

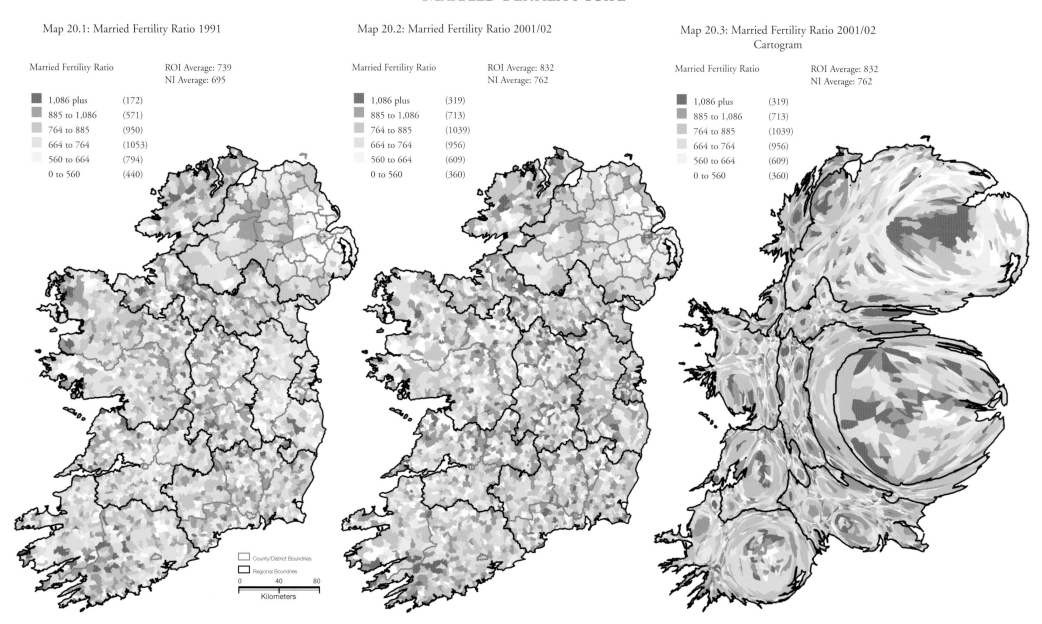

Map 20.1: Married Fertility Ratio 1991

Married Fertility Ratio

ROI Average: 739
NI Average: 695

■	1,086 plus	(172)
■	885 to 1,086	(571)
▨	764 to 885	(950)
▨	664 to 764	(1053)
▨	560 to 664	(794)
□	0 to 560	(440)

Map 20.2: Married Fertility Ratio 2001/02

Married Fertility Ratio

ROI Average: 832
NI Average: 762

■	1,086 plus	(319)
■	885 to 1,086	(713)
▨	764 to 885	(1039)
▨	664 to 764	(956)
▨	560 to 664	(609)
□	0 to 560	(360)

Map 20.3: Married Fertility Ratio 2001/02
Cartogram

Married Fertility Ratio

ROI Average: 832
NI Average: 762

■	1,086 plus	(319)
■	885 to 1,086	(713)
▨	764 to 885	(1039)
▨	664 to 764	(956)
▨	560 to 664	(609)
□	0 to 560	(360)

County/District Boundries
Regional Boundries

0   40   80
Kilometers

The geography of married fertility patterns (Map 20.1) differs slightly from that for overall fertility in that higher values in rural areas were replicated in urban settings. More significantly the rates (this time expressed as the number of children aged 0 to 4 per 1,000 married females aged 15 to 44) were almost twice as high as for overall fertility in both jurisdictions. The average rate was higher in the South than in the North for both 1991 (739 to 695) and 2001/02 (832 to 762) with this gap increasing slightly (Map 20.2). The change between the two periods shows a significant increase, again slightly higher in the Republic at 12.59% as opposed to 9.7% in the North. Despite the increasing number of people co-habiting and giving birth out of wedlock, it appears that the association

Map 20.4: Married Fertility Ratio Change
1991–2001/02

1991 - 2001/02 Change

ROI Average: +12.59%
NI Average: +9.70%

- ■ Major Increase
- ▨ Medium Increase
- ▨ Minor Increase
- Minor Decrease
- Medium Decrease
- ▨ Major Decrease

Map 20.5: Married Fertility Ratio Change
1991–2001/02 Cartogram

1991 - 2001/02 Change

ROI Average: +12.59%
NI Average: +9.70%

- ■ Major Increase
- ▨ Medium Increase
- ▨ Minor Increase
- Minor Decrease
- Medium Decrease
- ▨ Major Decrease

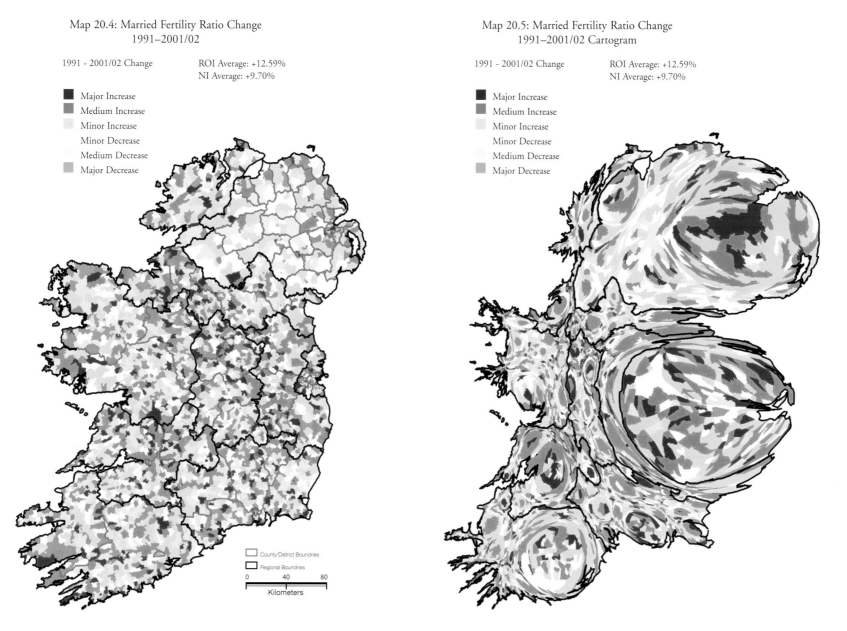

County/District Boundries
Regional Boundries

0   40   80
Kilometers

between marriage and fertility remains strong. While it is difficult to pick out any clear pattern of change from the standard choropleth map (Map 20.4), the cartogram (Map 20.5) shows that the areas with the greatest increase included inner-city Belfast and the inner suburbs of Dublin and Cork. This may reflect immigration into inner city areas and the increase in new immigrant families. Where decrease in married fertility existed, it seemed to be primarily in rural areas.

MARRIED PERSONS AS A PERCENTAGE OF TOTAL POPULATION

Map 21.1: % Married 1991

% Married - 15/16 plus

ROI Average: 51.43%
NI Average: 58.10%

■	58 plus	(775)
■	53 to 58	(1241)
■	50 to 53	(888)
■	47 to 50	(470)
□	40 to 47	(442)
□	9 to 40	(164)

Map 21.2: % Married 2001/02

% Married - 15/16 plus

ROI Average: 47.07
NI Average: 51.12

■	58 plus	(437)
■	53 to 58	(1166)
■	50 to 53	(869)
■	47 to 50	(621)
□	40 to 47	(574)
□	9 to 40	(329)

Map 21.3: % Married 2001/02 cartogram

% Married - 15/16 plus

ROI Average: 47.07
NI Average: 51.12

■	58 plus	(437)
■	53 to 58	(1166)
■	50 to 53	(869)
■	47 to 50	(621)
□	40 to 47	(574)
□	9 to 40	(329)

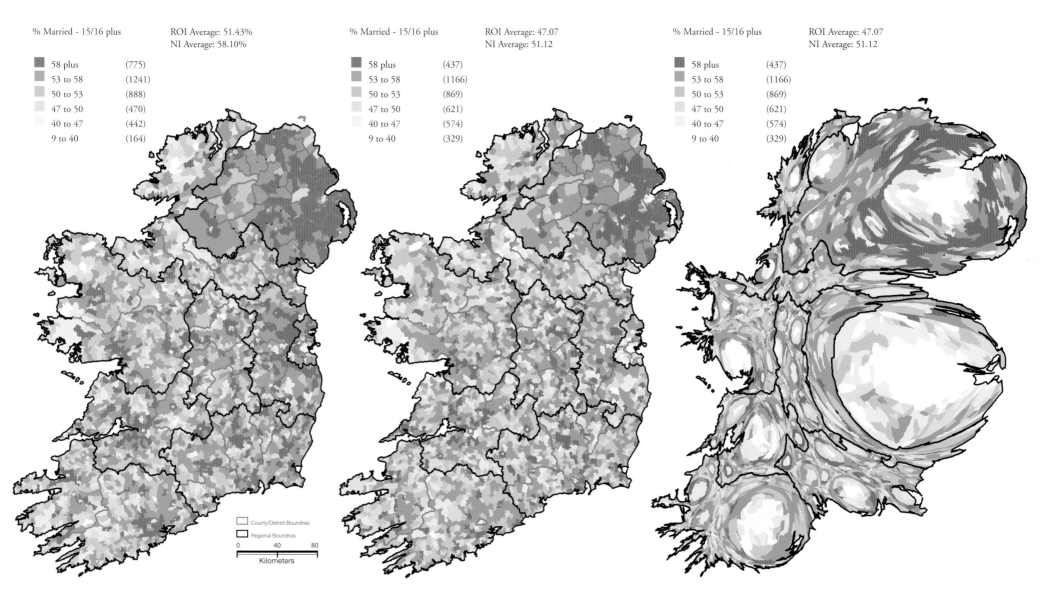

County/District Boundries
Regional Boundries

0   40   80
Kilometers

The maps for the percentage of the population who are married seem to show strong suburban and commuting belt geographies (Map 21.1 and Map 21.2). The converse was also true whereby marriage rates were lower in city centres and remoter rural areas that reflected the younger and older demographic mixes respectively of those areas. The rates were higher in both periods in the North, though the gap at 6.67% in 1991 had reduced to 4.05% in 2001/02. More generally the figures did show an overall decline in this period which may reflect wider reductions in married proportions against those cohabiting and divorced. The figures for the inner city parts of Belfast, Dublin and other cities such as Galway and Derry were consistently low (Map 21.3). Changes between 1991 and

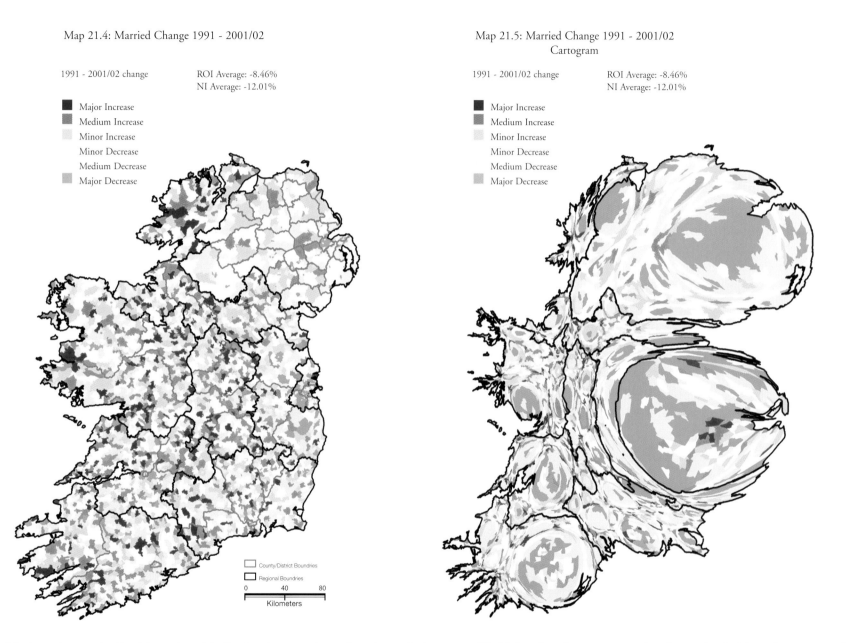

Map 21.4: Married Change 1991 - 2001/02

1991 - 2001/02 change

ROI Average: -8.46%
NI Average: -12.01%

■ Major Increase
▨ Medium Increase
□ Minor Increase
Minor Decrease
Medium Decrease
▨ Major Decrease

County/District Boundries

Regional Boundries

0   40   80
Kilometers

Map 21.5: Married Change 1991 - 2001/02
Cartogram

1991 - 2001/02 change

ROI Average: -8.46%
NI Average: -12.01%

■ Major Increase
▨ Medium Increase
□ Minor Increase
Minor Decrease
Medium Decrease
▨ Major Decrease

2001/02 exhibited an urban-rural split with continued decline in urban areas (apart from the south city centre of Dublin) and any increases were primarily associated with rural settings. Declines were also noted in the suburban edges of most of the remaining cities and small towns (Map 21.5). This may have been associated with younger, less traditional populations where cohabitation is initially preferred to marriage.

SINGLE, SEPARATED, WIDOWED AND DIVORCED PERSONS AS A PERCENTAGE OF TOTAL POPULATION

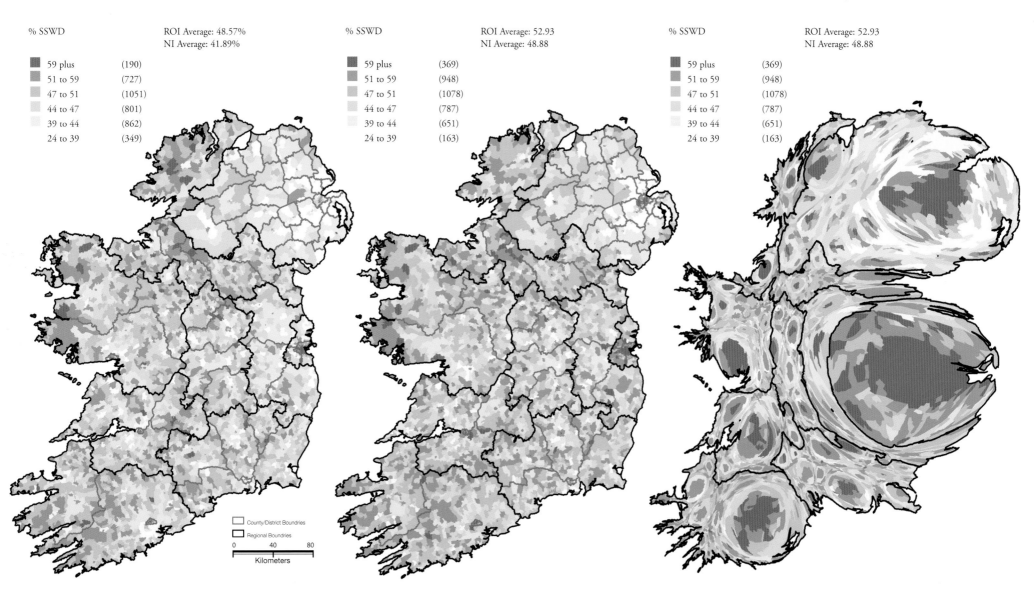

Map 22.1: % SSWD 1991

% SSWD

ROI Average: 48.57%
NI Average: 41.89%

■	59 plus	(190)
■	51 to 59	(727)
■	47 to 51	(1051)
■	44 to 47	(801)
■	39 to 44	(862)
■	24 to 39	(349)

Map 22.2: % SSWD 2001/02

% SSWD

ROI Average: 52.93
NI Average: 48.88

■	59 plus	(369)
■	51 to 59	(948)
■	47 to 51	(1078)
■	44 to 47	(787)
■	39 to 44	(651)
■	24 to 39	(163)

Map 22.3: % SSWD 2001/02 Cartogram

% SSWD

ROI Average: 52.93
NI Average: 48.88

■	59 plus	(369)
■	51 to 59	(948)
■	47 to 51	(1078)
■	44 to 47	(787)
■	39 to 44	(651)
■	24 to 39	(163)

County/District Boundries

Regional Boundries

0   40   80
Kilometers

In contrast to the maps of the proportion of population married, one would expect to see the opposite pattern in the maps of the percentages of the population who were single, separated, widowed or divorced. This was indeed the case with the highest clustering of single, separated, widowed and divorced residents in the inner urban areas. This was best exemplified in Map 22.3 where the cartogram vividly highlights those concentrations. There were pockets of higher percentages in rural areas and one of the dangers of an amalgamated category such as this is that quite separate patterns are aggregated together. It was also not unreasonable to assume that concentrations in rural areas are more associated with high percentages of the widowed within the wider category. As the previous set of

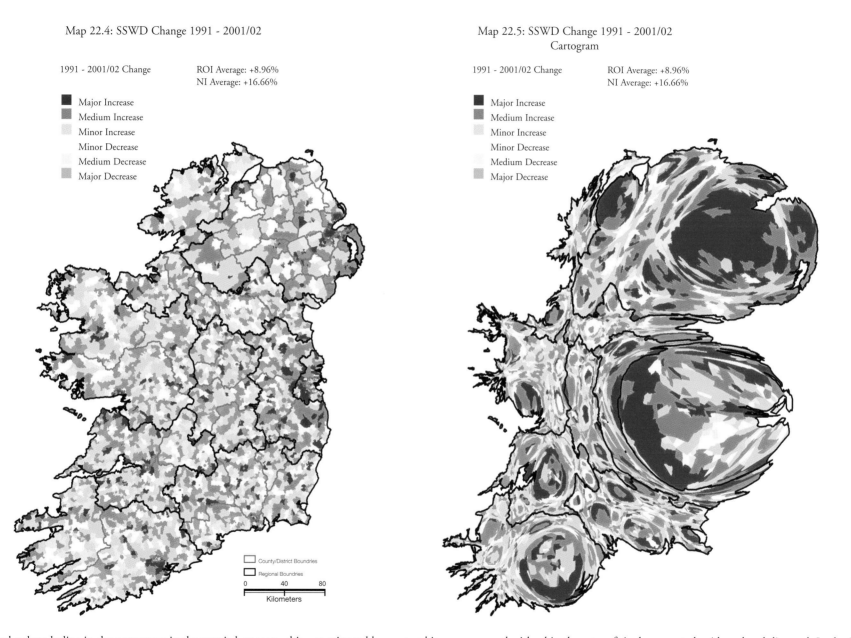

Map 22.4: SSWD Change 1991 - 2001/02

1991 - 2001/02 Change

ROI Average: +8.96%
NI Average: +16.66%

■ Major Increase
■ Medium Increase
□ Minor Increase
Minor Decrease
Medium Decrease
■ Major Decrease

County/District Boundries
Regional Boundries

0   40   80
Kilometers

Map 22.5: SSWD Change 1991 - 2001/02
Cartogram

1991 - 2001/02 Change

ROI Average: +8.96%
NI Average: +16.66%

■ Major Increase
■ Medium Increase
□ Minor Increase
Minor Decrease
Medium Decrease
■ Major Decrease

maps reflected a slow decline in the percentage in the married category, this was mirrored by a general increase across the island in the rates of single, separated, widowed and divorced. In the South there was an increase from 48.57% to 52.93% between 1991 and 2002 while in the North the figures were lower in 1991 at 41.89% but were catching up fast by 2001 with an average rate of 48.88%. This was also confirmed by the change maps (Map 22.4 and Map 22.5) where the rate of increase in the North was, at 16.66%, well above the rate of 8.96% in the South. In Belfast and Derry this was a feature of inner city areas whereas the pattern was more dispersed in the Southern cities.

ROMAN CATHOLICS AS A PERCENTAGE OF TOTAL POPULATION

Map 23.1: % Catholic 1991

Map 23.2: % Catholic 2001/02

Map 23.3: % Catholic 2001/02 Cartogram

% Roman Catholics

ROI Average: 91.60%
NI Average: 38.40%

	% Roman Catholics	
	95 plus	(1328)
	90 to 95	(1296)
	81 to 90	(635)
	60 to 81	(288)
	26 to 60	(176)
	0 to 26	(257)

% Roman Catholics

ROI Average: 88.40%
NI Average: 40.25%

	% Roman Catholics	
	95 plus	(779)
	90 to 95	(1436)
	81 to 90	(927)
	60 to 81	(416)
	26 to 60	(186)
	0 to 26	(252)

% Roman Catholics

ROI Average: 88.40%
NI Average: 40.25%

	% Roman Catholics	
	95 plus	(779)
	90 to 95	(1436)
	81 to 90	(927)
	60 to 81	(416)
	26 to 60	(186)
	0 to 26	(252)

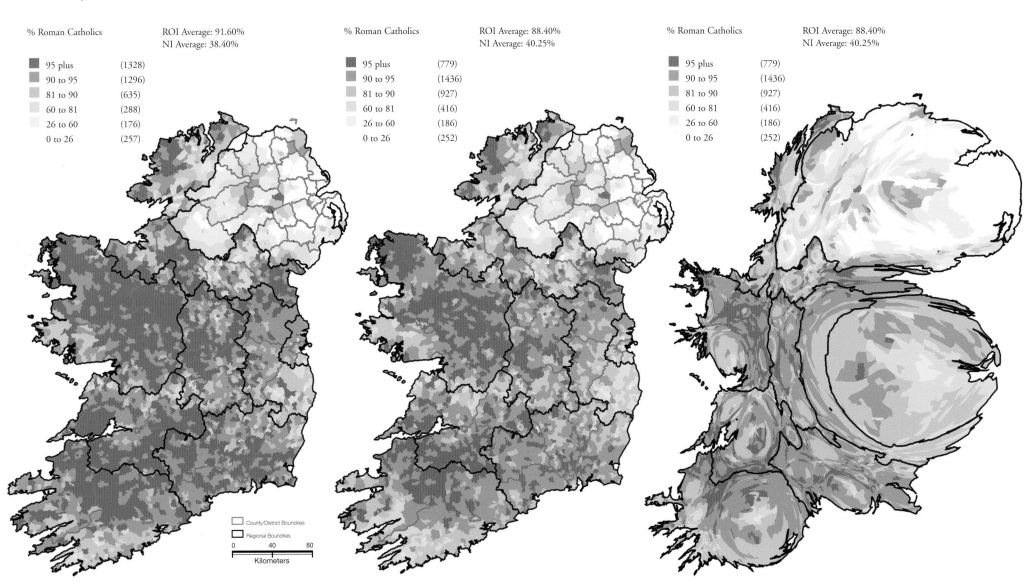

County/District Boundries
Regional Boundries

0   40   80
Kilometers

The most obvious characteristic of Maps 23.1 and 23.2 is the difference between Northern Ireland and the Republic of Ireland, with consistently higher proportions of Catholics in the South. In the North, the well known east-west differential, with a predominantly Catholic west and predominantly Protestant east, is notable. The smallest Catholic percentages in the Republic of Ireland include parts of the extreme south west, south of Dublin and close to the border with Northern Ireland. The cartogram (Map 23.3) indicates clearly the predominantly Protestant east of Northern Ireland and the comparatively small proportion of Catholics in Dublin. The cartograms of absolute and relative change (Maps 23.4 and 23.5) represent only ten years of change, and the figures are generally small.

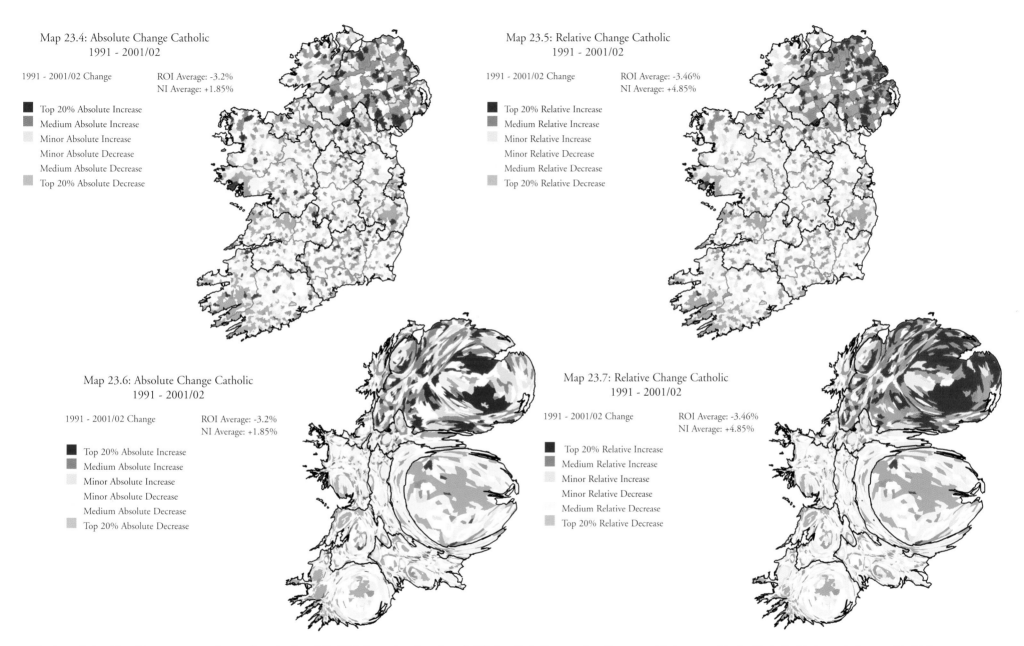

Map 23.4: Absolute Change Catholic
1991 - 2001/02

1991 - 2001/02 Change   ROI Average: -3.2%
                               NI Average: +1.85%

■ Top 20% Absolute Increase
▨ Medium Absolute Increase
░ Minor Absolute Increase
  Minor Absolute Decrease
  Medium Absolute Decrease
▨ Top 20% Absolute Decrease

Map 23.5: Relative Change Catholic
1991 - 2001/02

1991 - 2001/02 Change   ROI Average: -3.46%
                               NI Average: +4.85%

■ Top 20% Relative Increase
▨ Medium Relative Increase
░ Minor Relative Increase
  Minor Relative Decrease
  Medium Relative Decrease
▨ Top 20% Relative Decrease

Map 23.6: Absolute Change Catholic
1991 - 2001/02

1991 - 2001/02 Change   ROI Average: -3.2%
                               NI Average: +1.85%

■ Top 20% Absolute Increase
▨ Medium Absolute Increase
░ Minor Absolute Increase
  Minor Absolute Decrease
  Medium Absolute Decrease
▨ Top 20% Absolute Decrease

Map 23.7: Relative Change Catholic
1991 - 2001/02

1991 - 2001/02 Change   ROI Average: -3.46%
                               NI Average: +4.85%

■ Top 20% Relative Increase
▨ Medium Relative Increase
░ Minor Relative Increase
  Minor Relative Decrease
  Medium Relative Decrease
▨ Top 20% Relative Decrease

Northern Ireland is subject to greater change than the Republic. This is partly a function of differing Catholic as against Protestant birth rates, with the Catholic birth rate being notably higher.
In addition, the decline in religious identity is a bigger factor in the Protestant community than in the Catholic community (this assertion is supported by a range of recent surveys). Changes to the
religious composition in the South in recent years are partly a function of immigration, with a growing proportion of, for example, Muslims and Orthodox Christians.

PERSONS IN PRINCIPLE PROTESTANT DENOMINATIONS

Map 24.1: % Protestant and Others 1991

% Protestant Denominations & Others

ROI Average: 4.20%
NI Average: 50.60%

	41 plus	(377)
	12 to 41	(385)
	4 to 12	(888)
	3 to 4	(332)
	1 to 3	(1072)
	0 to 1	(926)

Map 24.2: % Protestant and Others 2001/02

% Protestant Denominations & Others

ROI Average: 6.10%
NI Average: 45.80%

	41 plus	(368)
	12 to 41	(462)
	4 to 12	(1425)
	3 to 4	(493)
	1 to 3	(988)
	0 to 1	(260)

Map 24.3: % Protestant and Others 2001/02 Cartogram

% Protestant Denominations & Others

ROI Average: 6.10%
NI Average: 45.80%

	41 plus	(368)
	12 to 41	(462)
	4 to 12	(1425)
	3 to 4	(493)
	1 to 3	(988)
	0 to 1	(260)

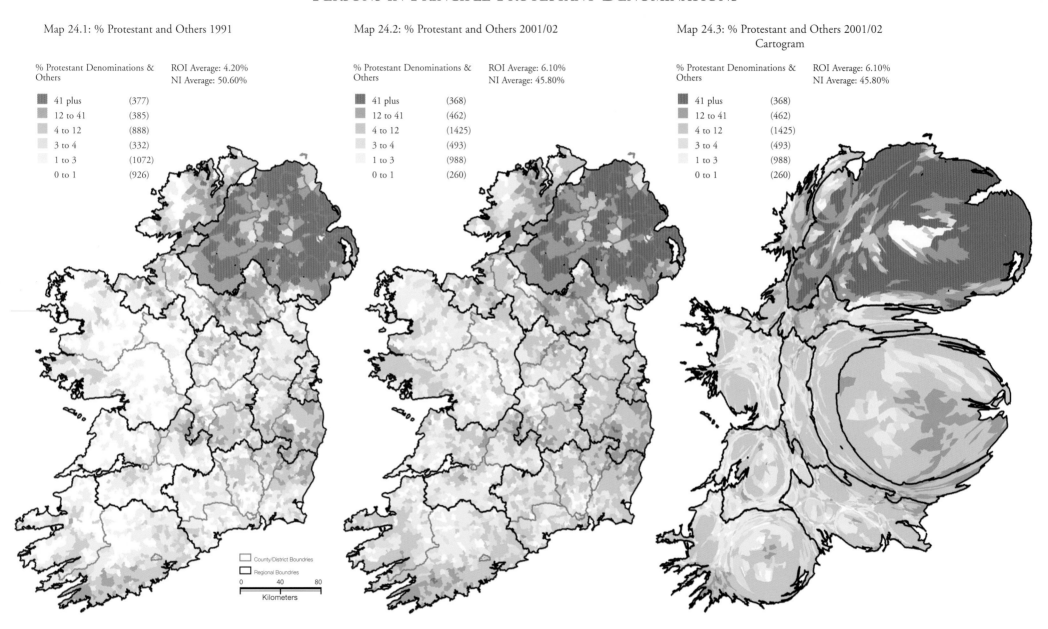

County/District Boundries
Regional Boundries

0   40   80
Kilometers

Map 24.1 is largely the reverse of the 1991 map of Catholics (Map 23.1), given that the population comprises almost exclusively Catholics or members of some Protestant denomination. Northern Ireland (and to some degree other parts of the north of Ireland) clearly stands apart from the rest of the island. In parts of the west coast of the Republic of Ireland, the Protestant population is very small indeed. There is very little change between 1991 and 2001/02, however there is a greater proportion of individuals who did not subscribe to any religion in 2001/02 than 1991. The cartogram, by highlighting religion with respect to population density, increases the contrast between the North and South. The cartogram of absolute change, shows that there are a number of areas in Northern

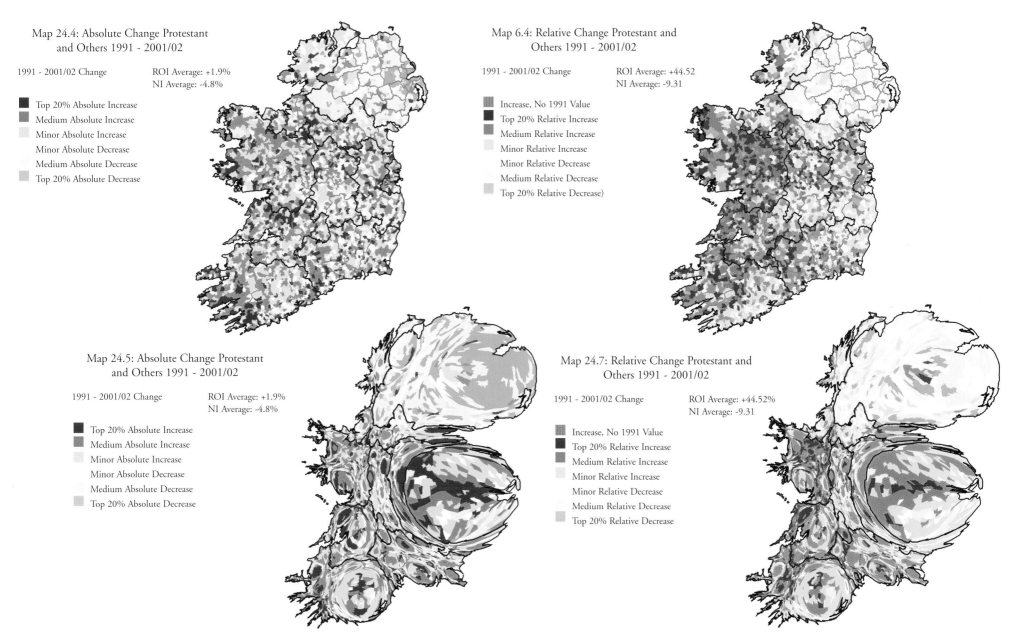

Map 24.4: Absolute Change Protestant
and Others 1991 - 2001/02

1991 - 2001/02 Change

ROI Average: +1.9%
NI Average: -4.8%

■ Top 20% Absolute Increase
▨ Medium Absolute Increase
▧ Minor Absolute Increase
Minor Absolute Decrease
Medium Absolute Decrease
▧ Top 20% Absolute Decrease

Map 6.4: Relative Change Protestant and
Others 1991 - 2001/02

1991 - 2001/02 Change

ROI Average: +44.52
NI Average: -9.31

▨ Increase, No 1991 Value
■ Top 20% Relative Increase
▨ Medium Relative Increase
▧ Minor Relative Increase
Minor Relative Decrease
Medium Relative Decrease
▧ Top 20% Relative Decrease)

Map 24.5: Absolute Change Protestant
and Others 1991 - 2001/02

1991 - 2001/02 Change

ROI Average: +1.9%
NI Average: -4.8%

■ Top 20% Absolute Increase
▨ Medium Absolute Increase
▧ Minor Absolute Increase
Minor Absolute Decrease
Medium Absolute Decrease
▧ Top 20% Absolute Decrease

Map 24.7: Relative Change Protestant and
Others 1991 - 2001/02

1991 - 2001/02 Change

ROI Average: +44.52%
NI Average: -9.31

▨ Increase, No 1991 Value
■ Top 20% Relative Increase
▨ Medium Relative Increase
▧ Minor Relative Increase
Minor Relative Decrease
Medium Relative Decrease
▧ Top 20% Relative Decrease

Ireland where the number of Protestants has declined. In contrast, in the Republic there were fairly uniform (although small) increases in the percentage of Protestants and others. Amongst the most interesting features of the change cartograms are the DEDs in the west of Ireland which had, according to the 1991 Census, no members of Protestant denominations or other religions, but did by the time of the 2002 Census. In these same areas, there are many areas with a large relative increase in members of these groups, no doubt affected by international immigration.

PERSONS OF NO RELIGION OR NOT STATED

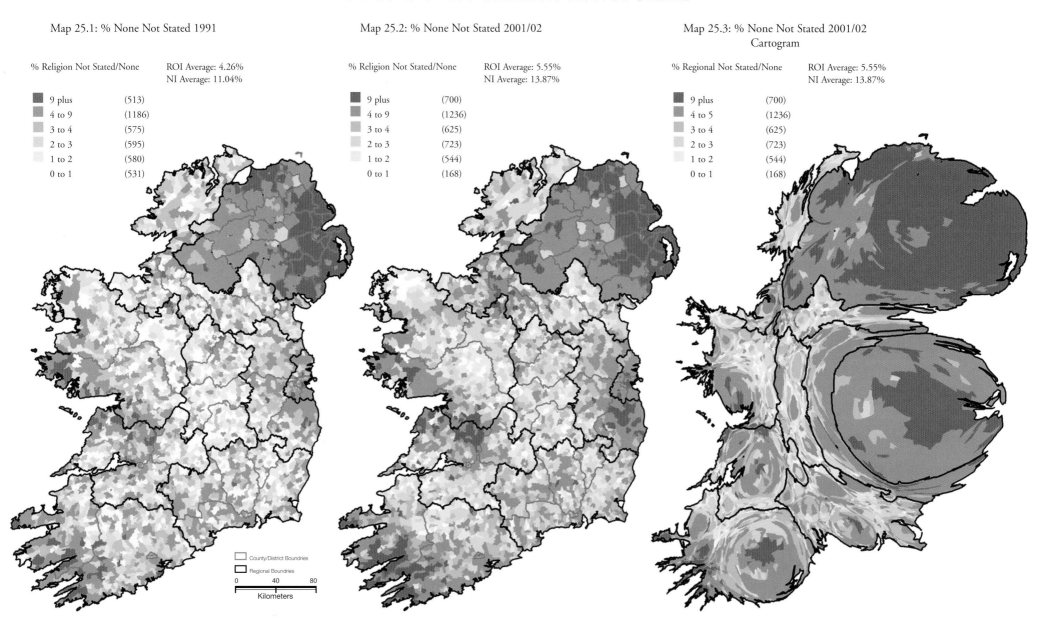

Map 25.1: % None Not Stated 1991

% Religion Not Stated/None   ROI Average: 4.26%
                                    NI Average: 11.04%

■	9 plus	(513)
■	4 to 9	(1186)
■	3 to 4	(575)
■	2 to 3	(595)
■	1 to 2	(580)
□	0 to 1	(531)

Map 25.2: % None Not Stated 2001/02

% Religion Not Stated/None   ROI Average: 5.55%
                                    NI Average: 13.87%

■	9 plus	(700)
■	4 to 9	(1236)
■	3 to 4	(625)
■	2 to 3	(723)
■	1 to 2	(544)
□	0 to 1	(168)

Map 25.3: % None Not Stated 2001/02
Cartogram

% Regional Not Stated/None   ROI Average: 5.55%
                                    NI Average: 13.87%

■	9 plus	(700)
■	4 to 5	(1236)
■	3 to 4	(625)
■	2 to 3	(723)
■	1 to 2	(544)
□	0 to 1	(168)

County/District Boundries
Regional Boundries

0   40   80
Kilometers

As with the previous maps of religion, there is a noticeable contrast between Northern Ireland and the Republic of Ireland in the numbers of people who declared no religion or did not state their religion. In Northern Ireland, there is a notable distinction between the east and west, with a larger proportion of none or not-stated religion in the east. Given that the east of Northern Ireland is predominantly Protestant, this supports the assertion that individuals with a Protestant background are less likely to label themselves as Protestants, whereas those with a Catholic background may be more likely to identify themselves as Catholics. In the South the largest concentrations of people in the 'no religion or not stated' classes are in south Dublin, the south west and the mid west.

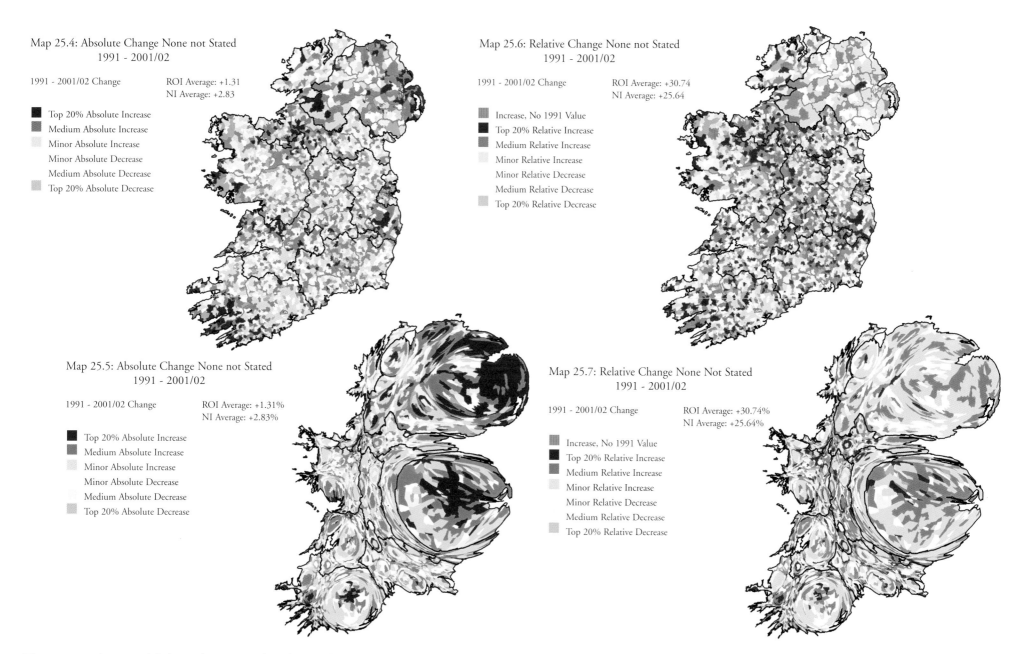

Map 25.4: Absolute Change None not Stated
1991 - 2001/02

1991 - 2001/02 Change

ROI Average: +1.31
NI Average: +2.83

■ Top 20% Absolute Increase
■ Medium Absolute Increase
  Minor Absolute Increase
  Minor Absolute Decrease
  Medium Absolute Decrease
  Top 20% Absolute Decrease

Map 25.6: Relative Change None not Stated
1991 - 2001/02

1991 - 2001/02 Change

ROI Average: +30.74
NI Average: +25.64

  Increase, No 1991 Value
■ Top 20% Relative Increase
  Medium Relative Increase
  Minor Relative Increase
  Minor Relative Decrease
  Medium Relative Decrease
  Top 20% Relative Decrease

Map 25.5: Absolute Change None not Stated
1991 - 2001/02

1991 - 2001/02 Change

ROI Average: +1.31%
NI Average: +2.83%

■ Top 20% Absolute Increase
■ Medium Absolute Increase
  Minor Absolute Increase
  Minor Absolute Decrease
  Medium Absolute Decrease
  Top 20% Absolute Decrease

Map 25.7: Relative Change None Not Stated
1991 - 2001/02

1991 - 2001/02 Change

ROI Average: +30.74%
NI Average: +25.64%

  Increase, No 1991 Value
■ Top 20% Relative Increase
  Medium Relative Increase
  Minor Relative Increase
  Minor Relative Decrease
  Medium Relative Decrease
  Top 20% Relative Decrease

The cartogram (Map 25.3) helps to demonstrate the urban/rural distinction, with more people in this class in urban areas such as Dublin, Cork and Belfast. Maps 25.4 and 25.5 highlight that change across the island is spatially variable, with little evidence of distinct regional concentrations of increase or decrease in members of these classes. However, the areas with the largest absolute increase in people with no religion or with no religion stated are large urban areas. There are many areas in the South which in 1991 had no individuals in these categories, but did in 2002, suggesting growing secularisation.

POPULATION AGED OVER THREE ABLE TO SPEAK IRISH

Map 26.1: % 3+ Speaks Irish,1991

% 3+ Speaks Irish   ROI Average: 32.6%
NI Average: 8.7%

- 51 plus   (141)
- 34 to 51   (1400)
- 28 to 34   (918)
- 21 to 28   (960)
- 10 to 21   (446)
- 0 to 10   (385)

Map 26.2: % 3+ Speaks Irish, 2001/02

% 3+ Speaks Irish   ROI Average: 41.9%
NI Average: 6.6%

- 51 plus   (634)
- 34 to 51   (2310)
- 28 to 34   (322)
- 21 to 28   (116)
- 10 to 21   (178)
- 0 to 10   (436)

Map 26.3: % 3+ Speaks Irish, 2001/02
Cartogram

% 3+ Speaks Irish   ROI Average: 41.9%
NI Average: 6.6%

- 51 plus   (634)
- 34 to 51   (2310)
- 28 to 34   (322)
- 21 to 28   (116)
- 10 to 21   (178)
- 0 to 10   (436)

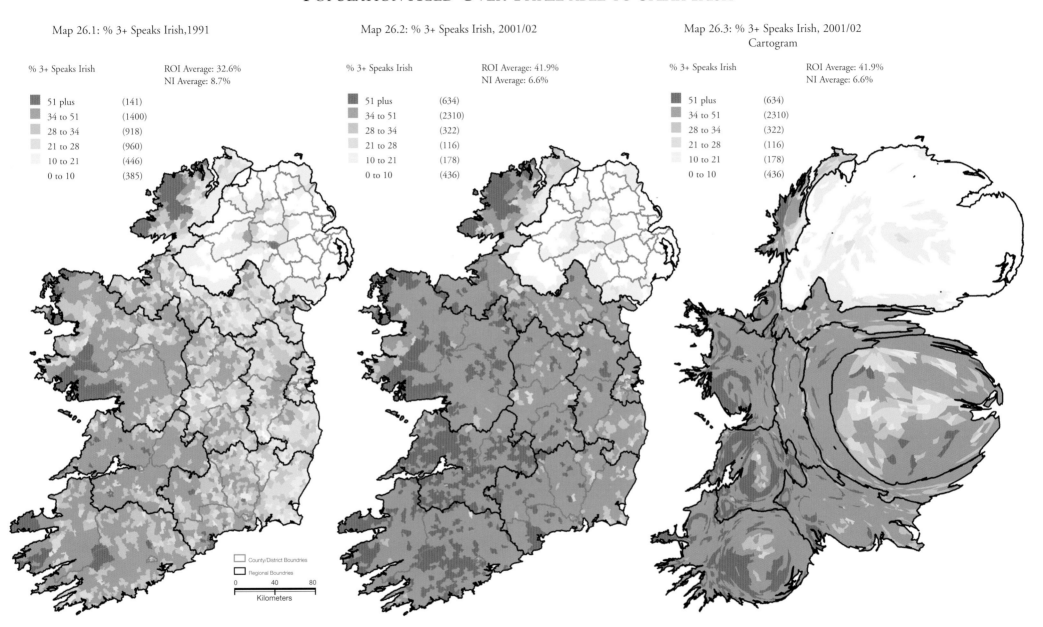

County/District Boundries
Regional Boundries

0   40   80
Kilometers

In Maps 26.1 and 26.2, predictably there is a clear distinction between those speaking Irish in the Republic of Ireland and Northern Ireland, and between the predominantly rural west and the east. Gaeltacht areas such as west County Donegal, west County Mayo, west County Galway and County Kerry are clearly identifiable. There is some evidence of a greater proportion of Irish speakers in Northern Ireland near to the border with the Republic, but the numbers are still relatively low at 10-21%. The cartograms of change reveal an increase in the percentage of Irish speakers in the South

Map 26.4: Absolute Change 3+ Speaks Irish,
1991-2001/02

1991 - 2001/02 Change ROI Average: +9.3%
         NI Average: -2.1%

- Top 20% Absolute Increase
- Medium Absolute Increase
- Minor Absolute Increase
- Minor Absolute Decrease
- Medium Absolute Decrease
- Top 20% Absolute Decrease

Map 26.5: Relative Change 3+ Speaks Irish,
1991-2001/02

1991 - 2001/02 Change ROI Average: +28.5%
         NI Average: -24.1%

- Top 20% Relative Increase
- Medium RelativeIncrease
- Minor Relative Increase
- Minor Relative Decrease
- Medium RelativeDecrease
- Top 20% Relative Decrease

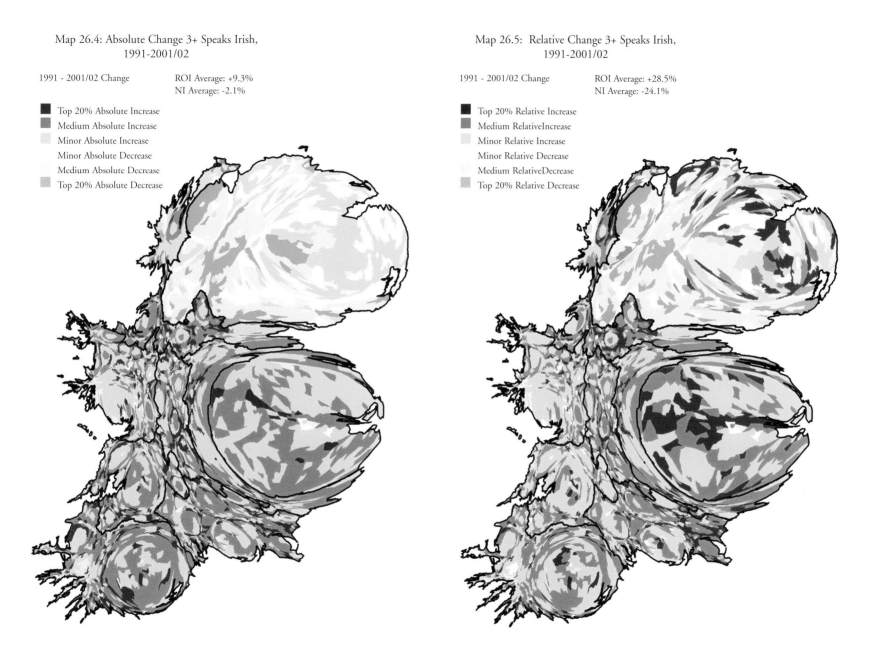

(9.3%) and a decline in the North (-2.1%). Despite an overall fall in the North, there are some increases in the proportion of Irish speakers in areas around Belfast Lough and on parts of the north coast. In the South, the relative growth in Irish speakers is evident across the country, but more strongly in the east than in the west. This is due to the smaller base of Irish speakers in the east of the Republic, where there has been greater scope for proportional increases.

Chapter 4: Housing, Travel and Transport

HOUSEHOLD WITH 0 CAR

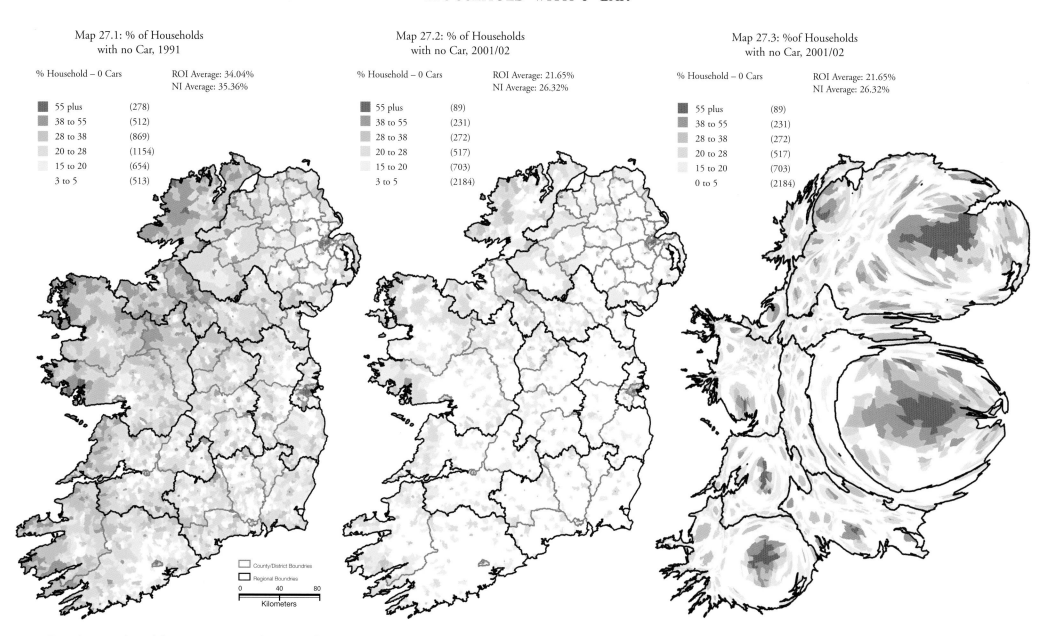

Map 27.1: % of Households
with no Car, 1991

% Household – 0 Cars

ROI Average: 34.04%
NI Average: 35.36%

■	55 plus	(278)
■	38 to 55	(512)
■	28 to 38	(869)
■	20 to 28	(1154)
■	15 to 20	(654)
■	3 to 5	(513)

Map 27.2: % of Households
with no Car, 2001/02

% Household – 0 Cars

ROI Average: 21.65%
NI Average: 26.32%

■	55 plus	(89)
■	38 to 55	(231)
■	28 to 38	(272)
■	20 to 28	(517)
■	15 to 20	(703)
■	3 to 5	(2184)

Map 27.3: %of Households
with no Car, 2001/02

% Household – 0 Cars

ROI Average: 21.65%
NI Average: 26.32%

■	55 plus	(89)
■	38 to 55	(231)
■	28 to 38	(272)
■	20 to 28	(517)
■	15 to 20	(703)
■	0 to 5	(2184)

County/District Boundries
Regional Boundries

0   40   80
Kilometers

In an increasingly mobile society, car ownership is a useful indicator of both lifestyle and income. Some localities have populations that need to travel significant distances to use services. Map 27.1 shows a clear east-west pattern and a distinctive urban-rural divide in terms of car availability on the island in 1991. The higher percentage of households without a car increases with distance from the east coast and the highest levels are found in remote rural areas on the Atlantic coast, notably in pockets of Donegal, Mayo, Sligo, Galway, Clare and Kerry but also in the north-west and central border areas. A predictable exception to this pattern is the large urban centres of Dublin and Belfast and this undoubtedly is a measure of the significant household numbers in central areas with low car

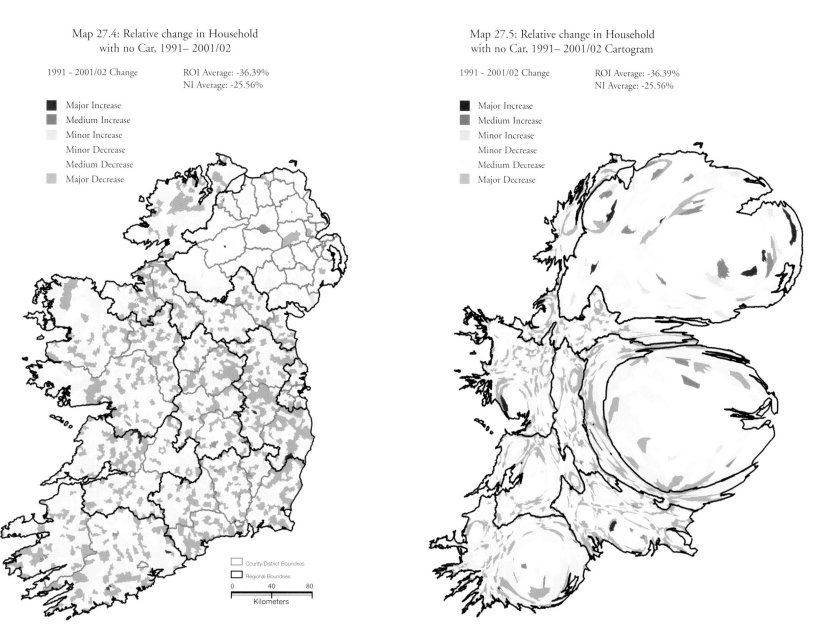

Map 27.4: Relative change in Household
with no Car, 1991– 2001/02

1991 - 2001/02 Change   ROI Average: -36.39%
                             NI Average: -25.56%

■ Major Increase
■ Medium Increase
□ Minor Increase
  Minor Decrease
  Medium Decrease
■ Major Decrease

Map 27.5: Relative change in Household
with no Car, 1991– 2001/02 Cartogram

1991 - 2001/02 Change   ROI Average: -36.39%
                             NI Average: -25.56%

■ Major Increase
■ Medium Increase
□ Minor Increase
  Minor Decrease
  Medium Decrease
■ Major Decrease

□ County/District Boundries
□ Regional Boundries

0   40   80
Kilometers

ownership due to good public transport and access to services. Map 27.2 displays a similar pattern for 2001/02 but the average percentage rate of households without any car has fallen from about a third of all households across the island in 1991 to just above a quarter (26.32%) in the North and a fifth (21.65) in the Republic. The cartogram for 2001/02 (Map 27.3) highlights the magnitude of the urban contribution to these patterns. Map 27.4 illustrates the variation of change across island and highlights clearly the greater levels of change in the Republic. The cartogram (Map 27.5) suggests that the areas with highest growth for non car households are found in the suburbs of larger towns particularly in the North.

HOUSEHOLDS WITH 2 CARS

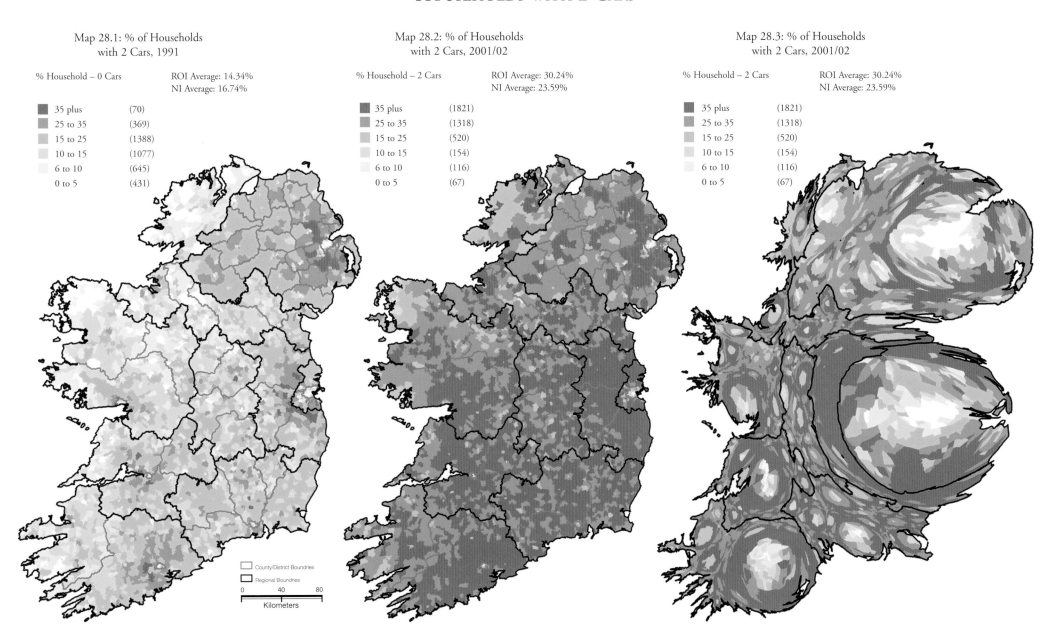

Map 28.1: % of Households
with 2 Cars, 1991

% Household – 0 Cars

ROI Average: 14.34%
NI Average: 16.74%

■	35 plus	(70)
■	25 to 35	(369)
■	15 to 25	(1388)
□	10 to 15	(1077)
□	6 to 10	(645)
□	0 to 5	(431)

Map 28.2: % of Households
with 2 Cars, 2001/02

% Household – 2 Cars

ROI Average: 30.24%
NI Average: 23.59%

■	35 plus	(1821)
■	25 to 35	(1318)
■	15 to 25	(520)
□	10 to 15	(154)
□	6 to 10	(116)
□	0 to 5	(67)

Map 28.3: % of Households
with 2 Cars, 2001/02

% Household – 2 Cars

ROI Average: 30.24%
NI Average: 23.59%

■	35 plus	(1821)
■	25 to 35	(1318)
■	15 to 25	(520)
□	10 to 15	(154)
□	6 to 10	(116)
□	0 to 5	(67)

County/District Boundries
Regional Boundries

0   40   80
Kilometers

Settlement patterns and levels of prosperity are key influences on multiple car ownership. The distribution of dual car households in 1991 reflects the expected pattern of high rates for commuting zones in cities and towns (which tend to have higher income levels than non urban areas). Northern Ireland, which has a higher average rate (16.74%) than the Republic of Ireland (14.34%), also has a more obvious cluster pattern of two car households. The geography and intensity of this pattern also appears to reflect the catchments of its well-defined urban network which is much higher than the more dispersed urban system of the Republic. However, the spatial distribution for 2001/02 depicts a remarkable change. Whilst the distribution for Northern Ireland shows an intensification of the

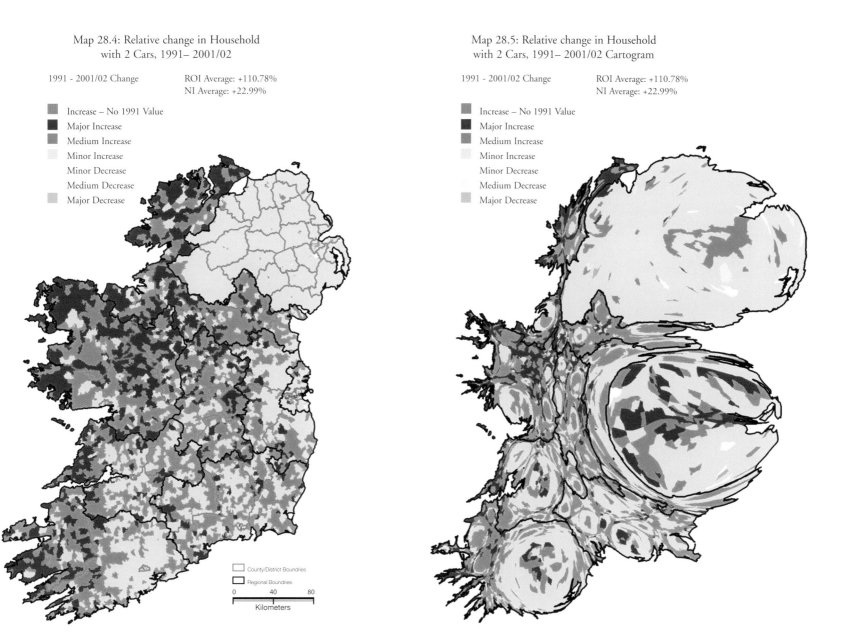

Map 28.4: Relative change in Household
with 2 Cars, 1991– 2001/02

1991 - 2001/02 Change ROI Average: +110.78%
NI Average: +22.99%

Increase – No 1991 Value
Major Increase
Medium Increase
Minor Increase
Minor Decrease
Medium Decrease
Major Decrease

County/District Boundries
Regional Boundries
0   40   80
Kilometers

Map 28.5: Relative change in Household
with 2 Cars, 1991– 2001/02 Cartogram

1991 - 2001/02 Change ROI Average: +110.78%
NI Average: +22.99%

Increase – No 1991 Value
Major Increase
Medium Increase
Minor Increase
Minor Decrease
Medium Decrease
Major Decrease

previous pattern, virtually all areas in the Republic show saturation coverage for dual car households (Donegal, west Mayo and parts of west Kerry are the main exceptions). The cartogram (Map 28.3) highlights the difference in growth levels in the two jurisdictions between 1991 and 2001/2 when the Republic of Ireland's average for dual car households doubled to 30.24% compared to the more modest increase for Northern Ireland of 23.59%. While Map 28.4 suggests a pattern of greatest increase over the decade in the counties along the Atlantic corridor and midlands, the cartogram highlights some interesting urban corridor patterns and the massive change levels that have occurred in and around Dublin region.

WORKFORCE TRAVELLING LESS THAN 2 MILES

Map 29.1: % of Workforce
travelling < 2 Miles. 2001/02

Approx < 2 Miles

ROI Average: 14.89%
NI Average: 30.99%

■	38 plus	(255)
■	21 to 38	(498)
■	11 to 21	(780)
■	5 to 11	(1439)
■	3 to 5	(618)
■	0 to 53	(406)

Map 29.2: % of Workforce
travelling < 2 Miles. 2001/02

Approx < 2 Miles

ROI Average: 14.89%
NI Average: 30.99%

■	38 plus	(255)
■	21 to 38	(498)
■	11 to 21	(780)
■	5 to 11	(1439)
■	3 to 5	(618)
■	0 to 53	(406)

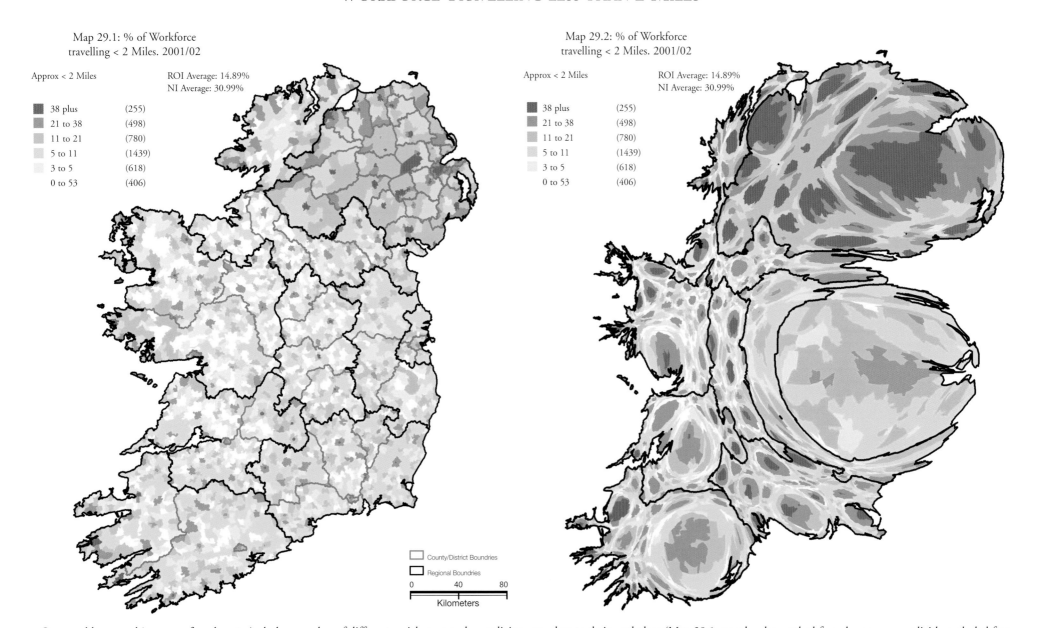

County/District Boundries
Regional Boundries

0   40   80
Kilometers

One would expect this group of workers to include a number of different social groups who are living very close to their workplace (Map 29.1; people who worked from home were explicitly excluded from this figure). While one does see the expected highest rates for these groups in city centres, particularly in the North, the rates were slightly lower than might be expected in the city centres of Cork and Dublin. This may reflect population densities which tend to be higher in inner cities in the North, as well as a wider range of employment opportunity for local residents beyond their immediate locale. The clustering in the North was also reflected in the much higher average rate for workers travelling 0 to 2 miles to work. At 30.99% the figure for the North was over twice that of the South at 14.89%. Both maps also showed relatively high rates in some of the smaller cities and provincial towns. This was in part explained by the size of those towns which would rarely be more than 2 miles in circumference. As these data were only collected in the South for the first time in 2002, it was impossible to produce change data from 1991 and this applies to all the subsequent travel to work maps as well.

Workforce Travelling between 2 Miles and 5 Miles

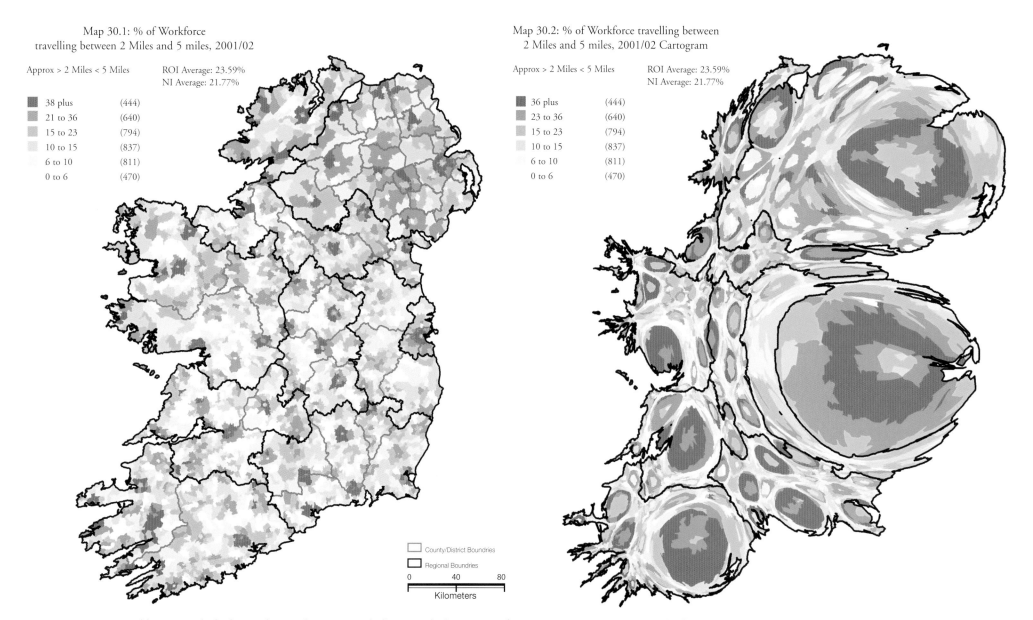

Map 30.1: % of Workforce
travelling between 2 Miles and 5 miles, 2001/02

Approx > 2 Miles < 5 Miles

ROI Average: 23.59%
NI Average: 21.77%

■	38 plus	(444)
■	21 to 36	(640)
■	15 to 23	(794)
■	10 to 15	(837)
■	6 to 10	(811)
■	0 to 6	(470)

Map 30.2: % of Workforce travelling between
2 Miles and 5 miles, 2001/02 Cartogram

Approx > 2 Miles < 5 Miles

ROI Average: 23.59%
NI Average: 21.77%

■	36 plus	(444)
■	23 to 36	(640)
■	15 to 23	(794)
■	10 to 15	(837)
■	6 to 10	(811)
■	0 to 6	(470)

☐ County/District Boundries
☐ Regional Boundries

0   40   80
Kilometers

Map 30.1, as one would expect with the longer distance being mapped, illustrates the beginnings of a concentric pattern at 2 to 5 miles from the centres of urban areas where there are denser concentrations of employment. This pattern is visible for the larger cities but is also clearly visible for all urban centres including smaller towns such as Cavan, Coleraine and Clonmel. In the cartogram (Map 30.2) the larger cities of Dublin and Belfast showed clustering in suburban areas within the city perimeters, whereas in the smaller cities, this pattern was outside the city boundaries given the relatively smaller commuting distances associated with Cork and Galway. These areas were likely to have included people using public transport where it was available. The rates were generally lower in the rural areas, even for those close to the towns and cities. Unlike the higher levels of short-range travel in the North, the average rates were much closer for in this case with the rates in the South at 23.59% being only slightly higher than for the North at 21.77%.

63

WORKFORCE TRAVELLING BETWEEN 5 MILES AND 10 MILES

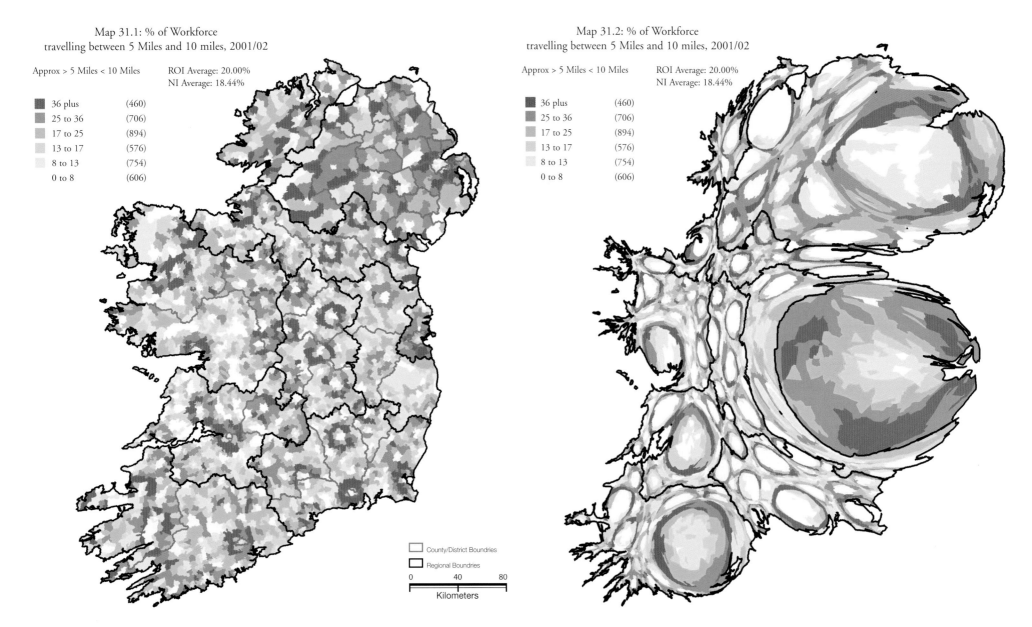

Map 31.1: % of Workforce
travelling between 5 Miles and 10 miles, 2001/02

Approx > 5 Miles < 10 Miles

ROI Average: 20.00%
NI Average: 18.44%

■	36 plus	(460)
■	25 to 36	(706)
■	17 to 25	(894)
■	13 to 17	(576)
■	8 to 13	(754)
■	0 to 8	(606)

Map 31.2: % of Workforce
travelling between 5 Miles and 10 miles, 2001/02

Approx > 5 Miles < 10 Miles

ROI Average: 20.00%
NI Average: 18.44%

■	36 plus	(460)
■	25 to 36	(706)
■	17 to 25	(894)
■	13 to 17	(576)
■	8 to 13	(754)
■	0 to 8	(606)

☐ County/District Boundries

☐ Regional Boundries

0   40   80
Kilometers

When the data for the percentage of workers who travelled more than five and less than ten miles to work is mapped (Map 31.1), the concentric ring pattern of commuting is further emphasised. This distance includes commuters in the outer suburbs of the bigger cities, although it is a visible pattern in all urban areas including county towns such as Kilkenny and Mullingar thus highlighting the continuing role of such towns as local employment foci. This was less clearly visible as a pattern in the North though it is visible to an extent in the cartogram (Map 31.2). The average rates for both North (21.77%) and South (23.59%) are similar. The number of people commuting between 10 and 15 miles to work is about half the number commuting 5 to 10 miles (South 11.71%; North 9.55%). The concentric ring pattern is again visible, but around a smaller number of towns, highlighting the local nature of some labour markets as opposed to the great pull and importance of others.

WORKFORCE TRAVELLING BETWEEN 10 MILES AND 15 MILES

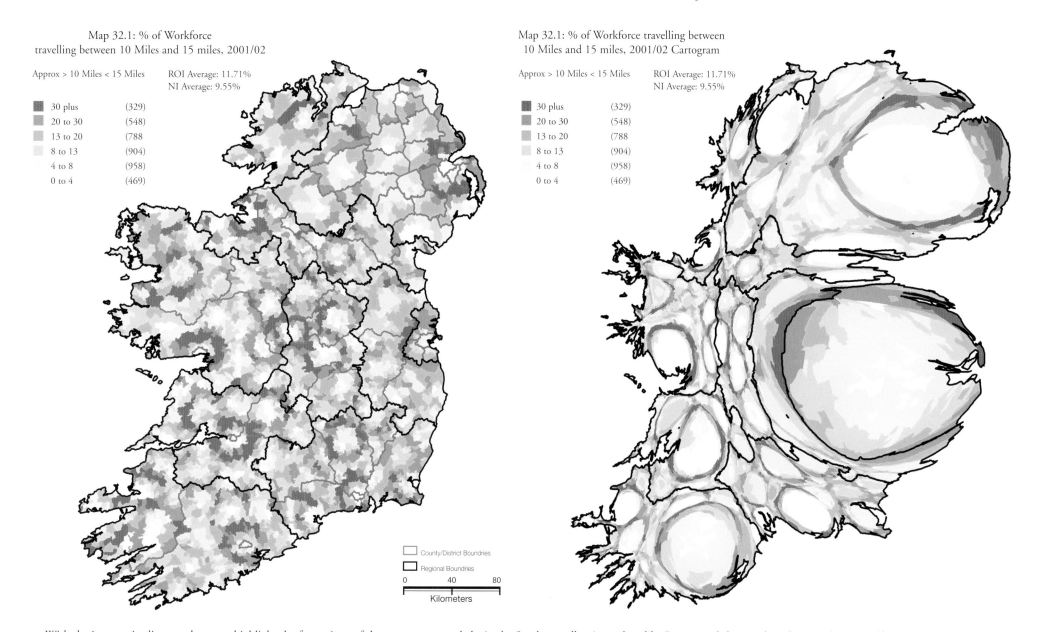

Map 32.1: % of Workforce
travelling between 10 Miles and 15 miles, 2001/02

Approx > 10 Miles < 15 Miles

ROI Average: 11.71%
NI Average: 9.55%

■	30 plus	(329)
▪	20 to 30	(548)
▪	13 to 20	(788
▫	8 to 13	(904)
▫	4 to 8	(958)
▫	0 to 4	(469)

Map 32.1: % of Workforce travelling between
10 Miles and 15 miles, 2001/02 Cartogram

Approx > 10 Miles < 15 Miles

ROI Average: 11.71%
NI Average: 9.55%

■	30 plus	(329)
▪	20 to 30	(548)
▪	13 to 20	(788
▫	8 to 13	(904)
▫	4 to 8	(958)
▫	0 to 4	(469)

☐ County/District Boundries

☐ Regional Boundries

0   40   80
Kilometers

With the increase in distance the maps highlight the formations of the new commuter belts in the South as well as in pockets like Bangor and the North Ards areas close to Belfast (Map 32.1). The typologies of such places are often characterised by young, mixed professional populations, new housing developments, and relatively high fertility rates. The cartogram (Map 32.2) identifies well the quite narrow clustering of highest rates in the suburban and fringes around the larger cities. Here, where public transport exists it is heavily used, but travel becomes increasing reliant on car use. Interestingly commuting belts intersect but do not overlap suggesting that there is a single dominant node in each area.

WORKFORCE TRAVELLING BETWEEN 15 MILES AND 30 MILES

Map 33.1: % of Workers Travelling between 15 miles and 30 miles

Approx > 15 Miles < 30 Miles

ROI Average: 12.51%
NI Average: 8.54%

■	35 plus	(315)
■	24 to 35	(553)
■	16 to 24	(809)
■	10 to 16	(834)
■	5 to 10	(780)
■	0 to 5	(705)

Map 33.2: % of Workers Travelling between 15 miles and 30 miles

Approx > 15 miles < 30 Miles

ROI Average: 12.51%
NI Average: 8.54%

■	35 plus	(315)
■	24 to 35	(553)
■	16 to 24	(809)
■	10 to 16	(834)
■	5 to 10	(780)
■	0 to 5	(705)

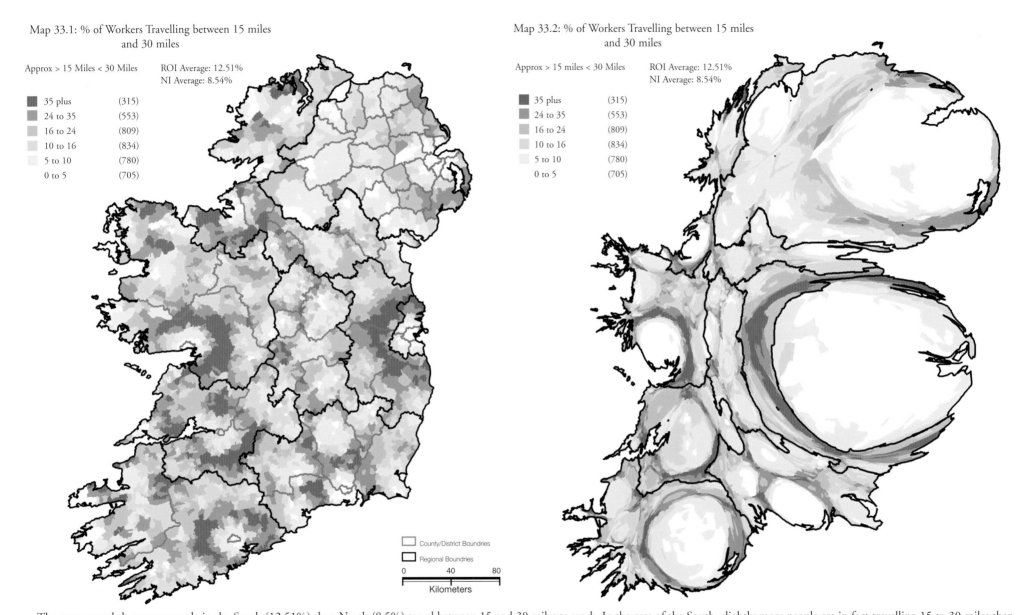

County/District Boundries

Regional Boundries

0   40   80
Kilometers

The maps reveal that more people in the South (12.51%) than North (8.5%) travel between 15 and 30 miles to work. In the case of the South, slightly more people are in fact travelling 15 to 30 miles than 10 to 15 miles per commute, a finding that runs counter to the distance decay effect one might expect to find. This might partly be explained by a shift in scale from 5 miles to 15 miles, but nonetheless significant numbers of people are commuting long distances. In particular there are high levels of commuting around Dublin and Galway, as well as other larger cities such as Limerick, Cork, Waterford and Sligo. Typically smaller satellite towns like Leixlip, Ashbourne, and Tuam form part of this commuter belt and this is also reflected in the gradual peri-urbanisation of rural areas around the major towns. Moreover, the pattern is evident in counties that previously would have had low commuter rates such as Tipperary, Laois, Offaly and Cavan and, to a lesser extent, districts like Ballycastle and Downpatrick in the North. Again the cartogram (Map 33.2) emphasises the spatial concentration of these commuting populations in concentric districts around the main centres of employment.

WORKFORCE TRAVELLING 30 MILES PLUS

Map 34.1: % of Workers Travelling 30+ Miles

Map 34.2: % of Workers Travelling
30 Miles Cartogram

Approx 30 plus Miles

ROI Average: 6.10%
NI Average: 4.03%

■	20 plus	(274)
	13 to 20	(610)
	9 to 13	(670)
	6 to 9	(738)
	3 to 6	(732)
	0 to 3	(972)

Approx 30 plus Miles

ROI Average: 6.10%
NI Average: 4.03%

■	20 plus	(274)
	13 to 20	(610)
	9 to 13	(670)
	6 to 9	(738)
	3 to 6	(732)
	0 to 3	(972)

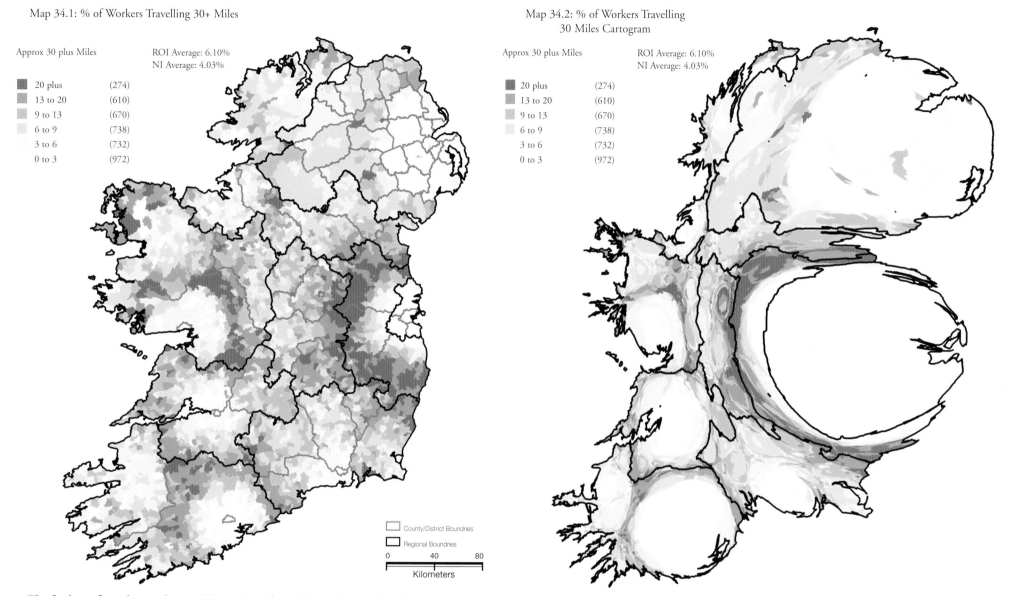

County/District Boundries
Regional Boundries

0   40   80
Kilometers

The final set of travel to work maps (Map 34.1 and 34.2) show the numbers of people commuting over 30 miles to work. While significant numbers of the population are undertaking such commutes (4.03%, North; 6.10%, South) a distance decay effect is evident. The concentric circle pattern is now most evident in the South, showing the outer ranges of commutes to large centres, in particular Dublin, Cork and Galway. The counties surrounding these centres, such as Meath, Kildare, Wicklow and Louth around Dublin have many areas where over 20% of the population are commuting long distances each day, placing significant pressure onto the roads and public transport. While difficult to disaggregate, there may be a number of other types of workers who travel more than 60 miles each day for work such as mobile workers or people who are resident in one location at weekends and who work in a fixed location the rest of the week. The latter group in particular might make up a significant minority of this category. In all of the distance to work maps no account is taken for cross-border flows specifically, though this might be an interesting area for future analysis and for census question design.

HOUSEHOLDS OWNER OCCUPIED

Map 35.1: % Households - Owner Occupied,
1991

% Households - Owner
Occupied

ROI Average: 79.27%
NI Average: 62.41%

- 93 plus (891)
- 88 to 93 (1090)
- 81 to 88 (876)
- 69 to 81 (588)
- 46 to 69 (336)
- 1 to 46 (199)

Map 35.2: % Households - Owner Occupied,
2001/02

% Households - Owner
Occupied

ROI Average: 77.42%
NI Average: 69.61%

- 93 plus (561)
- 88 to 93 (1182)
- 81 to 88 (1064)
- 69 to 81 (687)
- 46 to 69 (364)
- 6.5 to 46 (138)

Map 35.3: % Households - Owner Occupied,
2001/02

% Households - Owner
Occupied

ROI Average: 77.42%
NI Average: 69.61%

- 93 plus (561)
- 88 to 93 (1182)
- 81 to 88 (1064)
- 69 to 81 (687)
- 46 to 69 (364)
- 6.5 to 46 (138)

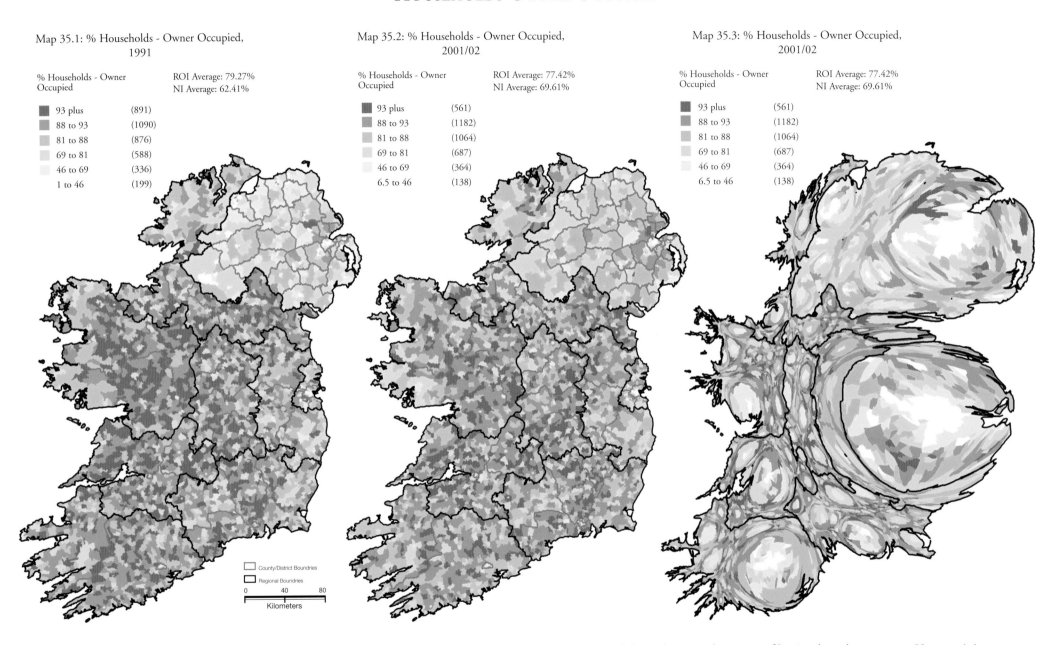

County/District Boundries

Regional Boundries

0   40   80
Kilometers

Owner occupancy is a deceptive category because it incorporates those who are already outright owners of dwellings and those who are in the process of buying through a mortgage. However, it is a useful tenure category for socio-economic comparison purposes when set alongside the non-owner (rented) categories. In 1991 there was a discernible difference of almost 17% in the pattern of owner occupiers for Northern Ireland (62.41%) and the Republic (79.27%). This disparity has reduced to less than 8% by 2001/02 as the average for the Republic decreased to 77.42% whilst the average for Northern Ireland increased to 69.61%. The cartogram (Map 35.3) illustrates more realistically the spatial pattern of owner occupancy. It shows that the Dublin region and Northern Ireland between

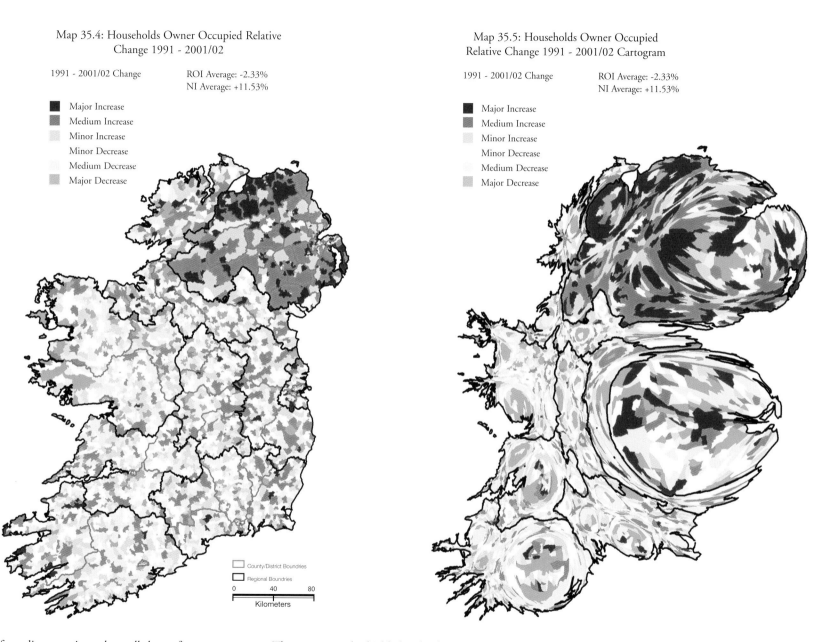

Map 35.4: Households Owner Occupied Relative
Change 1991 - 2001/02

1991 - 2001/02 Change

ROI Average: -2.33%
NI Average: +11.53%

■ Major Increase
▨ Medium Increase
▫ Minor Increase
  Minor Decrease
  Medium Decrease
▨ Major Decrease

Map 35.5: Households Owner Occupied
Relative Change 1991 - 2001/02 Cartogram

1991 - 2001/02 Change

ROI Average: -2.33%
NI Average: +11.53%

■ Major Increase
▨ Medium Increase
▫ Minor Increase
  Minor Decrease
  Medium Decrease
▨ Major Decrease

□ County/District Boundries
▭ Regional Boundries

0   40   80
Kilometers

them account for a disproportionately small share of owner occupancy. The cartogram also highlights the distinctive patterns associated with central urban areas and surrounding suburbs which have low levels of owner occupancy along with rural areas. Map 35.4 summarises the intensity of change across the island and emphasises the high rate of change for Northern Ireland (11.53%) compared to the Republic (-2.33%). However, this map masks important patterns of change which are captured in the cartogram (Map 35.5) which shows patterns of variation within and between urban areas (particularly in Dublin and Cork) which reflect the significant population shifts and change of housing location and age structure in these areas.

HOUSEHOLDS OWNER OCCUPIED - OWNS OUTRIGHT

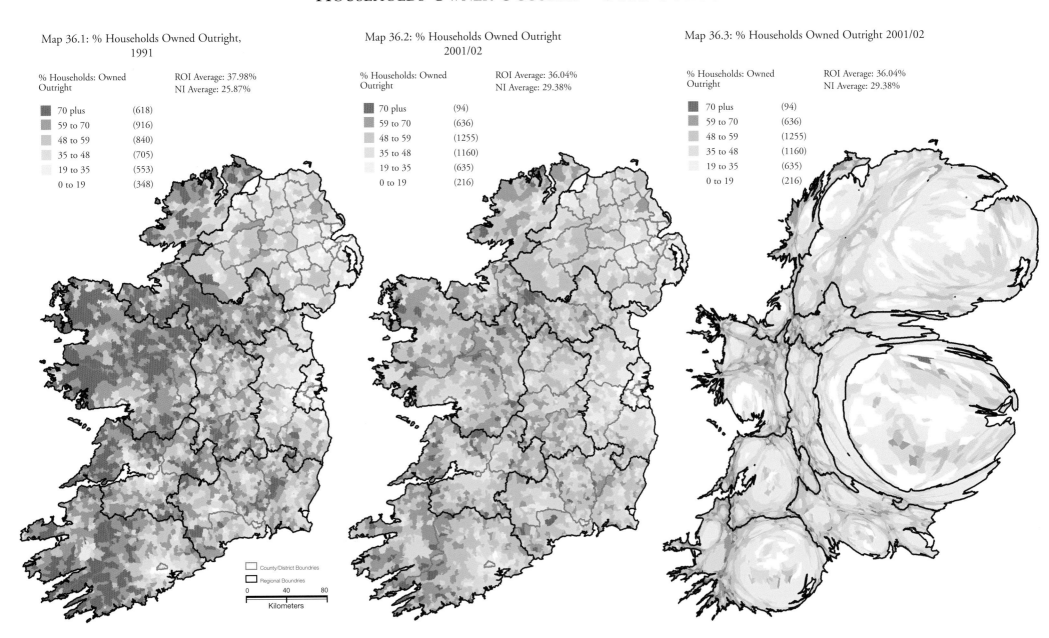

Map 36.1: % Households Owned Outright,
1991

% Households: Owned
Outright

ROI Average: 37.98%
NI Average: 25.87%

■	70 plus	(618)
■	59 to 70	(916)
■	48 to 59	(840)
■	35 to 48	(705)
■	19 to 35	(553)
	0 to 19	(348)

Map 36.2: % Households Owned Outright
2001/02

% Households: Owned
Outright

ROI Average: 36.04%
NI Average: 29.38%

■	70 plus	(94)
■	59 to 70	(636)
■	48 to 59	(1255)
■	35 to 48	(1160)
■	19 to 35	(635)
	0 to 19	(216)

Map 36.3: % Households Owned Outright 2001/02

% Households: Owned
Outright

ROI Average: 36.04%
NI Average: 29.38%

■	70 plus	(94)
■	59 to 70	(636)
■	48 to 59	(1255)
■	35 to 48	(1160)
■	19 to 35	(635)
	0 to 19	(216)

County/District Boundries
Regional Boundries

0   40   80
Kilometers

The percentage of houses owned outright (i.e. without a loan or mortgage) in 1991 was less than half that of the wider category of owner occupier in the period 2001/02 for both Northern Ireland (25.87% compared to 64.21%) and the Republic (37.98% as against 79.27%). Map 36.1 shows rural areas, particularly in western and border areas of in the Republic, have the highest rates of outright ownership. This clear pattern is no longer evident a decade later as revealed by Map 36.2. During this period the slight decrease in the Republic (to 36.04%) and the slight increase in Northern Ireland (to 29.38%) translate into a much more diffuse spatial distribution for high ownership levels. The extent of rural ownership levels is placed in more meaningful context by the cartogram at Map 36.3

Map 36.4: Households Owned Outright Relative Change
1991 - 2001/02

1991 - 2001/02 Change

ROI Average: -5.10%
NI Average: +13.56%

- Major Increase
- Medium Increase
- Minor Increase
- Minor Decrease
- Medium Decrease
- Major Decrease

County/District Boundries
Regional Boundries

0   40   80
Kilometers

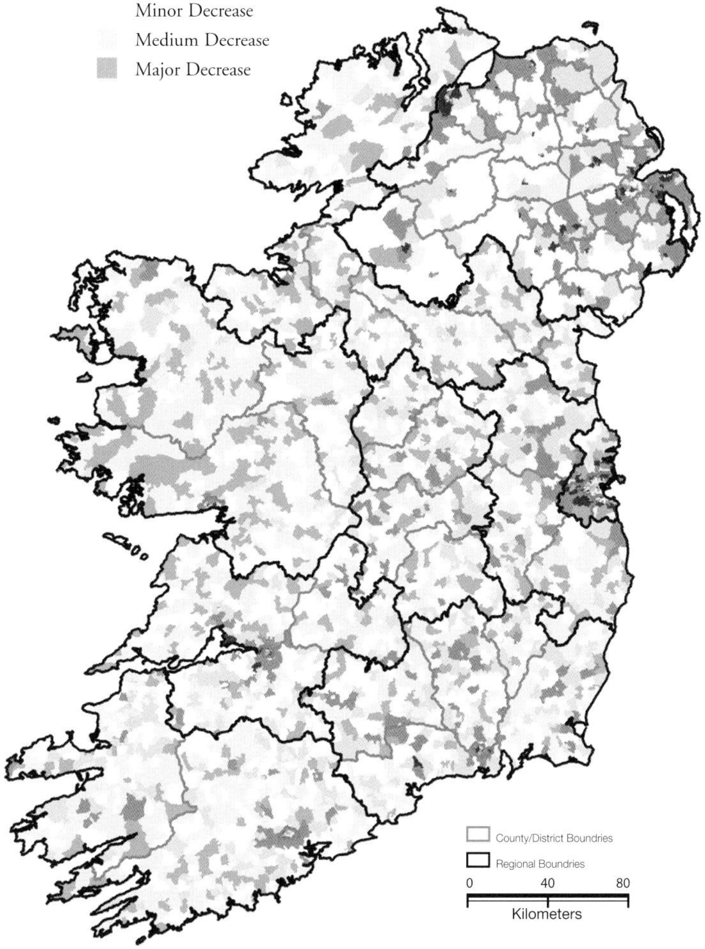

Map 36.5: Households Owned Outright Relative Change
1991 - 2001/02 Cartogram

1991 - 2001/02 Change

ROI Average: -5.10%
NI Average: +13.56%

- Major Increase
- Medium Increase
- Minor Increase
- Minor Decrease
- Medium Decrease
- Major Decrease

which shows the greater contribution made to the overall total by the urban areas. These are physically smaller in area but account for a disproportionately larger proportion of actual population ownership than the spatially dispersed and physically larger pockets in rural areas. Indeed, as shown by Map 36.4 and confirmed more clearly by the cartogram at Map 36.5, the suburban peripheries of urban areas are the main areas of fast growth in outright ownership for both the Republic (which experienced an overall decline rate of -5.1% for the decade) and Northern Ireland (which had an overall growth rate of 13.56%).

HOUSEHOLDS WITH LOANS AND MORTGAGES

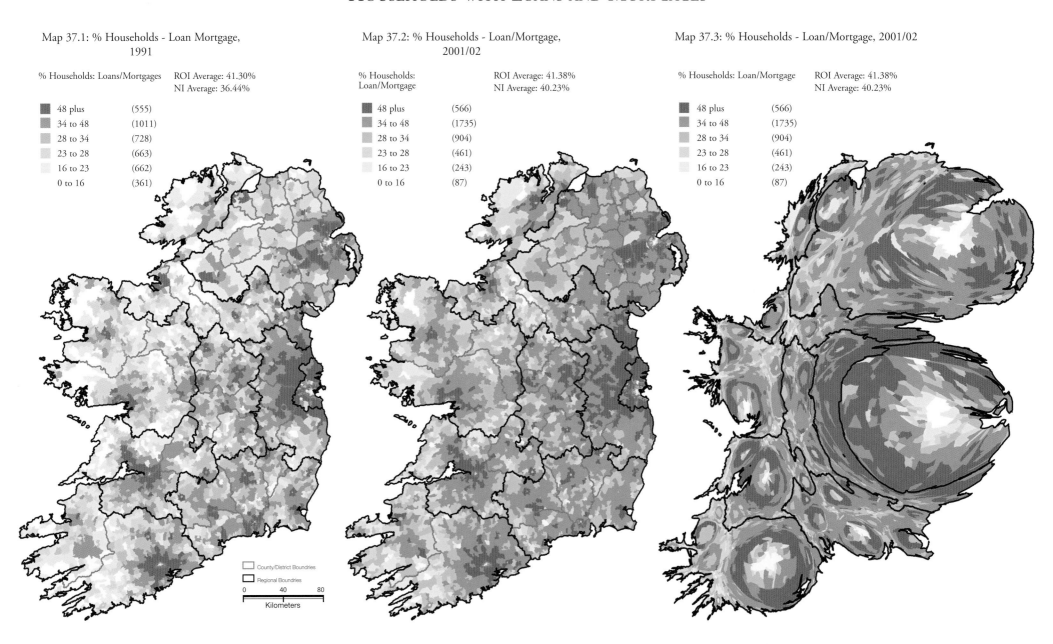

Map 37.1: % Households - Loan Mortgage, 1991

% Households: Loans/Mortgages		ROI Average: 41.30% NI Average: 36.44%
■	48 plus	(555)
■	34 to 48	(1011)
■	28 to 34	(728)
■	23 to 28	(663)
■	16 to 23	(662)
	0 to 16	(361)

Map 37.2: % Households - Loan/Mortgage, 2001/02

% Households: Loan/Mortgage		ROI Average: 41.38% NI Average: 40.23%
■	48 plus	(566)
■	34 to 48	(1735)
■	28 to 34	(904)
■	23 to 28	(461)
■	16 to 23	(243)
	0 to 16	(87)

Map 37.3: % Households - Loan/Mortgage, 2001/02

% Households: Loan/Mortgage		ROI Average: 41.38% NI Average: 40.23%
■	48 plus	(566)
■	34 to 48	(1735)
■	28 to 34	(904)
■	23 to 28	(461)
■	16 to 23	(243)
	0 to 16	(87)

County/District Boundries
Regional Boundries

0   40   80
Kilometers

Maps at 37.1 and 37.2 are effectively inverse images of those presented for outright ownership. The spatial distribution shows low levels of mortgaged housing in rural areas and highest levels in the commuter catchments of the urban areas. Interestingly, in the decade between 1991 and 2001/02, the percentage gap between Northern Ireland and the Republic for mortgage-based ownership has fallen from approximately 5% to 1% as the rates in both jurisdictions converge on an overall average of about 41%. The cartogram (Map 37.3) for 2001/02 affirms the huge role of the commuter footprint, particularly in and around Dublin, in accounting for absolute levels of home ownership linked to loans/mortgages. Ironically, despite the high levels of mortgage-owned homes in the urban

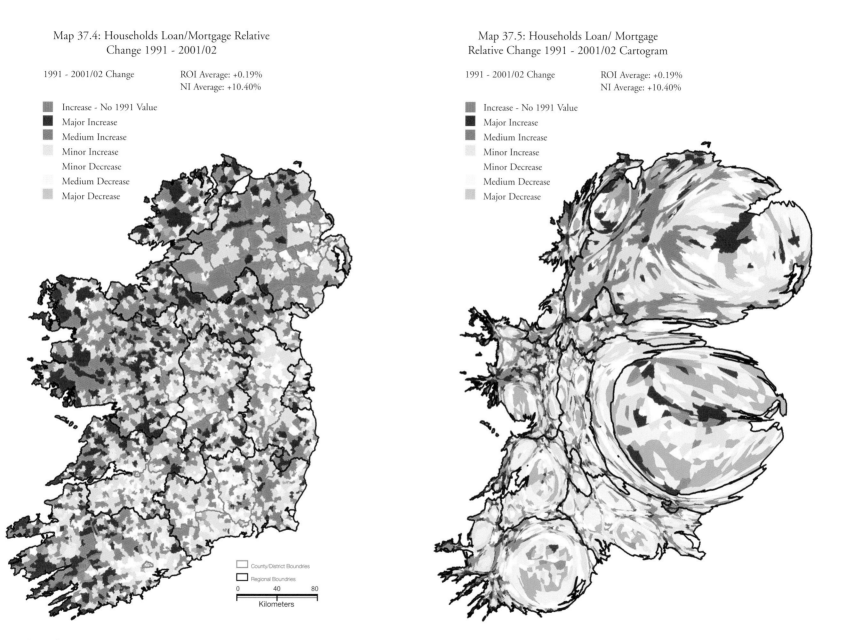

Map 37.4: Households Loan/Mortgage Relative
Change 1991 - 2001/02

1991 - 2001/02 Change   ROI Average: +0.19%
                             NI Average: +10.40%

Increase - No 1991 Value
Major Increase
Medium Increase
Minor Increase
Minor Decrease
Medium Decrease
Major Decrease

County/District Boundries
Regional Boundries

0   40   80
Kilometers

Map 37.5: Households Loan/ Mortgage
Relative Change 1991 - 2001/02 Cartogram

1991 - 2001/02 Change   ROI Average: +0.19%
                             NI Average: +10.40%

Increase - No 1991 Value
Major Increase
Medium Increase
Minor Increase
Minor Decrease
Medium Decrease
Major Decrease

centres in the Republic of Ireland, it is the rural areas that display the fastest rates of growth over the decade 1991-2001/02. Average growth rates were static in the Republic at 0.19% but expanded significantly by a rate of 10.4% in Northern Ireland. However, in both jurisdictions a broadly similar a pattern of rate change is discernible. The suburbs of the main cities experienced considerable decreases (particularly in the Republic) whilst the central city areas, commuter zones and rural areas grew along with distinctive city centre to edge corridors in Dublin and Belfast.

HOUSEHOLDS RENTED PRIVATELY

Map 38.1: % Households - Rented Private, 1991

% Households: Rented Private   ROI Average: 7.98%
   NI Average: 5.56%

- 16 plus   (166)
- 7 to 16   (412)
- 5 to 7   (463)
- 2 to 5   (1419)
- 0 to 2   (1014)
- 0 to 0   (506)

Map 38.2: % Households - Rented Private 2001/02

% Households: Rented Private   ROI Average: 11.05%
   NI Average: 6.65%

- 16 plus   (256)
- 7 to 16   (765)
- 5 to 7   (640)
- 2 to 5   (1563)
- 0 to 2   (567)
- 0 to 0   (206)

Map 38.3: % Households - Rented Private 2001/02

% Households: Rented Private   ROI Average: 11.05%
   NI Average: 6.65%

- 16 plus   (256)
- 7 to 16   (765)
- 5 to 7   (640)
- 2 to 5   (1563)
- 0 to 2   (567)
- 0 to 0   (205)

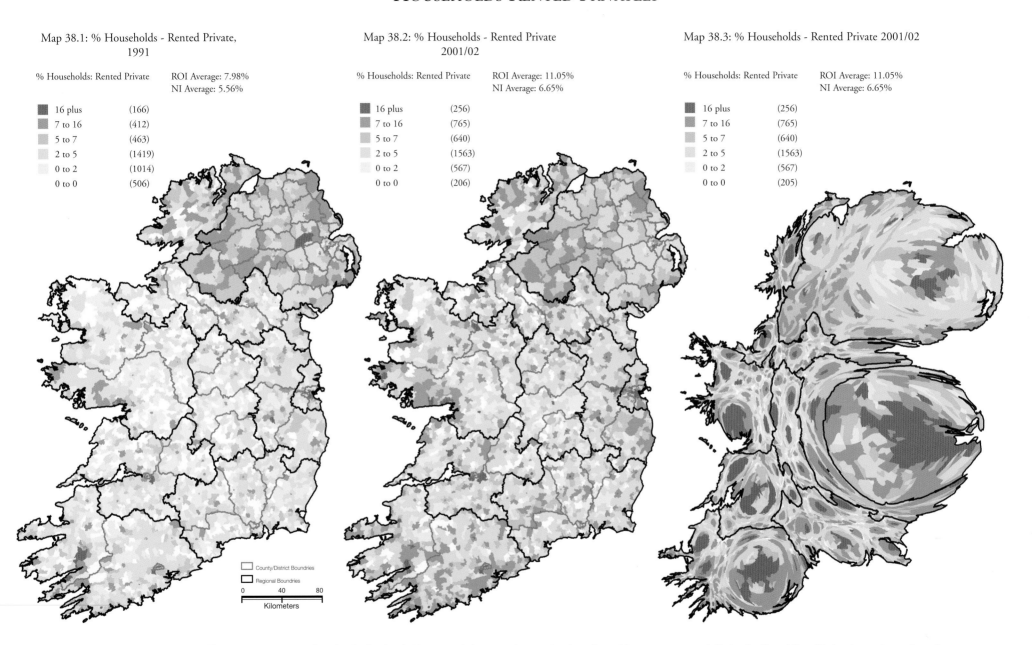

County/District Boundries
Regional Boundries

0   40   80
Kilometers

This has traditionally been a small tenure category on the island of Ireland. However, it is currently growing in scale and importance especially in the Republic of Ireland at a time when the percentage share of social rented dwellings as a proportion of overall tenure is declining. The average tenure share for private rental in the Republic grew from 7.98% in 1991 to 11.01% in 2002. The comparable tenure figures for Northern Ireland show a much smaller increase - from 5.56% to 6.65%. Despite the higher average levels of private rental housing in the Republic, the spatial distribution for this tenure for 1991 and 2001/02 (Maps 38.1 and 38.2) suggest a more diffuse distribution pattern in that jurisdiction. This apparent anomaly is explained by the cartogram (Map 38.3) which highlights the role of the major cities and other large urban centres in accounting for the bulk of this tenure category. Outside of these geographically widely distributed urban centres this tenure type was almost

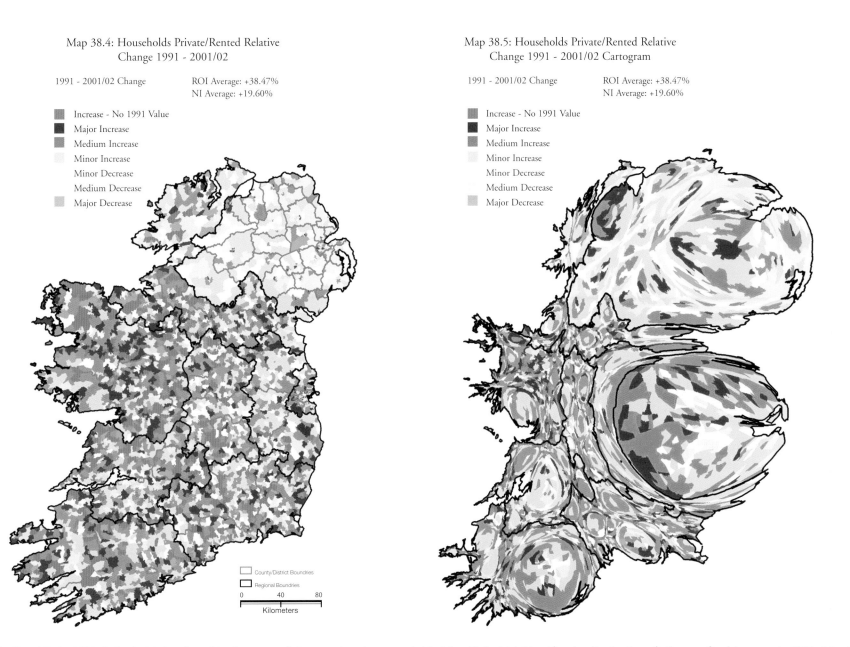

Map 38.4: Households Private/Rented Relative
Change 1991 - 2001/02

1991 - 2001/02 Change   ROI Average: +38.47%
                             NI Average: +19.60%

Increase - No 1991 Value
Major Increase
Medium Increase
Minor Increase
Minor Decrease
Medium Decrease
Major Decrease

County/District Boundries
Regional Boundries

0   40   80
Kilometers

Map 38.5: Households Private/Rented Relative
Change 1991 - 2001/02 Cartogram

1991 - 2001/02 Change   ROI Average: +38.47%
                             NI Average: +19.60%

Increase - No 1991 Value
Major Increase
Medium Increase
Minor Increase
Minor Decrease
Medium Decrease
Major Decrease

invisible in the Republic in 1991. Indeed, this is reflected in the extent of the green locations recorded in Map 38.4 which identifies the distribution of nil scores for this tenure in 1991. Map 38.5 highlights the extent to which urban areas (and particularly suburban areas in the Republic) account for the major growth rates between 1991 and 2001/2. It also reiterates the distinctive patterns that prevail for both the Republic and Northern Ireland and highlights the more widespread growth in the Republic. The latter had an average growth rate of 38.37% for the decade and was therefore almost twice the 19.60% average growth rate experienced in Northern Ireland between 1991 and 2001.

HOUSEHOLDS LOCAL AUTHORITY/SOCIAL RENTED AND OTHERS

Map 39.1: % Households - LA and Social
Rented, 1991

% Households: LA and
Social Rented

ROI Average: 12.74%
NI Average: 31.92%

	36 plus	(272)
	17 to 36	(514)
	10 to 17	(894)
	7 to 10	(662)
	4 to 7	(890)
	0 to 4	(748)

Map 39.2: % Households - LA and Social
Rented, 2001/02

% Households: LA and
Social Rented

ROI Average: 11.52%
NI Average: 23.74%

	36 plus	(150)
	17 to 36	(459)
	10 to 17	(1009)
	7 to 10	(784)
	4 to 7	(972)
	0 to 4	(632)

Map 39.3: % Households - LA and Social Rented,
2001/02

% Households: LA and
Social Rented

ROI Average: 11.52%
NI Average: 23.74%

	36 plus	(150)
	17 to 36	(459)
	10 to 17	(1009)
	7 to 10	(784)
	4 to 7	(972)
	0 to 4	(632)

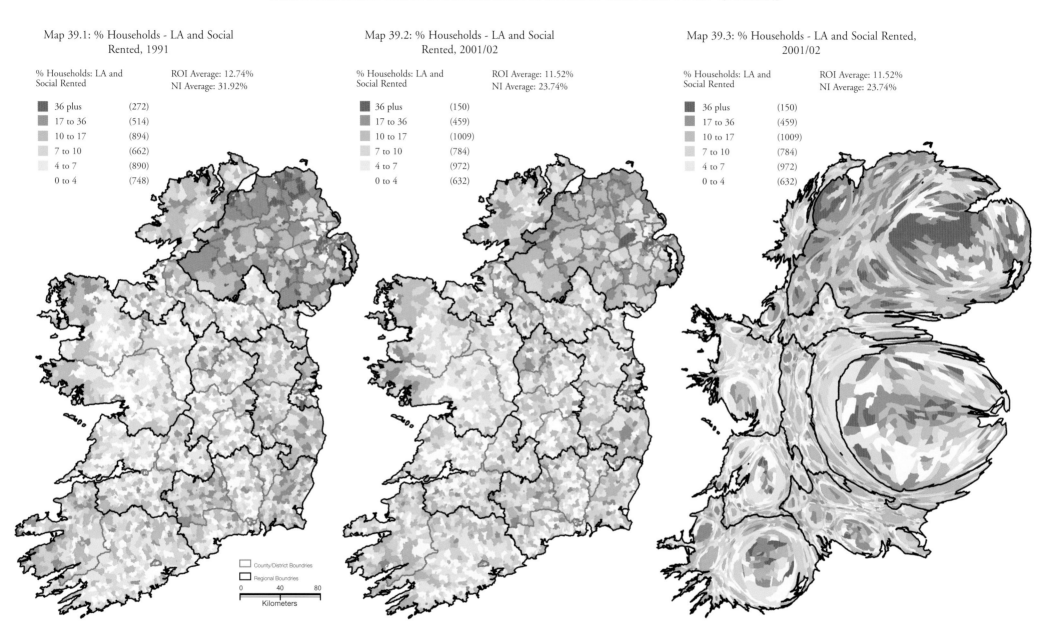

County/District Boundries
Regional Boundries

0   40   80
Kilometers

The geographical distribution of rented local authority and social housing is quite distinctive. This category of housing has a high but declining prevalence in Northern Ireland (31.92% of overall average tenure in 1991 compared to 23.74% in 2001). The percentage for the Republic of Ireland is lower but also declining, albeit less dramatically (from 12.74% of total tenures in 1991 to 11.52% in 2002). The distinct patterns of this tenure type on both parts of the island is illustrated in Maps 39.1 and 39.2 but are highlighted most clearly in the cartogram (Map 39.3). Clearly, urban areas

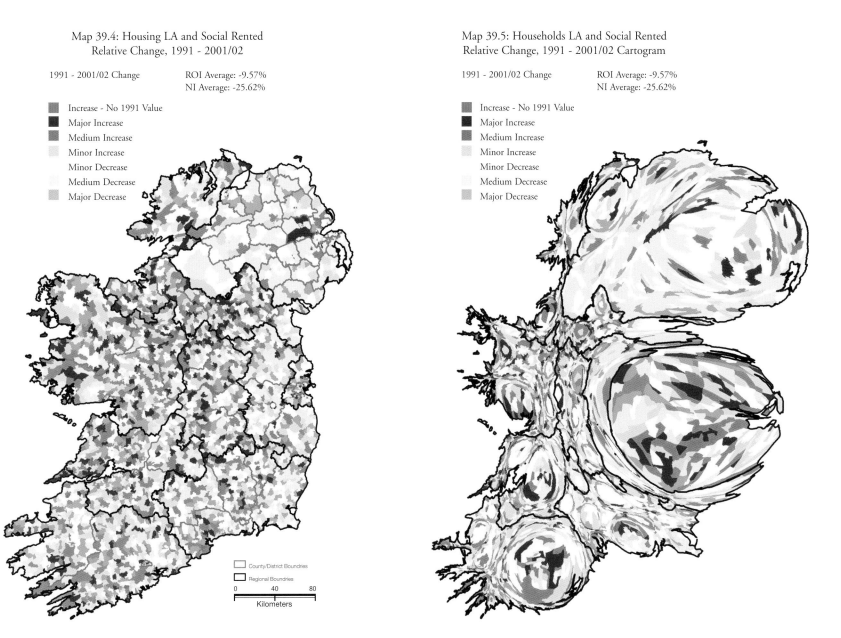

Map 39.4: Housing LA and Social Rented
Relative Change, 1991 - 2001/02

1991 - 2001/02 Change   ROI Average: -9.57%
                         NI Average: -25.62%

Increase - No 1991 Value
Major Increase
Medium Increase
Minor Increase
Minor Decrease
Medium Decrease
Major Decrease

County/District Boundries
Regional Boundries

0   40   80
Kilometers

Map 39.5: Households LA and Social Rented
Relative Change, 1991 - 2001/02 Cartogram

1991 - 2001/02 Change   ROI Average: -9.57%
                         NI Average: -25.62%

Increase - No 1991 Value
Major Increase
Medium Increase
Minor Increase
Minor Decrease
Medium Decrease
Major Decrease

account for the largest proportion of this housing tenure which tends to be located in city centre areas, particular suburbs and some of the sectoral corridors that connect specific suburbs to the town centres. This pattern is repeated in the rate of change maps (39.4 and 39.5), but with the north-south and urban-rural distinctiveness more clearly emphasised in the cartogram.

HOUSEHOLDS - CONVENTIONAL HOUSING

Map 40.1: % Conventional Housing, 2001/02

Map 40.2: % Conventional Housing, 2001/02

% Conventional Housing

ROI Average: 90.58%
NI Average: 91.18%

	99 plus	(743)
	97 to 99	(1443)
	94 to 97	(941)
	86 to 94	(555)
	65 to 86	(217)
	0 to 65	(97)

% Conventional Housing

ROI Average: 90.58%
NI Average: 91.18%

	99 plus	(743)
	97 to 99	(1443)
	94 to 97	(941)
	86 to 94	(555)
	65 to 86	(217)
	0 to 65	(97)

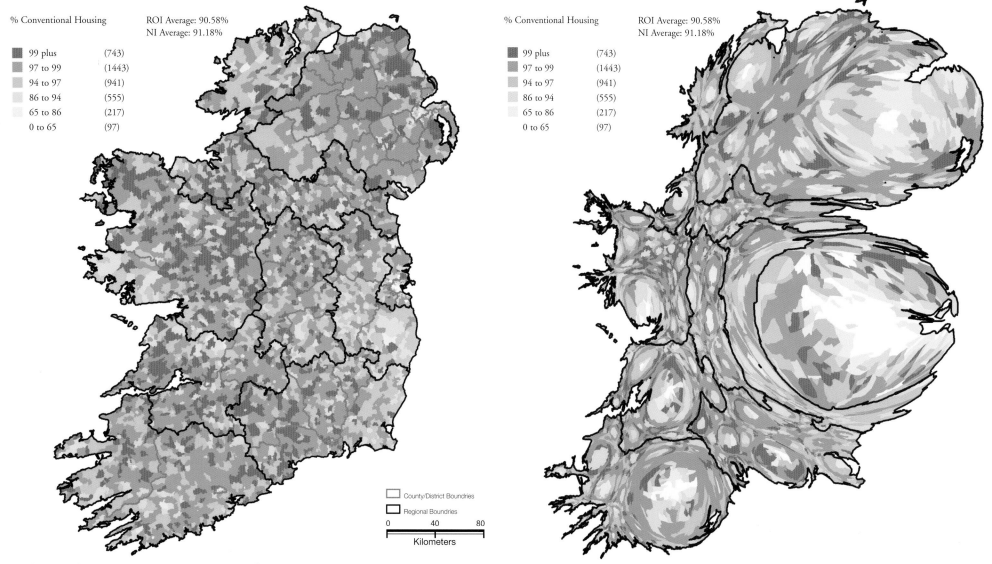

County/District Boundries

Regional Boundries

0   40   80
Kilometers

The type of housing that prevails in a country reflects economic and cultural priorities as well as cultural preferences. Conventional housing on the island of Ireland is comprised predominantly of single or two storey dwelling houses in one-off, detached, semi-detached and terrace style. Conventional housing accounted for nine out of every ten dwelling types on the island in 2001/02 with averages of 90.58% in the Republic and 91.18% in Northern Ireland. Map 40.1 suggests that some coastal areas depart from this trend. The cartogram at Map 40.2 confirms this pattern but reveals the far more significant influence of the urban dimension. The departure from the average of the major urban centres Cork, Limerick, Derry, Letterkenny, Galway, Waterford, and Sligo is evident but less clearly marked in terms of absolute numbers and average than Dublin and Belfast. A large proportion of dwellings in the two main cities have percentages of less than 66% conventional housing. Of course, in many respects this is to be expected as larger cities tend to have a greater mix of housing types. The Irish situation is, therefore, not unusual in this regard.

HOUSEHOLDS - APARTMENTS/FLATS

Map 41.1: % Flats/Apartments, 2001/02

% Flats/Apartments

ROI Average: 8.75%
NI Average: 8.53%

▓	23 plus	(154)
▓	3 to 13	(1014)
▓	2 to 3	(374)
░	1 to 2	(727)
	0 to 1	(689)
	0 to 0	(1038)

Map 41.2: % Flats/Apartments, 2001/02
Cartogram

% Flats/Apartments

ROI Average: 8.75%
NI Average: 8.53%

▓	23 plus	(154)
▓	3 to 23	(1014)
▓	2 to 3	(374)
░	1 to 2	(727)
	0 to 1	(689)
	0 to 0	(1038)

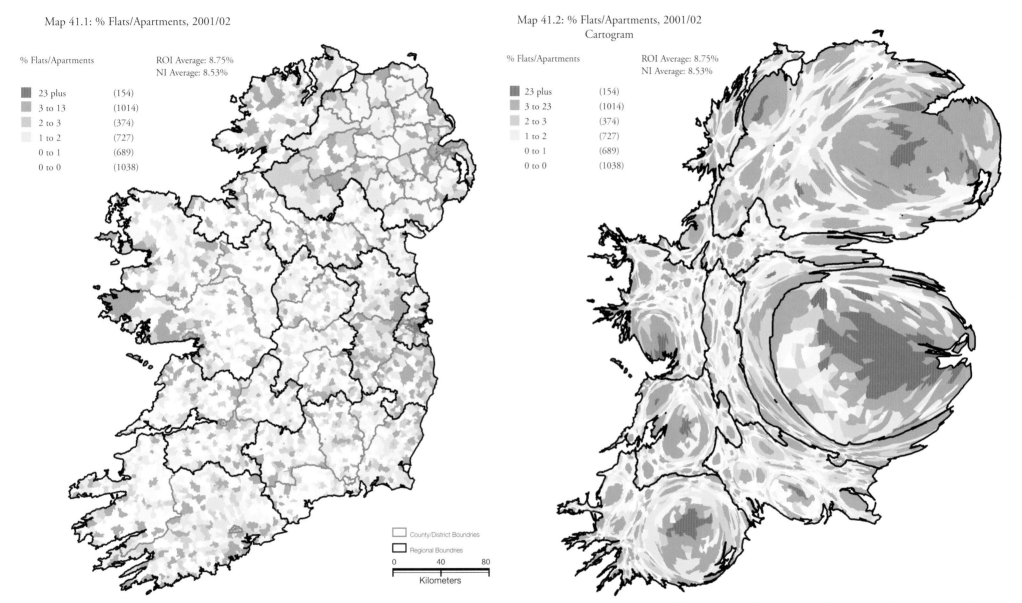

County/District Boundries

Regional Boundries

0   40   80
Kilometers

Map 41.1 shows the spatial distribution of flats/apartments across the island in 2001/2. It depicts an almost complete inverse image of the conventional housing map (Map 41.1) reflecting the small amount of this dwelling type (8.75% in the Republic and 8.53% in Northern Ireland). The restricted distribution of apartments / flats is highlighted by the cartogram at Map 41.2 which shows the extent to which their location is accounted for by urban settlements and by the larger centres in particular. The commuter belt corridors in the major cities and popular holiday locations such Connemara, North Clare, the Antrim Coast and many parts of County Wicklow also feature quite prominently.

HOUSEHOLDS - MOBILE/TEMPORARY HOUSING

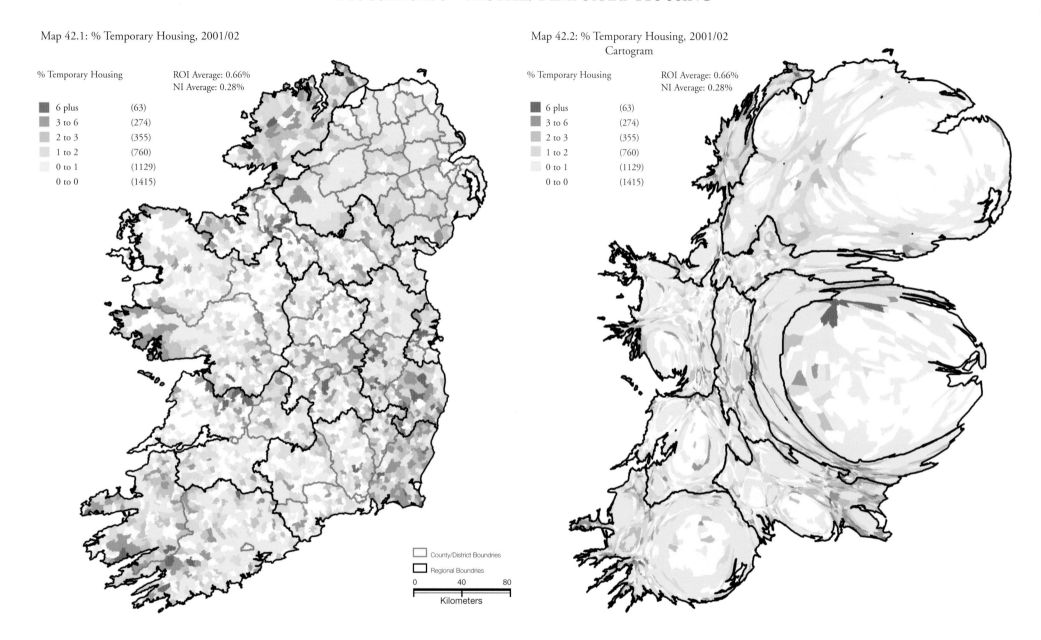

Map 42.1: % Temporary Housing, 2001/02

% Temporary Housing

ROI Average: 0.66%
NI Average: 0.28%

	6 plus	(63)
	3 to 6	(274)
	2 to 3	(355)
	1 to 2	(760)
	0 to 1	(1129)
	0 to 0	(1415)

Map 42.2: % Temporary Housing, 2001/02
Cartogram

% Temporary Housing

ROI Average: 0.66%
NI Average: 0.28%

	6 plus	(63)
	3 to 6	(274)
	2 to 3	(355)
	1 to 2	(760)
	0 to 1	(1129)
	0 to 0	(1415)

County/District Boundries

Regional Boundries

0   40   80
Kilometers

Temporary housing accommodation provides a useful indicator of emergency housing provision and can be a guide to both the extent and response to accommodation crises in the housing sector. Typically, this is a residual housing category which provides for travellers, refugees and immigrants as well as those in need of emergency shelter who are viewed as occupying temporary housing as a transition arrangement pending the provision of more permanent accommodation. The geographical distribution summarised in Map 42.1 indicates that the Republic of Ireland, with an average stock of 0.66%, has a proportion of temporary housing almost three times higher than Northern Ireland which has an average of 0.28%. The pattern of temporary housing has some interesting clustering with clear pockets of high rates found in west Galway, the southwest coast, the northwest and corridors radiating from Dublin to north Clare and from Dublin to Wexford.

Chapter 5: Economy

LABOUR FORCE PARTICIPATION RATE

Map 43.1: Labour Force Participation,1991

Labour Force Participation   ROI Average: 61.63%
NI Average: 69.36%

■	69 plus	(451)
■	64 to 69	(966)
■	61 to 64	(955)
□	58 to 61	(926)
□	53 to 58	(567)
	22 to 53	(115)

Map 43.2: Labour Force Participation, 2001/02

Labour Force Participation   ROI Average: 66.82%
NI Average: 65.78%

■	69 plus	(930)
■	64 to 69	(1740)
■	61 to 64	(748)
□	58 to 61	(365)
□	53 to 58	(135)
	22 to 53	(78)

Map 43.3: Labour Force Participation, 2001/02
Cartogram

Labour Force Participation   ROI Average: 66.82%
NI Average: 65.78%

■	69 plus	(930)
■	64 to 69	(1740)
■	61 to 64	(748)
□	58 to 61	(365)
□	53 to 58	(135)
	22 to 53	(78)

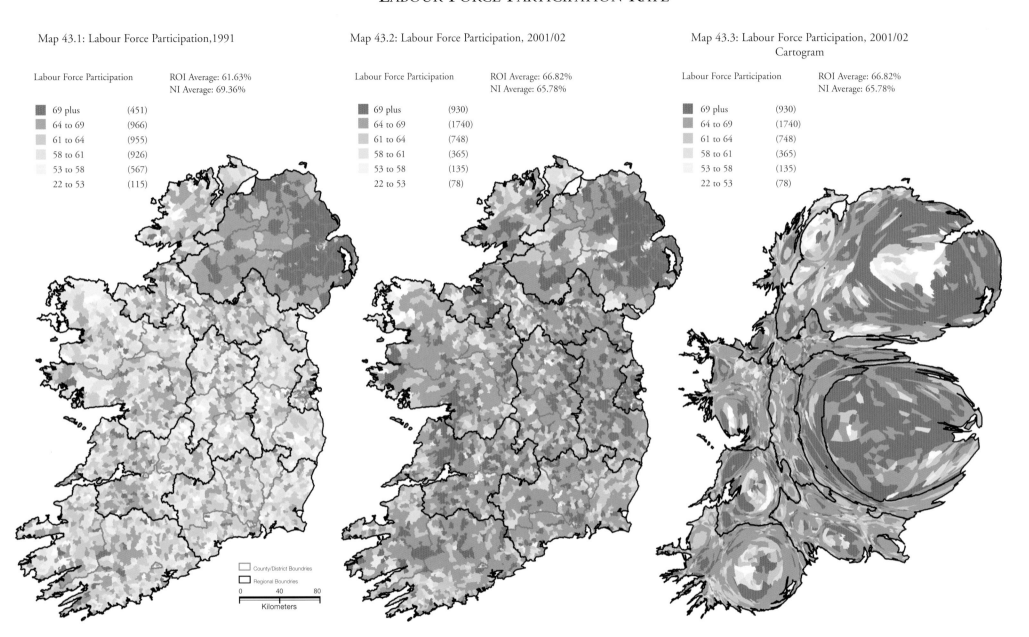

County/District Boundries
Regional Boundries

0   40   80
Kilometers

Map 43.1 suggests that, in 1991, labour force participation was greater in Northern Ireland (69.34%) than the Republic (61.63%). The participation rates in the Republic were highly spatially variable across the country due to local labour markets. Map 43.2 indicates that the 2002 labour force participation rates had increased in the South and were a little more spatially uniform in character. In Northern Ireland, an east-west distinction is clear, with high participation rates in the east, although the cartogram (Map 43.3) highlights a pocket of low participation in the centre of Belfast.

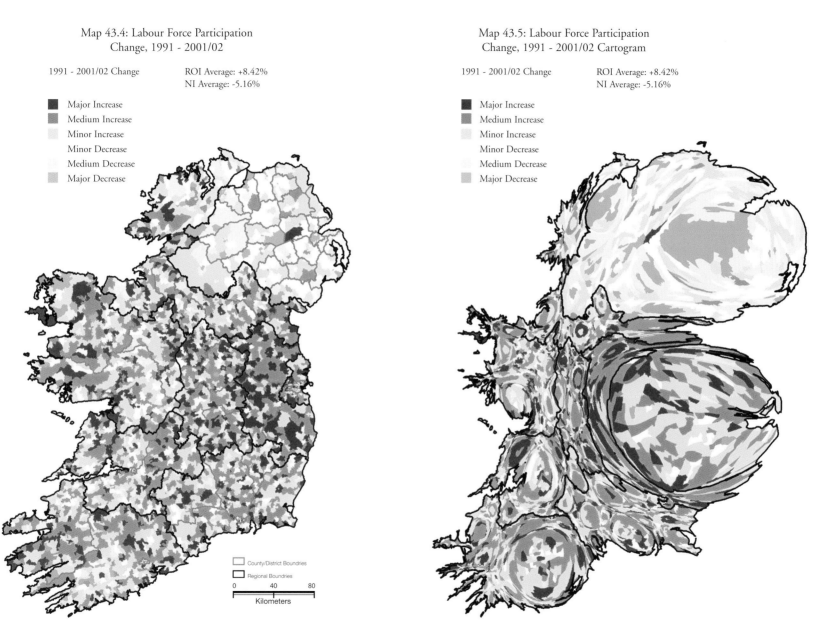

Map 43.4: Labour Force Participation
Change, 1991 - 2001/02

1991 - 2001/02 Change   ROI Average: +8.42%
                             NI Average: -5.16%

■ Major Increase
▨ Medium Increase
░ Minor Increase
  Minor Decrease
  Medium Decrease
▨ Major Decrease

▢ County/District Boundries
▢ Regional Boundries

0   40   80
     Kilometers

Map 43.5: Labour Force Participation
Change, 1991 - 2001/02 Cartogram

1991 - 2001/02 Change   ROI Average: +8.42%
                             NI Average: -5.16%

■ Major Increase
▨ Medium Increase
░ Minor Increase
  Minor Decrease
  Medium Decrease
▨ Major Decrease

The effect of the Celtic Tiger period is clearly demonstrated in Map 43.4, with a relatively large increase in labour force participation in the South from 1991 to 2002, although there are still pockets of low participation at the edges of Cork, Limerick and Galway. During the same period, there was a small decrease in participation in Northern Ireland, especially in Belfast and Derry/Londonderry. This is partly a function of manufacturing decline in those regions and consequent loss of jobs.

MALE LABOUR FORCE PARTICIPATION RATE

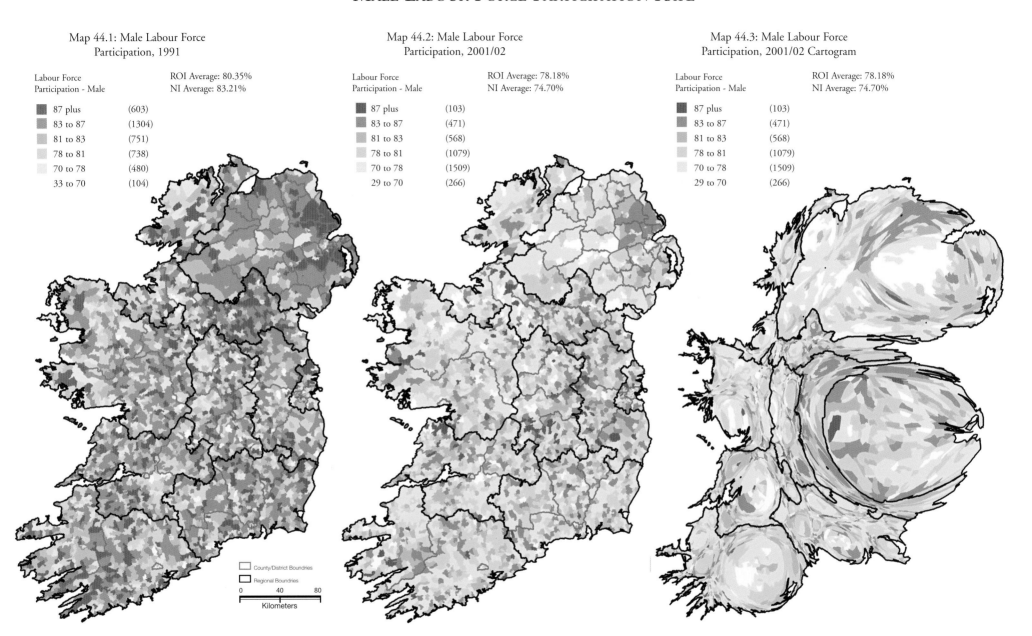

Map 44.1: Male Labour Force
Participation, 1991

Labour Force
Participation - Male

ROI Average: 80.35%
NI Average: 83.21%

87 plus	(603)
83 to 87	(1304)
81 to 83	(751)
78 to 81	(738)
70 to 78	(480)
33 to 70	(104)

County/District Boundries
Regional Boundries

0   40   80
Kilometers

Map 44.2: Male Labour Force
Participation, 2001/02

Labour Force
Participation - Male

ROI Average: 78.18%
NI Average: 74.70%

87 plus	(103)
83 to 87	(471)
81 to 83	(568)
78 to 81	(1079)
70 to 78	(1509)
29 to 70	(266)

Map 44.3: Male Labour Force
Participation, 2001/02 Cartogram

Labour Force
Participation - Male

ROI Average: 78.18%
NI Average: 74.70%

87 plus	(103)
83 to 87	(471)
81 to 83	(568)
78 to 81	(1079)
70 to 78	(1509)
29 to 70	(266)

Map 44.1 suggests that the distinction between Northern Ireland and the Republic is less marked when male labour force participation is considered than when both genders are taken together. The map is spatially heterogeneous, with only a few pockets of high or low participation, such as the east of Northern Ireland, that have a consistently high male labour force participation rate. There was a reduction in male labour force participation rates between 1991 and 2001/02 in both the Republic (-2.70%) and the North (-10.23%). The cartogram (Map 44.5) highlights in particular the decline

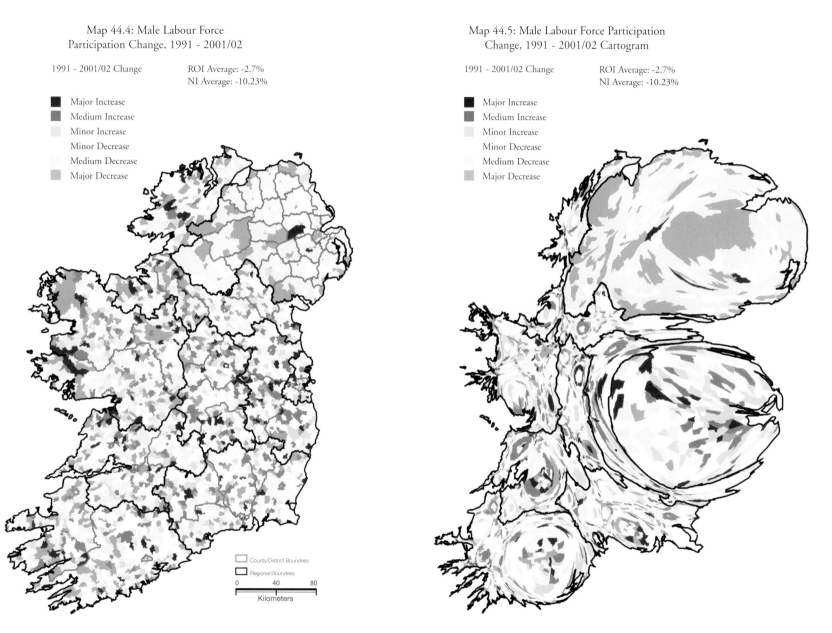

Map 44.4: Male Labour Force
Participation Change, 1991 - 2001/02

1991 - 2001/02 Change   ROI Average: -2.7%
                               NI Average: -10.23%

■ Major Increase
■ Medium Increase
  Minor Increase
  Minor Decrease
  Medium Decrease
■ Major Decrease

Map 44.5: Male Labour Force Participation
Change, 1991 - 2001/02 Cartogram

1991 - 2001/02 Change   ROI Average: -2.7%
                               NI Average: -10.23%

■ Major Increase
■ Medium Increase
  Minor Increase
  Minor Decrease
  Medium Decrease
■ Major Decrease

County/District Boundries
Regional Boundries

0   40   80
Kilometers

in male labour force participation in central Dublin, while the picture in Belfast is more mixed. The decline of heavy industry in Belfast, and Northern Ireland more widely, has clearly had an impact on male employment. In the South, the rise of female participation may have had a marginal impact on male participation in certain local labour markets.

FEMALE LABOUR FORCE PARTICIPATION RATE

Map 45.1: Female Labour Force
Participation, 1991

Labour Force
Participation - Female

ROI Average: 42.75%
NI Average: 55.77%

■	54 plus	(422)
■	44 to 54	(832)
	37 to 44	(1218)
	33 to 37	(673)
	27 to 33	(616)
	0 to 27	(219)

Map 45.2: Female Labour Force
Participation, 2001/02

Labour Force
Participation - Female

ROI Average: 55.36%
NI Average: 57.06%

■	54 plus	(1601)
■	44 to 54	(1902)
	37 to 44	(388)
	33 to 37	(63)
	27 to 33	(35)
	0 to 27	(7)

Map 45.3: Female Labour Force
Participation, 2001/02 Cartogram

Labour Force
Participation - Female

ROI Average: 55.36%
NI Average: 57.06%

■	54 plus	(1601)
■	44 to 54	(1902)
	37 to 44	(388)
	33 to 37	(63)
	27 to 33	(35)
	0 to 27	(7)

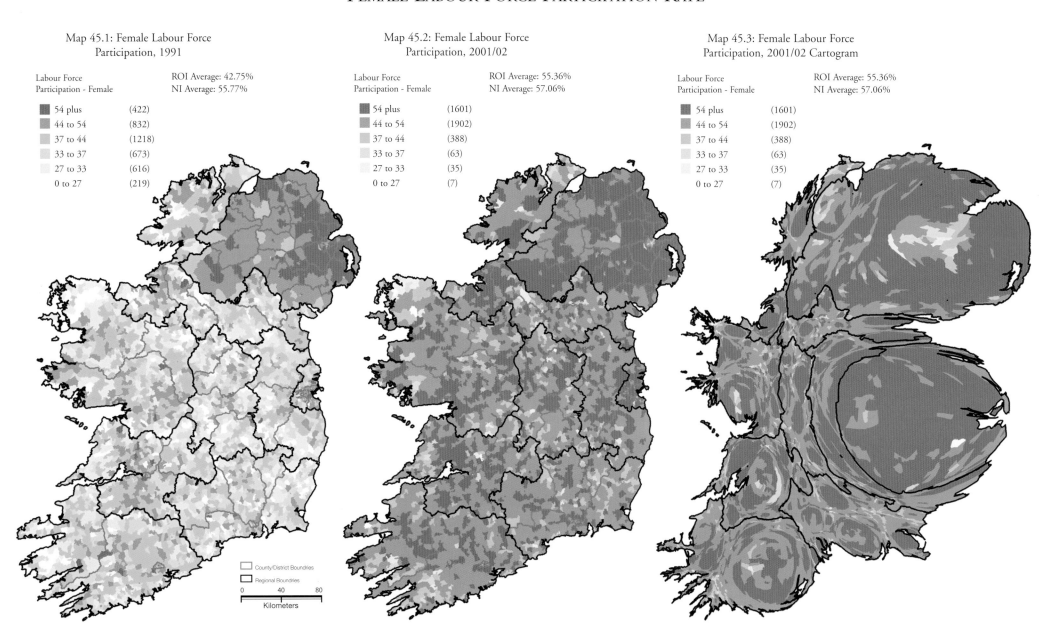

County/District Boundries
Regional Boundries

0   40   80
Kilometers

Map 45.1 reveals a very clear contrast between the female participation rate in the Republic of Ireland and Northern Ireland, with consistently higher participation rates in the North. Within Northern Ireland there is an east-west division with generally higher participation rates in the east and the major labour market in and around Belfast. Map 45.2 reveals that female participation grew enormously in the Republic between 1991 and 2002 (29.47%) and also grew in the west of Northern Ireland. While most of the South experienced some growth, it was particularly strong in areas surrounding the major cities. Given the low base of the Republic and the strong economic growth, one would expect more growth in the South. Female participation rates declined in both Belfast and Derry.

Map 45.4: Female Labour Force
Participation Change, 1991-2001/02

1991 - 2001/02 Change

ROI Average: +29.47%
NI Average: +2.31%

■ Major Increase
▨ Medium Increase
▫ Minor Increase
　 Minor Decrease
　 Medium Decrease
▨ Major Decrease

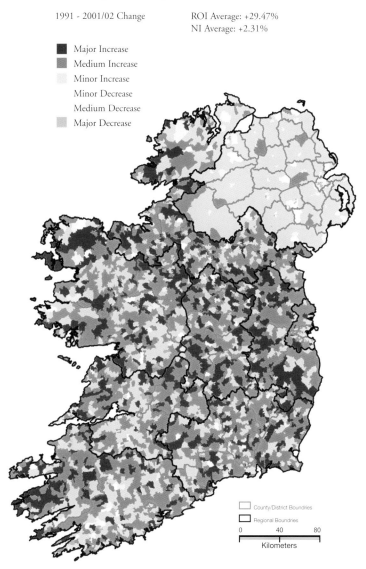

County/District Boundries
Regional Boundries

0　　40　　80
Kilometers

Map 45.4: Female Labour Force Participation
Change, 1991-2001/02 Cartogram

1991 - 2001/02 Change

ROI Average: +29.47%
NI Average: +2.31%

■ Major Increase
▨ Medium Increase
▫ Minor Increase
　 Minor Decrease
　 Medium Decrease
▨ Major Decrease

POPULATION CLASSED AS 'AT WORK'

Map 46.1: At Work, (15/16 - 64 years) 1991

% Population at Work

ROI Average: 50.99%
NI Average: 57.01%

■	61 plus	(440)
■	55 to 61	(1011)
■	51 to 55	(975)
■	47 to 51	(725)
■	40 to 47	(604)
	16 to 41	(225)

Map 46.2: At Work, (15/16 - 64 years) 2001/02

% Population at Work

ROI Average: 60.90%
NI Average: 61.20%

■	61 plus	(2002)
■	55 to 61	(1345)
■	51 to 55	(360)
■	47 to 51	(146)
■	40 to 47	(91)
	16 to 41	(52)

Map 46.3: At Work, (15/16 - 64 years) 2001/02 Cartogram

% Population at Work

ROI Average: 60.90%
NI Average: 61.20%

■	61 plus	(2002)
■	55 to 61	(1345)
■	51 to 55	(360)
■	47 to 51	(146)
■	40 to 47	(100)
	16 to 41	(43)

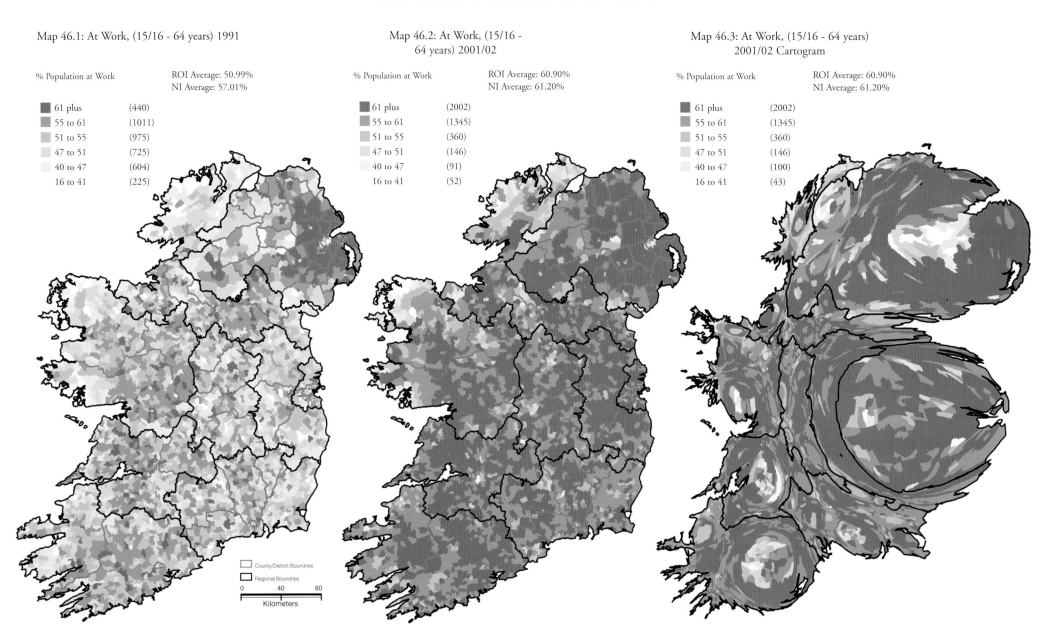

County/District Boundries
Regional Boundries

0   40   80
Kilometers

In 1991 the average number of people at work was 50.99% of the working age population in the Republic and 57.01% for Northern Ireland. Between 1991 to 2001/02, the percentage growth in the at work population in Republic (19.44%) more than doubled that of Northern Ireland (7.35%), so that the at work population in the North and South were approximately the same at 61.20% and 60.90% respectively. In 1991 the percent population at work shows a higher concentration of labour activity around Belfast.   By 2001, other parts of the province have grown to attain similar levels of

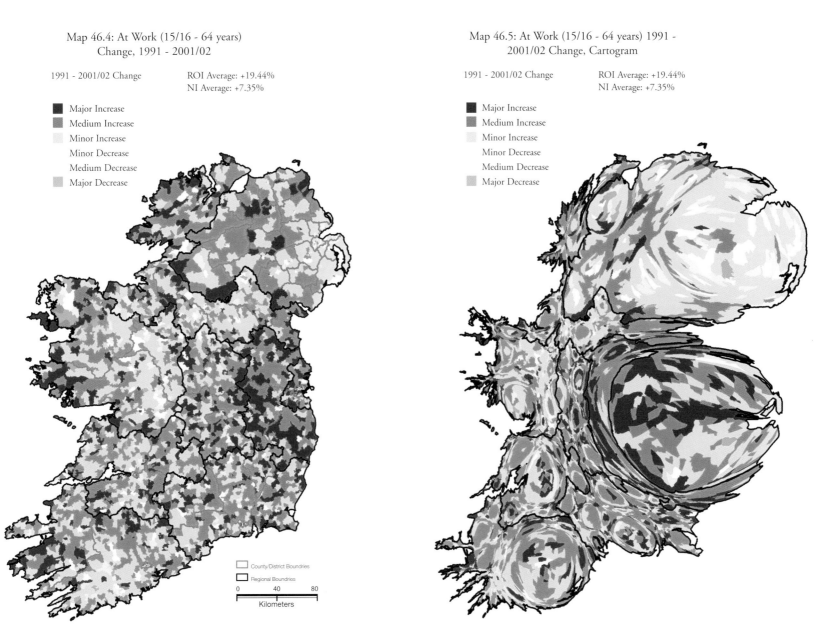

Map 46.4: At Work (15/16 - 64 years)
Change, 1991 - 2001/02

1991 - 2001/02 Change   ROI Average: +19.44%
                         NI Average: +7.35%

■ Major Increase
▨ Medium Increase
□ Minor Increase
  Minor Decrease
  Medium Decrease
▨ Major Decrease

Map 46.5: At Work (15/16 - 64 years) 1991 -
2001/02 Change, Cartogram

1991 - 2001/02 Change   ROI Average: +19.44%
                         NI Average: +7.35%

■ Major Increase
▨ Medium Increase
□ Minor Increase
  Minor Decrease
  Medium Decrease
▨ Major Decrease

□ County/District Boundries
▢ Regional Boundries

0   40   80
      Kilometers

at work percentages with the exception of Belfast city itself. The cartogram (Map 46.3) shows that significant portions of Belfast had at work populations of below 40%, replicated only in Derry, some parts of cities of Galway, Limerick, and Cork, and the Atlantic fringes of Donegal and west Mayo. The pattern of growth in the Republic is quite spatially heterogeneous, however, the strongest increase in the population at work occurs in Dublin and the surrounding counties, especially Meath, Kildare and Wicklow.

MALE POPULATION CLASSED AS 'AT WORK'

Map 47.1: Males Unemployed, (15/16 - 64 years) 1991

% Male Population Unemployed

ROI Average: 15.14%
NI Average: 16.03%

- 23 plus (511)
- 14 to 23 (1115)
- 12 to 14 (470)
- 10 to 12 (525)
- 7 to 10 (733)
- 0 to 7 (626)

Map 47.2: Males Unemployed, (15/16 - 64 years) 2001/02

% Male Population Unemployed

ROI Average: 7.39%
NI Average: 6.23%

- 23 plus (35)
- 14 to 23 (230)
- 12 to 14 (139)
- 10 to 12 (263)
- 7 to 10 (712)
- 0 to 7 (2617)

Map 47.3: Males Unemployed, (15/16 - 64 years) 2001/02 Cartogram

% Male Population Unemployed

ROI Average: 7.39%
NI Average: 6.23%

- 23 plus (35)
- 14 to 23 (230)
- 12 to 14 (139)
- 10 to 12 (263)
- 7 to 10 (712)
- 0 to 7 (2617)

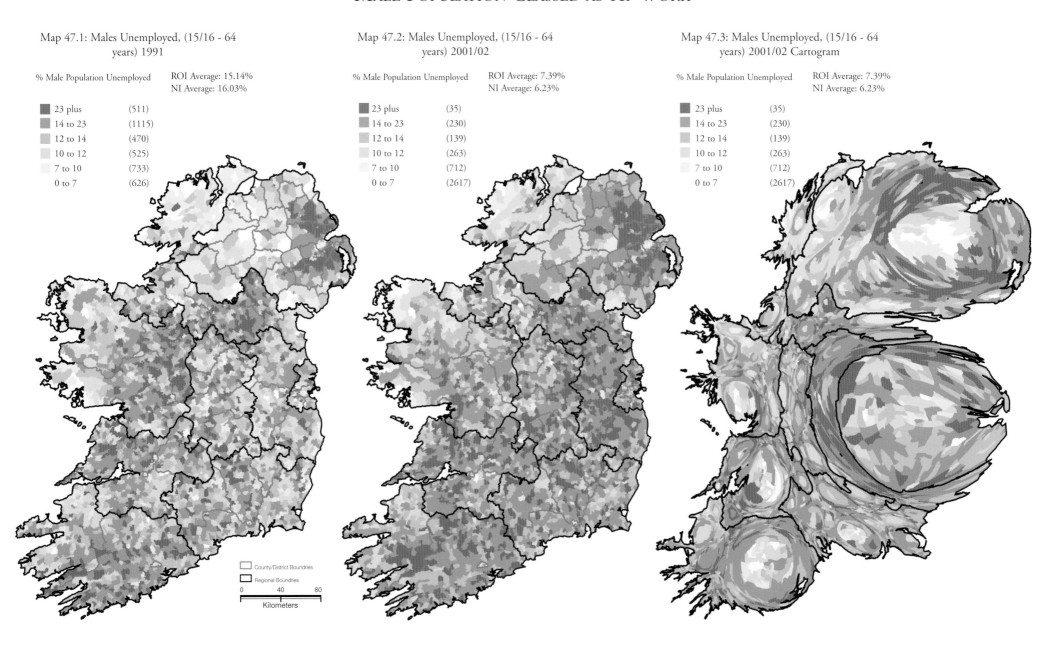

County/District Boundries
Regional Boundries

0 40 80
Kilometers

As with the total population at work, concentrations of high male at work percentages are found around Belfast in 1991, with many areas having more than 73% of males at work. The pattern in the Republic is less pronounced with more diffuse and sporadic concentrations. Both jurisdictions have a very similar average rate of at work males (65.2%, South; 65.39% North). Between 1991 and 2001 the rate of males at work population in the workforce grew 8.57% in the Republic and 4.79% in the North, consequently the rate of males at work became slightly higher in the South.

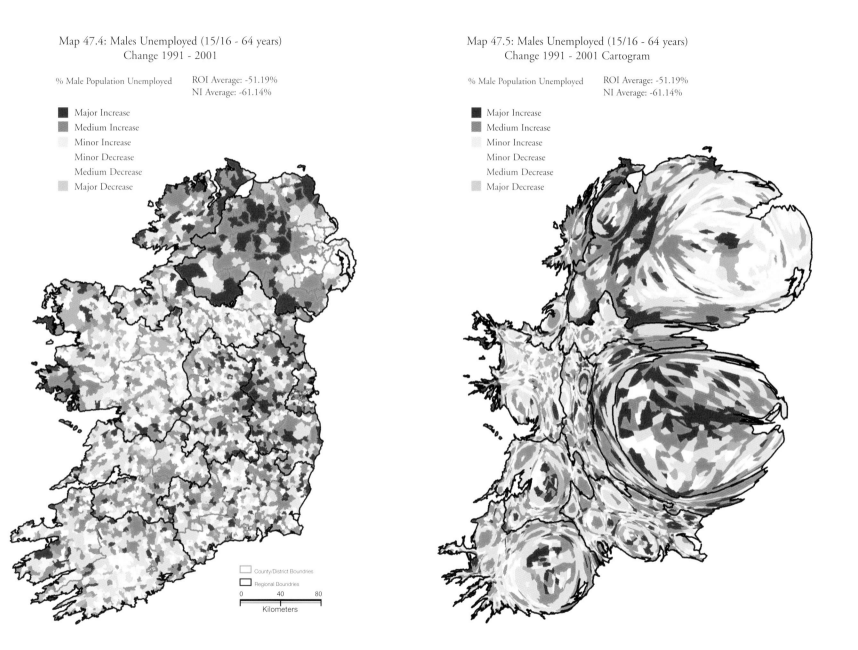

Map 47.4: Males Unemployed (15/16 - 64 years)
Change 1991 - 2001

% Male Population Unemployed   ROI Average: -51.19%
NI Average: -61.14%

■ Major Increase
▨ Medium Increase
□ Minor Increase
  Minor Decrease
  Medium Decrease
▨ Major Decrease

Map 47.5: Males Unemployed (15/16 - 64 years)
Change 1991 - 2001 Cartogram

% Male Population Unemployed   ROI Average: -51.19%
NI Average: -61.14%

■ Major Increase
▨ Medium Increase
□ Minor Increase
  Minor Decrease
  Medium Decrease
▨ Major Decrease

☐ County/District Boundries
☐ Regional Boundries

0   40   80
Kilometers

However, the Republic experienced more spatially concentrated decreases in percent male at work rates especially in west Mayo, west Sligo, Leitrim, Roscommon, Cavan and Monaghan. This was counter-balanced by a growth in and around Dublin. In Northern Ireland, there was strong growth in the west of the province and south Belfast, but a moderate decrease in areas surrounding Belfast. At work rates for males were lower in all of the principal towns and cities than their surrounds, with rates below 50% in 2001/02 evident in Belfast, Derry, Galway, Limerick and Cork.

FEMALE POPULATION CLASSED AS 'AT WORK'

Map 48.1: Females At Work, (15/16 - 64
years) 1991

% Female Population At Work

ROI Average: 36.62%
NI Average: 48.78%

■	49 plus	(373)
■	40 to 49	(696)
■	34 to 40	(958)
	29 to 34	(977)
	23 to 29	(682)
	0 to 23	(294)

Map 48.2: Females At Work, (15/16 - 64
years) 2001/02

% Female Population At Work

ROI Average: 50.92%
NI Average: 54.09%

■	49 plus	(1878)
■	40 to 49	(1624)
■	34 to 40	(361)
	29 to 34	(89)
	23 to 29	(33)
	0 to 23	(11)

Map 48.3: Females At Work, (15/16 - 64
years) 2001/02 Cartogram

% Female Population At Work

ROI Average: 50.92%
NI Average: 54.09%

■	49 plus	(1878)
■	40 to 49	(1624)
■	34 to 40	(361)
	29 to 34	(89)
	23 to 29	(33)
	0 to 23	(11)

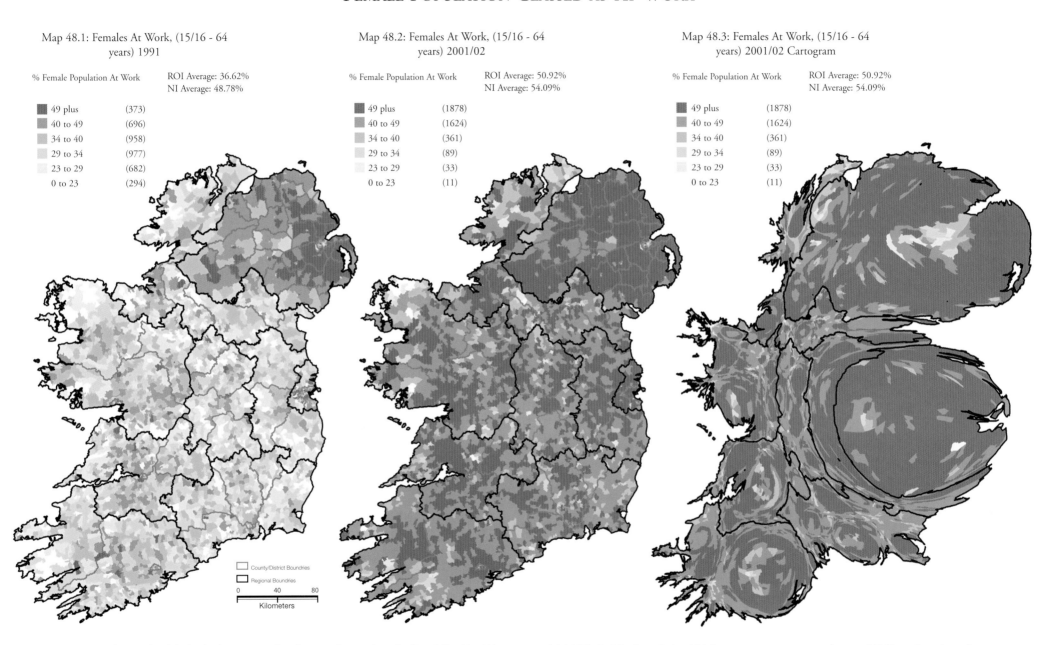

County/District Boundries
Regional Boundries

0   40   80
Kilometers

In 1991 Northern Ireland had a higher average female at work rate than the Republic, 48.78% as opposed 36.32%. In Northern Ireland higher rates are concentrated around Belfast, though are lower in the city itself, while no equivalent concentration existed in the South. By 2001/02, the Republic had similar average rates to Northern Ireland, 50.92% and 54.09% respectively, given the high rates of growth in female participation in the Celtic Tiger economy. Indeed, between 1991 and 2001/02 the rate of females at work grew by 39.05% in the Republic and 10.89% in the North. No specific

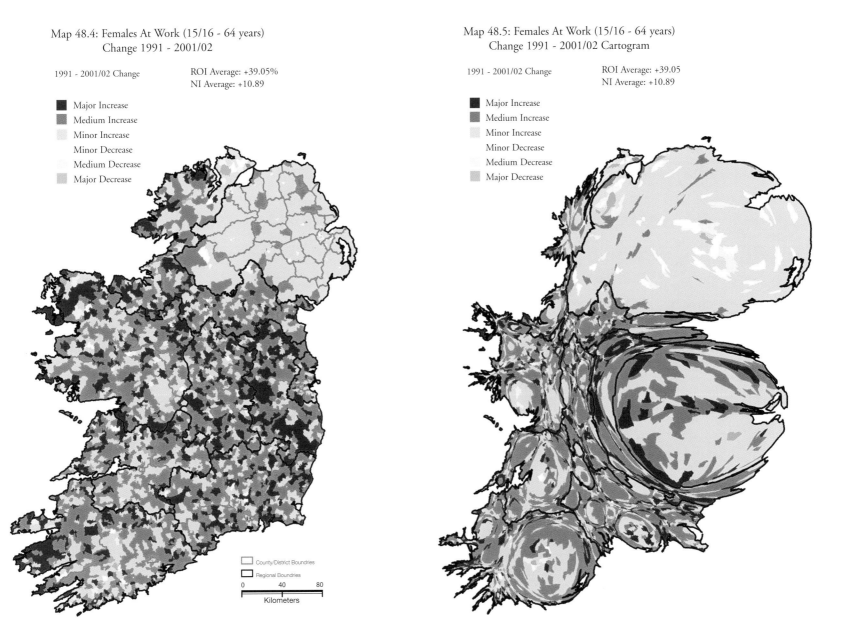

Map 48.4: Females At Work (15/16 - 64 years)
Change 1991 - 2001/02

1991 - 2001/02 Change

ROI Average: +39.05%
NI Average: +10.89

■ Major Increase
■ Medium Increase
□ Minor Increase
Minor Decrease
Medium Decrease
■ Major Decrease

Map 48.5: Females At Work (15/16 - 64 years)
Change 1991 - 2001/02 Cartogram

1991 - 2001/02 Change

ROI Average: +39.05
NI Average: +10.89

■ Major Increase
■ Medium Increase
□ Minor Increase
Minor Decrease
Medium Decrease
■ Major Decrease

□ County/District Boundries
□ Regional Boundries

0   40   80
Kilometers

concentration of higher rates of females at work is apparent in the North or South in 2001/02, although concentrations of lower female at work rates exist in west Mayo, north Donegal and Belfast city. Given the general pattern of growth of females at work, in contrast to males, there are only a few isolated areas where at work rates decreased.

LABOUR FORCE CLASSED AS 'AT WORK'

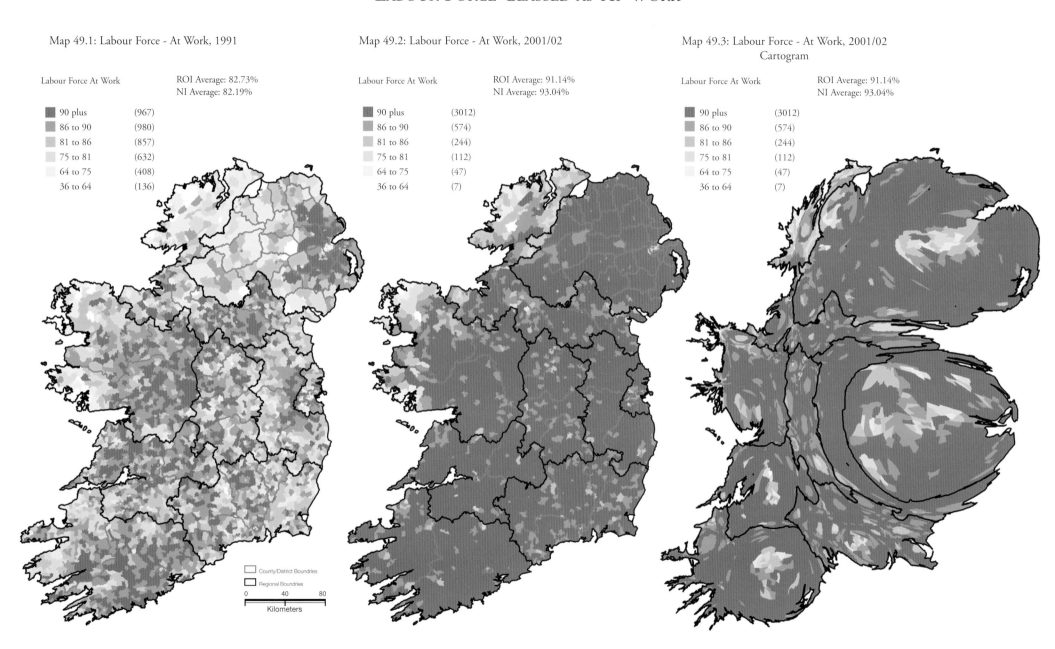

Map 49.1: Labour Force - At Work, 1991

Labour Force At Work

ROI Average: 82.73%
NI Average: 82.19%

■	90 plus	(967)
■	86 to 90	(980)
■	81 to 86	(857)
■	75 to 81	(632)
■	64 to 75	(408)
■	36 to 64	(136)

Map 49.2: Labour Force - At Work, 2001/02

Labour Force At Work

ROI Average: 91.14%
NI Average: 93.04%

■	90 plus	(3012)
■	86 to 90	(574)
■	81 to 86	(244)
■	75 to 81	(112)
■	64 to 75	(47)
■	36 to 64	(7)

Map 49.3: Labour Force - At Work, 2001/02
Cartogram

Labour Force At Work

ROI Average: 91.14%
NI Average: 93.04%

■	90 plus	(3012)
■	86 to 90	(574)
■	81 to 86	(244)
■	75 to 81	(112)
■	64 to 75	(47)
■	36 to 64	(7)

County/District Boundries
Regional Boundries

0   40   80
Kilometers

In 1991 there was no noticeable difference between the average labour force at work rates for the Republic (82.73%) and Northern Ireland (82.19%), yet there are distinct differences in spatial patterns. In Northern Ireland there is a higher rate of labour force at work in the commuter belt surrounding Belfast, while in the Republic higher rates are evident in the west midlands, south west, and surrounding Dublin. By 2001/02 the Northern Ireland average rate had reached 93.04% and the Republic rate 91.14%, with the majority of the island experiencing rates of more than 90% of the labour

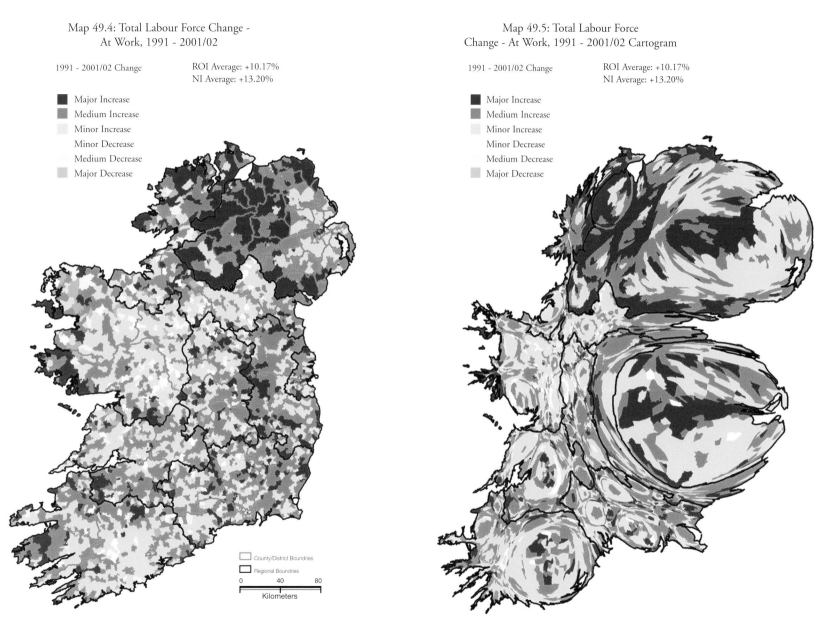

Map 49.4: Total Labour Force Change -
At Work, 1991 - 2001/02

1991 - 2001/02 Change

ROI Average: +10.17%
NI Average: +13.20%

■ Major Increase
▨ Medium Increase
▫ Minor Increase
Minor Decrease
Medium Decrease
▨ Major Decrease

□ County/District Boundries
▢ Regional Boundries

0   40   80
Kilometers

Map 49.5: Total Labour Force
Change - At Work, 1991 - 2001/02 Cartogram

1991 - 2001/02 Change

ROI Average: +10.17%
NI Average: +13.20%

■ Major Increase
▨ Medium Increase
▫ Minor Increase
Minor Decrease
Medium Decrease
▨ Major Decrease

force at work. The major exception to this trend are Donegal and the western reaches of Mayo and Galway, central Belfast, and parts of Dublin, Limerick and Cork. In Northern Ireland, the major increase in the percent of labour force occurred in Belfast city and to the west and south of the province. In the Republic, percentage change is less spatially concentrated, with the exception of central Dublin.

Male Labour Force Classed as 'At Work'

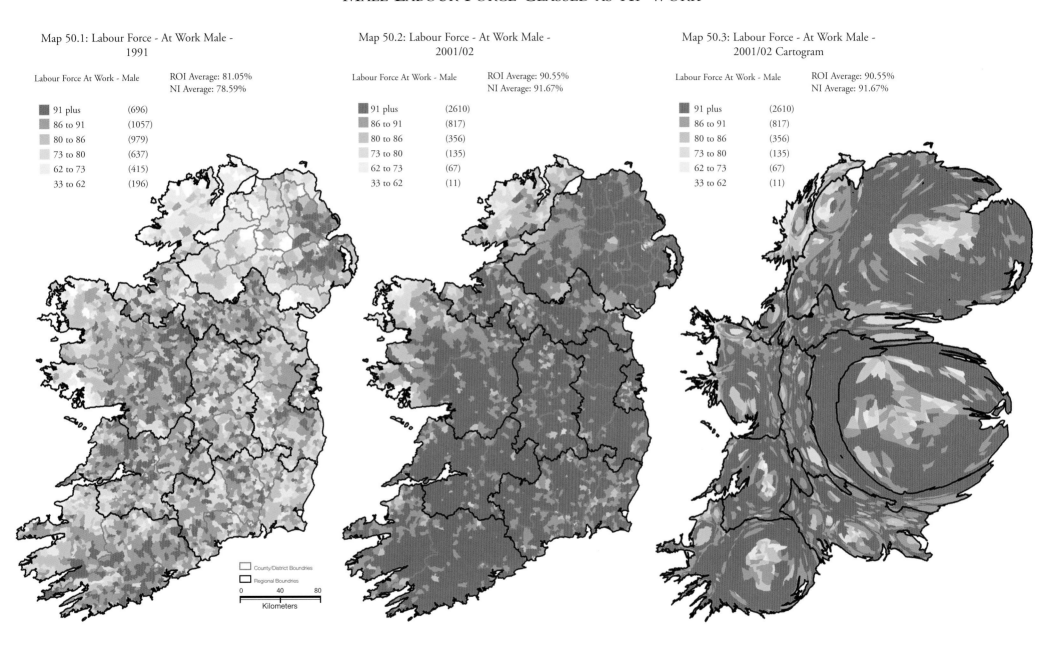

Map 50.1: Labour Force - At Work Male -
1991

Labour Force At Work - Male

ROI Average: 81.05%
NI Average: 78.59%

■	91 plus	(696)
■	86 to 91	(1057)
■	80 to 86	(979)
□	73 to 80	(637)
□	62 to 73	(415)
□	33 to 62	(196)

Map 50.2: Labour Force - At Work Male -
2001/02

Labour Force At Work - Male

ROI Average: 90.55%
NI Average: 91.67%

■	91 plus	(2610)
■	86 to 91	(817)
■	80 to 86	(356)
□	73 to 80	(135)
□	62 to 73	(67)
□	33 to 62	(11)

Map 50.3: Labour Force - At Work Male -
2001/02 Cartogram

Labour Force At Work - Male

ROI Average: 90.55%
NI Average: 91.67%

■	91 plus	(2610)
■	86 to 91	(817)
■	80 to 86	(356)
□	73 to 80	(135)
□	62 to 73	(67)
□	33 to 62	(11)

County/District Boundries
Regional Boundries

0   40   80
Kilometers

The pattern for male labour force at work in both 1991 and 2001/02 is, as one might expect, very similar to the overall labour force distribution, with a higher concentration of male labour force at work around the Belfast area and a less spatially concentrated pattern in the Republic. By 2001/02 the pattern changes across the island with average rates of male labour force at work above 90% in the majority of areas with the exceptions of central Belfast, Derry, Donegal, west Mayo and parts of Dublin, Cork and Limerick. Between 1991 and 2001/02 the average increase in the percentage of

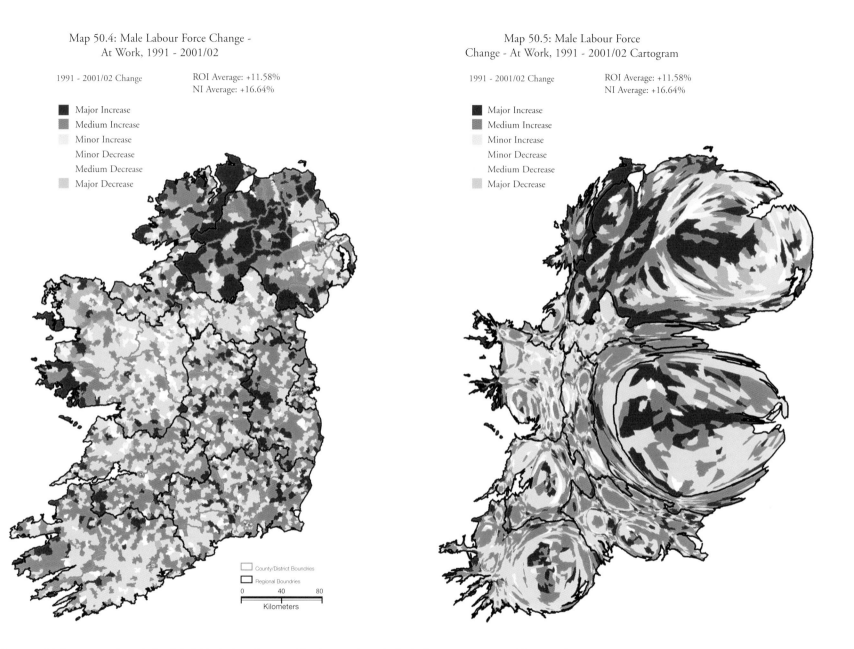

Map 50.4: Male Labour Force Change -
At Work, 1991 - 2001/02

1991 - 2001/02 Change   ROI Average: +11.58%
                               NI Average: +16.64%

■ Major Increase
▨ Medium Increase
☐ Minor Increase
  Minor Decrease
  Medium Decrease
▨ Major Decrease

☐ County/District Boundries
◻ Regional Boundries
0   40   80
        Kilometers

Map 50.5: Male Labour Force
Change - At Work, 1991 - 2001/02 Cartogram

1991 - 2001/02 Change   ROI Average: +11.58%
                               NI Average: +16.64%

■ Major Increase
▨ Medium Increase
☐ Minor Increase
  Minor Decrease
  Medium Decrease
▨ Major Decrease

male labour force was higher in Northern Ireland (16.64%) than the Republic (11.58%), with the highest increases in Belfast city, the west and south of the province. In the South the areas of increase are fairly evenly dispersed, with the cities of Dublin, Cork and Limerick showing concentrated pockets of growth. There are relatively few areas of decrease, mainly confined to some areas around Belfast and west Mayo.

FEMALE LABOUR FORCE CLASSED AS 'AT WORK'

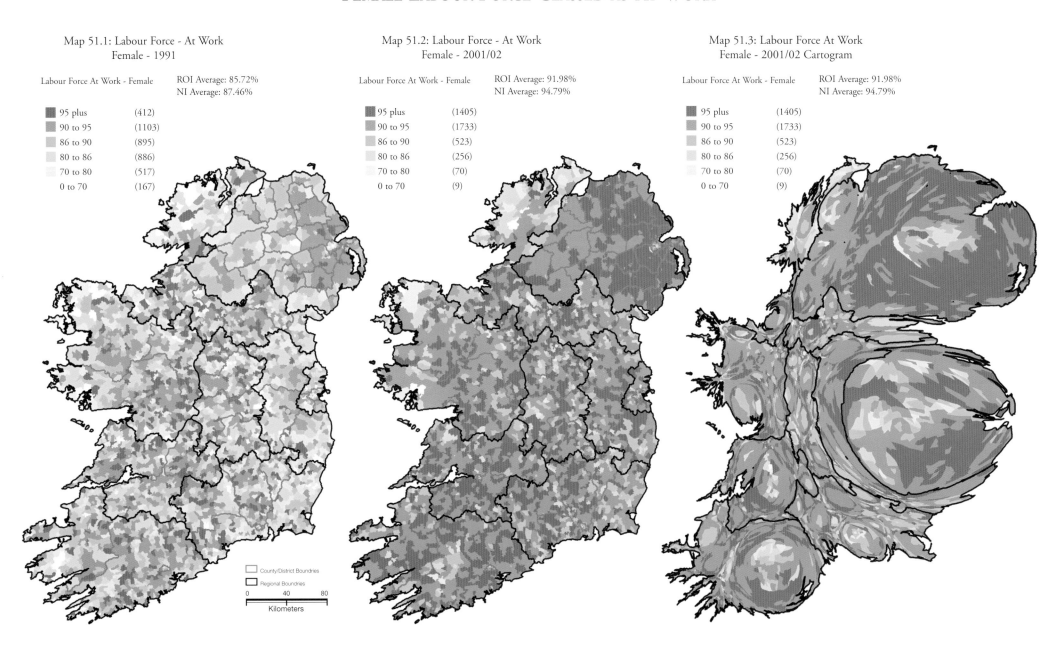

Map 51.1: Labour Force - At Work
Female - 1991

Labour Force At Work - Female

ROI Average: 85.72%
NI Average: 87.46%

■	95 plus	(412)
■	90 to 95	(1103)
■	86 to 90	(895)
■	80 to 86	(886)
■	70 to 80	(517)
■	0 to 70	(167)

Map 51.2: Labour Force - At Work
Female - 2001/02

Labour Force At Work - Female

ROI Average: 91.98%
NI Average: 94.79%

■	95 plus	(1405)
■	90 to 95	(1733)
■	86 to 90	(523)
■	80 to 86	(256)
■	70 to 80	(70)
■	0 to 70	(9)

Map 51.3: Labour Force At Work
Female - 2001/02 Cartogram

Labour Force At Work - Female

ROI Average: 91.98%
NI Average: 94.79%

■	95 plus	(1405)
■	90 to 95	(1733)
■	86 to 90	(523)
■	80 to 86	(256)
■	70 to 80	(70)
■	0 to 70	(9)

County/District Boundries
Regional Boundries

0   40   80
Kilometers

In 1991 the average female labour force at work was similar in Ireland and Northern Ireland with an average rate of 85.72% and 87.46% respectively. The pattern is broadly similar to the overall labour force participation rate, but less concentrated. By 2001, the average at work rate had increased to 94.79% in the North and 91.98% in the South, with the majority of areas above 90% at work.

As with the overall and male patterns, the exceptions were central Belfast, Derry, Donegal, west Mayo and parts of Dublin, Cork and Limerick. Growth between 1991 and 2001/02 was scattered across

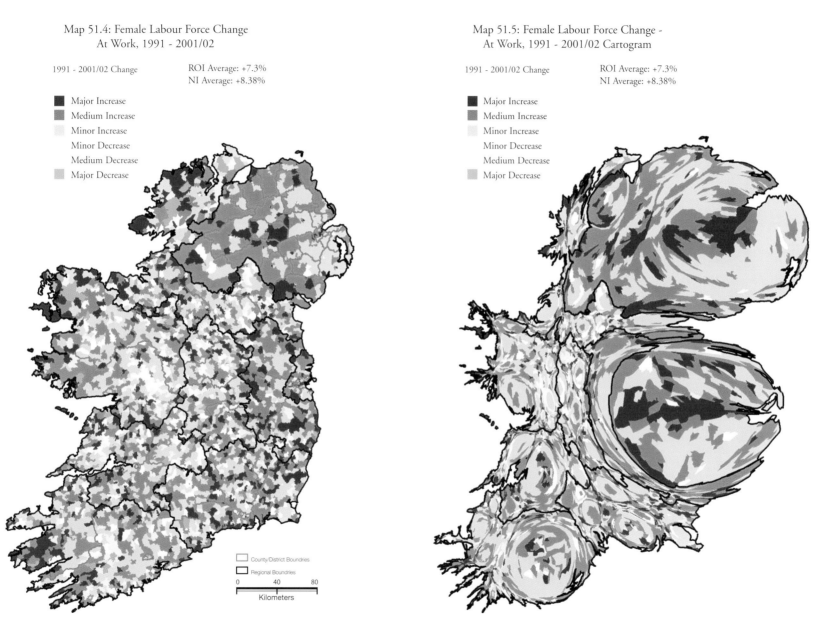

Map 51.4: Female Labour Force Change
At Work, 1991 - 2001/02

1991 - 2001/02 Change   ROI Average: +7.3%
                               NI Average: +8.38%

■ Major Increase
▨ Medium Increase
  Minor Increase
  Minor Decrease
  Medium Decrease
▨ Major Decrease

Map 51.5: Female Labour Force Change -
At Work, 1991 - 2001/02 Cartogram

1991 - 2001/02 Change   ROI Average: +7.3%
                               NI Average: +8.38%

■ Major Increase
▨ Medium Increase
  Minor Increase
  Minor Decrease
  Medium Decrease
▨ Major Decrease

County/District Boundries
Regional Boundries

0   40   80
Kilometers

the island, with notable areas of growth including west Cork, parts of Donegal, central Northern Ireland, Belfast city and central Dublin. No areas in Northern Ireland experienced a decrease between 1991 and 2001/02 of female labour force at work, but there was a broad scattering of areas lacking spatial concentration in the South.

POPULATION CLASSED AS 'UNEMPLOYED'

Map 52.1: 15/16 - 64 Unemployed, 1991

Map 52.2: 15/16 - 64 Unemployed, 2001/02

Map 52.3: 15/16 - 64 Unemployed, 2001/02
Cartogram

% Population Unemployed

ROI Average: 10.64%
NI Average: 10.99%

21 plus	(157)	
15 to 21	(411)	
11 to 15	(736)	
8 to 11	(962)	
6 to 8	(813)	
0 to 6	(901)	

% Population Unemployed

ROI Average: 5.92%
NI Average: 4.58%

21 plus	(8)	
15 to 21	(47)	
11 to 15	(167)	
8 to 11	(349)	
6 to 8	(587)	
0 to 6	(2838)	

% Population Unemployed

ROI Average: 5.92%
NI Average: 4.58%

21 plus	(8)	
15 to 21	(47)	
11 to 15	(167)	
8 to 11	(349)	
6 to 8	(587)	
0 to 6	(2838)	

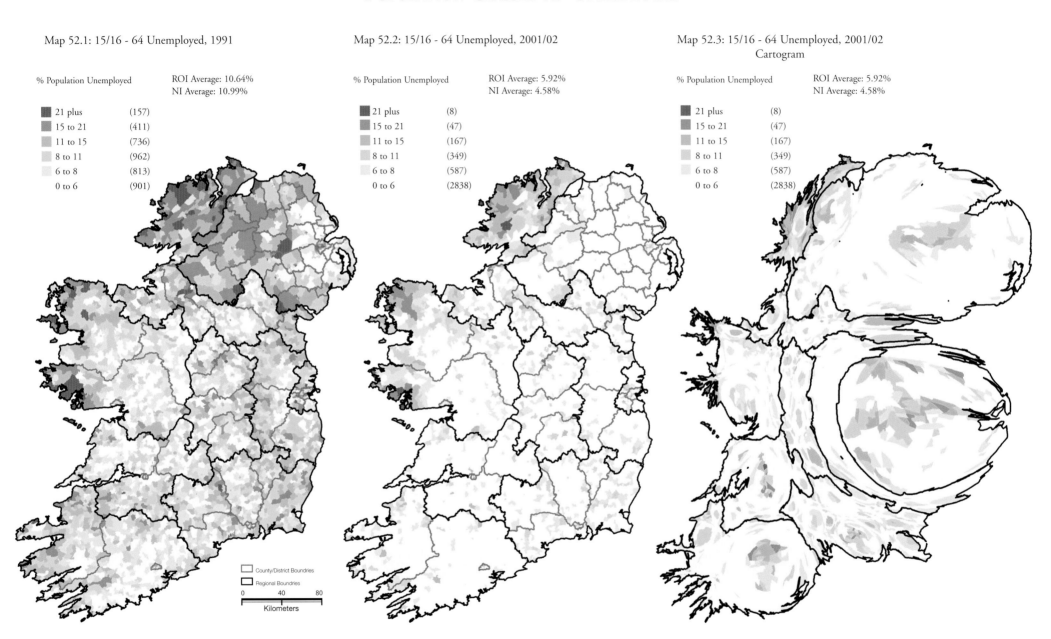

County/District Boundries

Regional Boundries

0   40   80

Kilometers

In 1991 the percent of population unemployed was broadly similar for Northern Ireland (10.99%) and the republic (10.64%). Within NI, rates exceeding 15% were experienced in Belfast city and in the west of the province in areas such as Portadown, Limavady, Strabane, Omagh and Cookstown. In the South, rates exceeding 15% unemployment were concentrated in Donegal, west Mayo and Galway. By 2001/02 employment rates had approximately halved in relative terms (by 58.33% and 44.36% respectively) to 4.58% in the North and 5.92% in the South. At this time, most of the

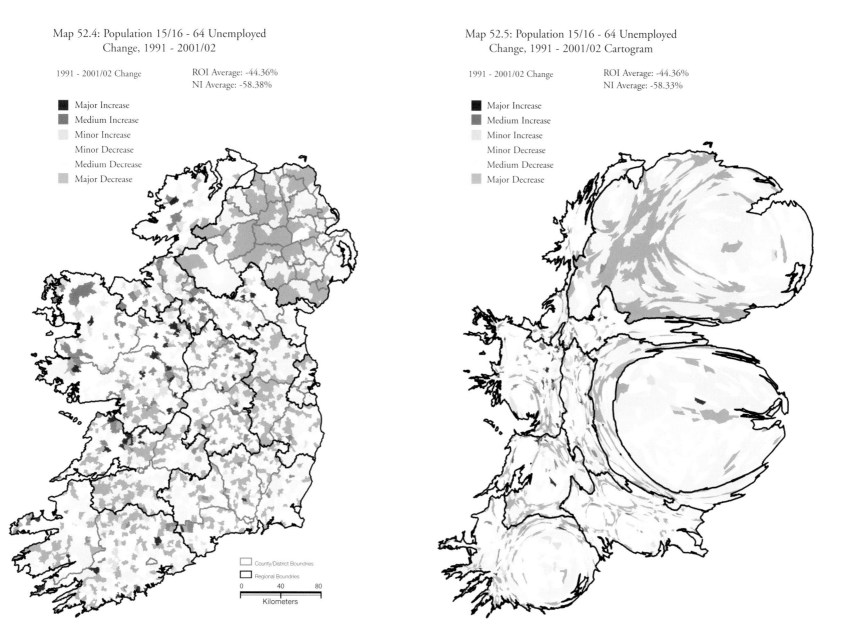

Map 52.4: Population 15/16 - 64 Unemployed
Change, 1991 - 2001/02

1991 - 2001/02 Change   ROI Average: -44.36%
                               NI Average: -58.38%

■ Major Increase
■ Medium Increase
  Minor Increase
  Minor Decrease
  Medium Decrease
■ Major Decrease

☐ County/District Boundries
☐ Regional Boundries

0   40   80
Kilometers

Map 52.5: Population 15/16 - 64 Unemployed
Change, 1991 - 2001/02 Cartogram

1991 - 2001/02 Change   ROI Average: -44.36%
                               NI Average: -58.33%

■ Major Increase
■ Medium Increase
  Minor Increase
  Minor Decrease
  Medium Decrease
■ Major Decrease

island had unemployment rates under 7% although clusters of high unemployment are still apparent in Donegal and west Mayo and Galway and, as the cartogram reveals, the cities of Belfast, Dublin, Cork and Limerick. Only a few places experienced unemployment gain, all in the Republic, and mostly in rural areas where the rural economy has experienced difficulties and decline.

MALE POPULATION CLASSED AS 'UNEMPLOYED'

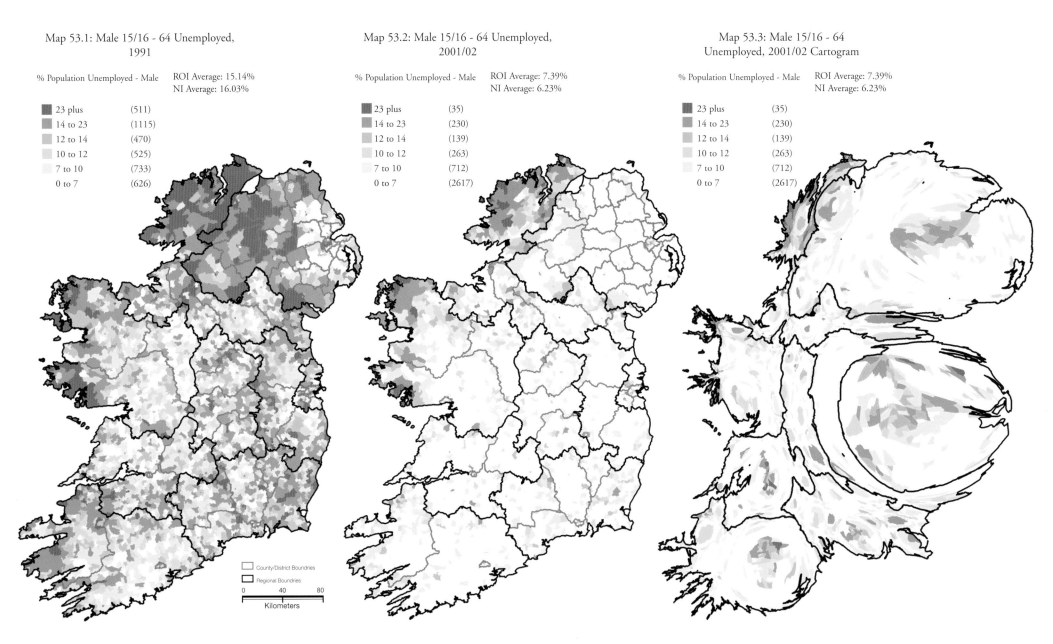

Map 53.1: Male 15/16 - 64 Unemployed,
1991

% Population Unemployed - Male   ROI Average: 15.14%
NI Average: 16.03%

■	23 plus	(511)
■	14 to 23	(1115)
■	12 to 14	(470)
■	10 to 12	(525)
■	7 to 10	(733)
	0 to 7	(626)

Map 53.2: Male 15/16 - 64 Unemployed,
2001/02

% Population Unemployed - Male   ROI Average: 7.39%
NI Average: 6.23%

■	23 plus	(35)
■	14 to 23	(230)
■	12 to 14	(139)
■	10 to 12	(263)
■	7 to 10	(712)
	0 to 7	(2617)

Map 53.3: Male 15/16 - 64
Unemployed, 2001/02 Cartogram

% Population Unemployed - Male   ROI Average: 7.39%
NI Average: 6.23%

■	23 plus	(35)
■	14 to 23	(230)
■	12 to 14	(139)
■	10 to 12	(263)
■	7 to 10	(712)
	0 to 7	(2617)

County/District Boundries
Regional Boundries

0   40   80
Kilometers

In 1991 the average percentage of unemployed males were similar at 15.14% in Northern Ireland and 16.03% in the Republic. In the North the areas with the highest rates include Belfast, south Armagh, Tyrone and Derry. In the Republic, Donegal and west Mayo and Galway, and parts of north Munster and east Leinster have high concentrations. By 2001/02 there was a significant relative decline in the levels of male unemployment in both the North (61.14%) and South (51.19%). This decrease occurs fairly evenly across Northern Ireland, but there are a scattering of areas experiencing

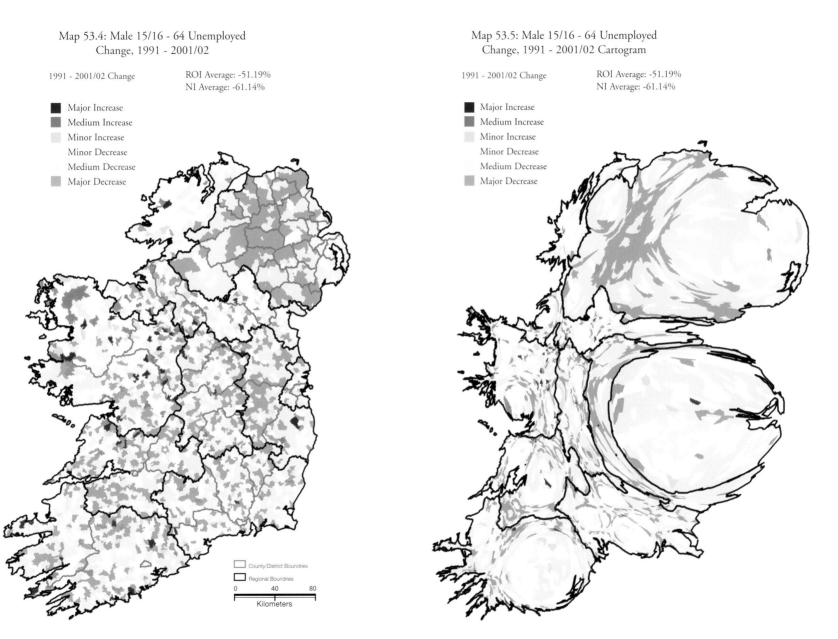

Map 53.4: Male 15/16 - 64 Unemployed
Change, 1991 - 2001/02

1991 - 2001/02 Change

ROI Average: -51.19%
NI Average: -61.14%

- Major Increase
- Medium Increase
- Minor Increase
- Minor Decrease
- Medium Decrease
- Major Decrease

Map 53.5: Male 15/16 - 64 Unemployed
Change, 1991 - 2001/02 Cartogram

1991 - 2001/02 Change

ROI Average: -51.19%
NI Average: -61.14%

- Major Increase
- Medium Increase
- Minor Increase
- Minor Decrease
- Medium Decrease
- Major Decrease

County/District Boundries
Regional Boundries

0   40   80

Kilometers

increase in the South, especially in rural areas. Despite the general pattern of decrease there are concentrations of male unemployment exceeding 14% in Belfast city, Derry, Donegal, west Mayo and Galway, and parts of Dublin, Galway and Limerick cities.

FEMALE POPULATION CLASSED AS 'UNEMPLOYED'

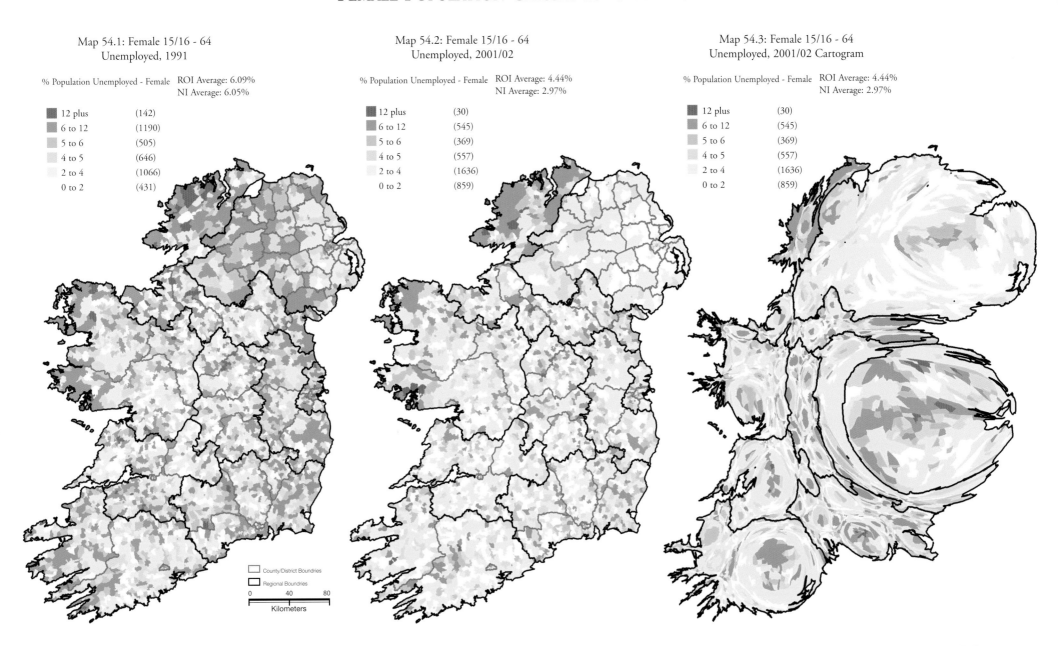

Map 54.1: Female 15/16 - 64
Unemployed, 1991

% Population Unemployed - Female   ROI Average: 6.09%
NI Average: 6.05%

12 plus	(142)
6 to 12	(1190)
5 to 6	(505)
4 to 5	(646)
2 to 4	(1066)
0 to 2	(431)

Map 54.2: Female 15/16 - 64
Unemployed, 2001/02

% Population Unemployed - Female   ROI Average: 4.44%
NI Average: 2.97%

12 plus	(30)
6 to 12	(545)
5 to 6	(369)
4 to 5	(557)
2 to 4	(1636)
0 to 2	(859)

Map 54.3: Female 15/16 - 64
Unemployed, 2001/02 Cartogram

% Population Unemployed - Female   ROI Average: 4.44%
NI Average: 2.97%

12 plus	(30)
6 to 12	(545)
5 to 6	(369)
4 to 5	(557)
2 to 4	(1636)
0 to 2	(859)

County/District Boundries
Regional Boundries
0   40   80
Kilometers

In 1991 the percent of unemployed females was 6.09% in the Republic and 6.05% in Northern Ireland. In part, the lower rates than males were due to a smaller number of women potentially being active participants in the work force. With the exception of a commuting ring around Belfast, female unemployment is relatively high across Northern Ireland. The pattern in the South is more diffuse, with little discernable concentration except along the western and eastern seaboards. By 2001/02, there is a significant relative drop (50.91%, North; 27.09% South) in female unemployment across the island, with the number of areas showing unemployment levels above 6% in both the Republic and Northern Ireland rapidly decreasing. The exceptions were the northwest and the principal

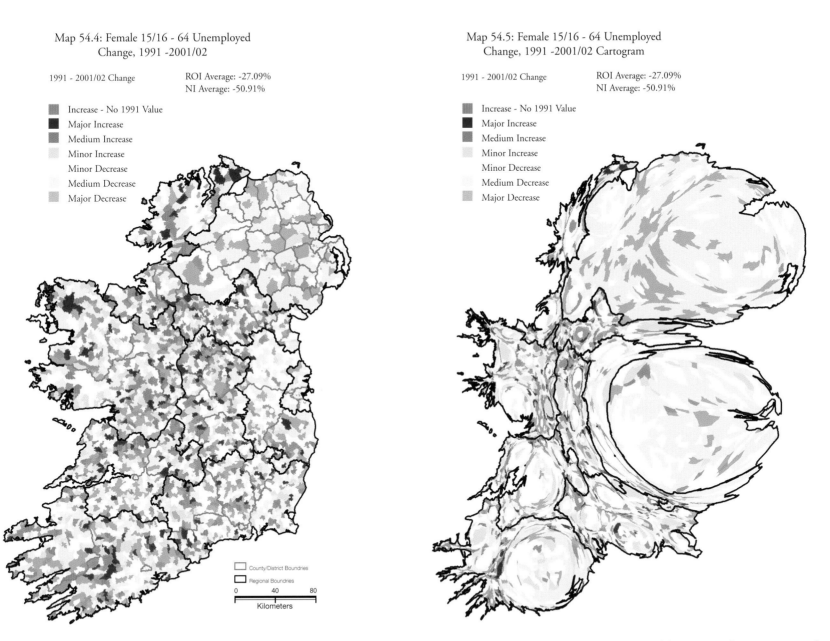

Map 54.4: Female 15/16 - 64 Unemployed
Change, 1991 -2001/02

1991 - 2001/02 Change

ROI Average: -27.09%
NI Average: -50.91%

Increase - No 1991 Value
Major Increase
Medium Increase
Minor Increase
Minor Decrease
Medium Decrease
Major Decrease

County/District Boundries
Regional Boundries

0   40   80
Kilometers

Map 54.5: Female 15/16 - 64 Unemployed
Change, 1991 -2001/02 Cartogram

1991 - 2001/02 Change

ROI Average: -27.09%
NI Average: -50.91%

Increase - No 1991 Value
Major Increase
Medium Increase
Minor Increase
Minor Decrease
Medium Decrease
Major Decrease

cities and towns in the South and Belfast in the North. Although rates of female unemployment decreased in almost all of Northern Ireland, in the Republic many rural areas experienced pockets of increase including a number areas shaded green that had no recorded female unemployment in 1991.

POPULATION CLASSED AS 'STUDENTS'

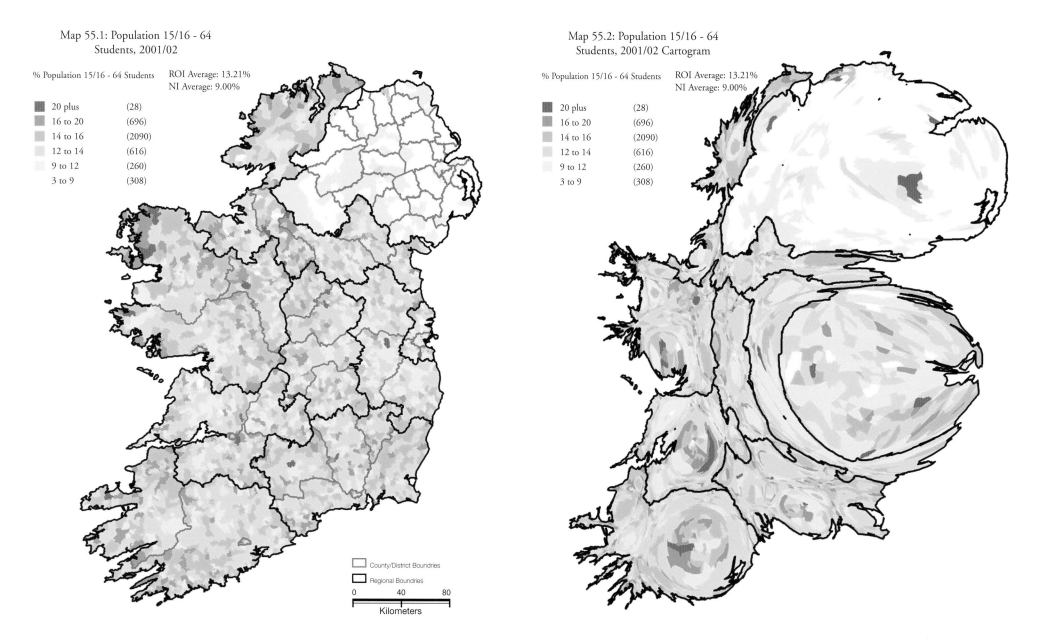

Map 55.1: Population 15/16 - 64
Students, 2001/02

% Population 15/16 - 64 Students   ROI Average: 13.21%
                                      NI Average: 9.00%

	20 plus	(28)
	16 to 20	(696)
	14 to 16	(2090)
	12 to 14	(616)
	9 to 12	(260)
	3 to 9	(308)

Map 55.2: Population 15/16 - 64
Students, 2001/02 Cartogram

% Population 15/16 - 64 Students   ROI Average: 13.21%
                                      NI Average: 9.00%

	20 plus	(28)
	16 to 20	(696)
	14 to 16	(2090)
	12 to 14	(616)
	9 to 12	(260)
	3 to 9	(308)

County/District Boundries

Regional Boundries

0   40   80
Kilometers

Comparison of the student population from 1991 to 2001 is problematic. In 1991 in Northern Ireland, students were recorded as resident at their vacation or home address. In 2001, students were counted at their term time address. Therefore, direct comparison between these figures has not been made here and only the 2001 (and 2002 in the Republic) figures are used. The most obvious feature of Map 55.1 is the marked difference between the Republic and Northern Ireland, with consistently higher proportions in the South (with the age range 15-64) than in the North (age range 16-64). In the cartogram (Map 55.2), the one notable peak in Belfast corresponds with the university area of south Belfast. Dublin, like the rest of the South, is extremely consistent in terms of proportions of students. Map 55.2 reveals areas with larger proportions of students in some areas including Cork and Limerick, both with large university communities.

NON-LABOUR FORCE CLASSED AS 'STUDENTS'

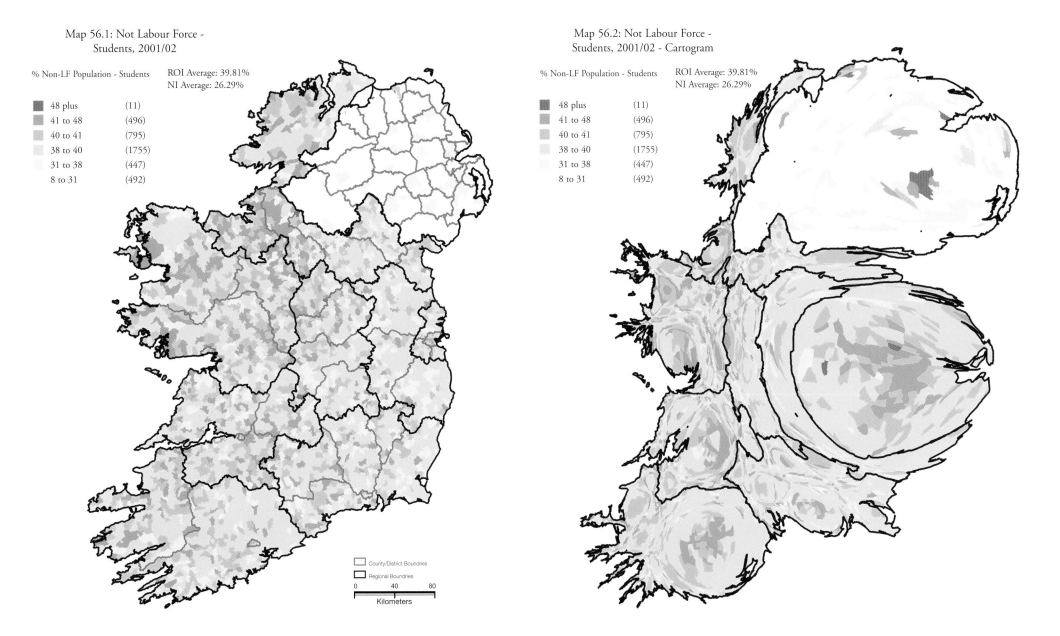

Map 56.1: Not Labour Force -
Students, 2001/02

% Non-LF Population - Students

ROI Average: 39.81%
NI Average: 26.29%

■	48 plus	(11)
■	41 to 48	(496)
■	40 to 41	(795)
▫	38 to 40	(1755)
▫	31 to 38	(447)
▫	8 to 31	(492)

Map 56.2: Not Labour Force -
Students, 2001/02 - Cartogram

% Non-LF Population - Students

ROI Average: 39.81%
NI Average: 26.29%

■	48 plus	(11)
■	41 to 48	(496)
■	40 to 41	(795)
▫	38 to 40	(1755)
▫	31 to 38	(447)
▫	8 to 31	(492)

▫ County/District Boundries
▫ Regional Boundries

0   40   80
Kilometers

Map 56.1 shows a marked contrast in the percentages of students who are not working as part of the labour force between the South and North, with much smaller proportions in the North. Tuition fees in the North are likely to be one reason for the larger percentage of students in the labour force in the North. The cartogram (Map 56.2) indicates areas of growth in students working in south Dublin, Galway, Cork and Limerick, all places with universities. In the west of Ireland there appear to more instances of areas with higher percentages of students not in the labour force than in the east, reflecting low student numbers and more restrictive labour markets. In Northern Ireland, the most notable increase in students not working is in south Belfast, where the largest proportion of students reside.

ECONOMIC DEPENDANCY RATIO

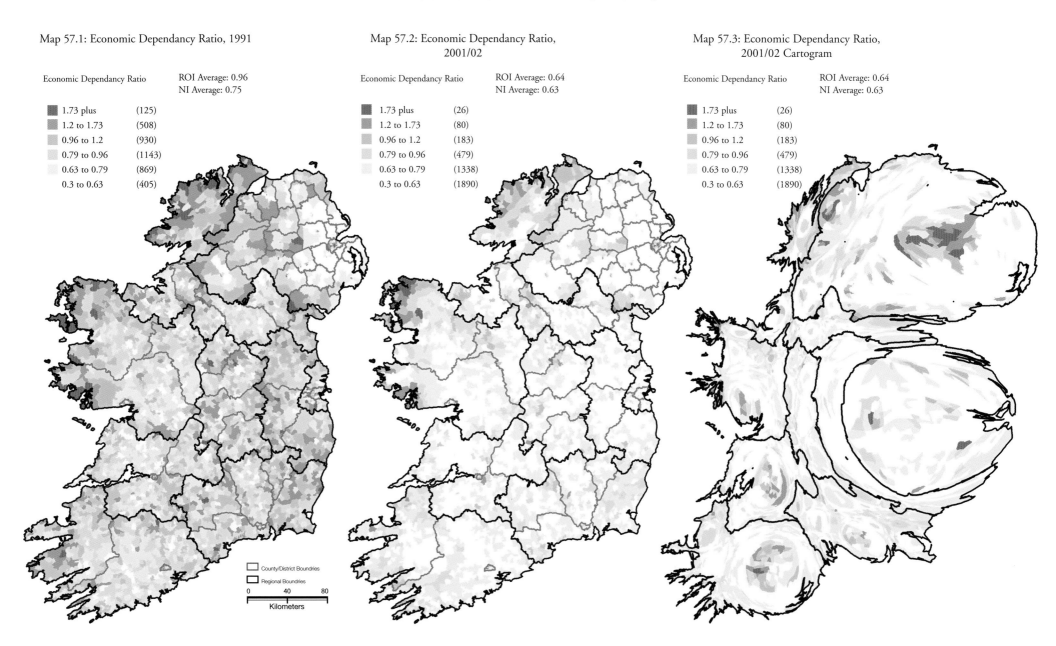

Map 57.1: Economic Dependancy Ratio, 1991

Economic Dependancy Ratio

ROI Average: 0.96
NI Average: 0.75

■	1.73 plus	(125)
■	1.2 to 1.73	(508)
▨	0.96 to 1.2	(930)
▨	0.79 to 0.96	(1143)
▨	0.63 to 0.79	(869)
□	0.3 to 0.63	(405)

County/District Boundries
Regional Boundries

0   40   80
Kilometers

Map 57.2: Economic Dependancy Ratio, 2001/02

Economic Dependancy Ratio

ROI Average: 0.64
NI Average: 0.63

■	1.73 plus	(26)
■	1.2 to 1.73	(80)
▨	0.96 to 1.2	(183)
▨	0.79 to 0.96	(479)
▨	0.63 to 0.79	(1338)
□	0.3 to 0.63	(1890)

Map 57.3: Economic Dependancy Ratio, 2001/02 Cartogram

Economic Dependancy Ratio

ROI Average: 0.64
NI Average: 0.63

■	1.73 plus	(26)
■	1.2 to 1.73	(80)
▨	0.96 to 1.2	(183)
▨	0.79 to 0.96	(479)
▨	0.63 to 0.79	(1338)
□	0.3 to 0.63	(1890)

The economic dependency ratio is calculated as the number of people 'not working' as a ratio of people 'at work' (in this case based on 15/16-64 population). People not working includes students, homemakers, the unemployed and those that have retired early. A ratio of 1.2 means that for every 100 people working, 120 people are not working. Given the Celtic Tiger years in the South and the enormous growth in the labour force, it is of little surprise the economic dependency ratio has fallen in most areas (Map 57.4), although there is a persistently high ratio in northwest Mayo, northwest Donegal, and some of the estates on the edges of Galway, Limerick and Cork (Map 57.2 and 57.3). In terms of change, there are a few outliers in rural areas which have seen an increase in the

Map 57.4: Economic Dependancy
Change, 1991 - 2001/02

1991 - 2001/02 Change   ROI Average: -33.33%
                               NI Average: -16%

■ Major Increase
▨ Medium Increase
░ Minor Increase
  Minor Decrease
  Medium Decrease
▨ Major Decrease

Map 57.5: Economic Dependancy
Change, 1991 - 2001/02 Cartogram

1991 - 2001/02 Change   ROI Average: -33.33%
                               NI Average: -16%

■ Major Increase
▨ Medium Increase
░ Minor Increase
  Minor Decrease
  Medium Decrease
▨ Major Decrease

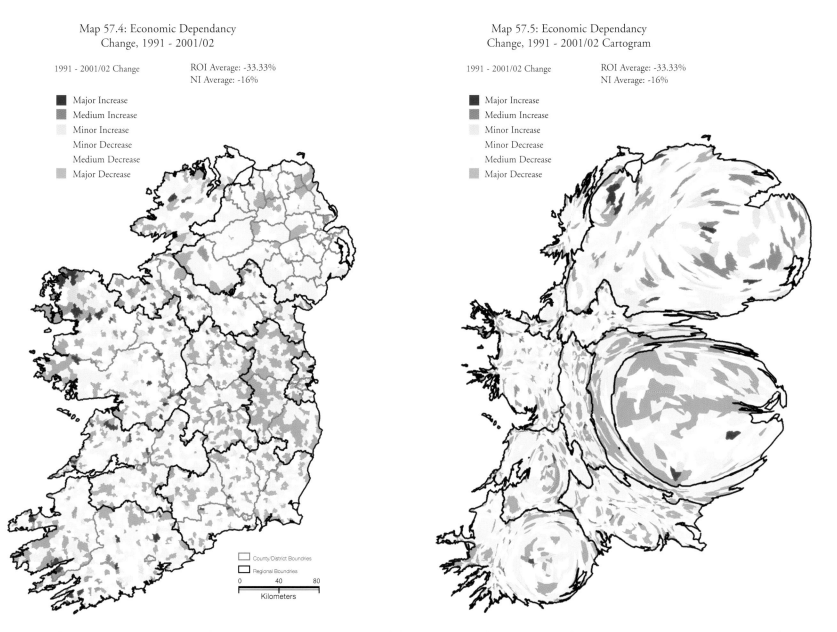

County/District Boundries
Regional Boundries
0   40   80
Kilometers

dependency ratio, especially in northwest Mayo and southwest Kerry, but these are in areas with low populations. The outlier in Dublin is caused by students congregated around University College Dublin. In the North the pattern is more mixed with the ratio falling in some areas and decreasing in others most likely as a result of local labour markets. The major increase in south Belfast is likely the result of the growth in Queen's University. There is however a persistently high ratio in west Belfast and Derry, with the ratio increasingly significantly in some parts of Derry.

INDUSTRY OF EMPLOYMENT CLASSED AS AGRICULTURE, HUNTING, FORESTRY AND FISHING

Map 58.1: IoE: AHFF, 1991

Map 58.2: IoE: AHFF, 2001/02

Map 58.3: IoE: AHFF, 2001/02 - Cartogram

% IoE: AHFF

ROI Average: 13.76%
NI Average: 4.25%

51 plus	(504)
39 to 51	(785)
27 to 39	(765)
17 to 27	(490)
5 to 17	(475)
0 to 5	(961)

% IoE: AHFF

ROI Average: 5.92%
NI Average: 3.01%

51 plus	(2)
39 to 51	(49)
27 to 39	(380)
17 to 27	(958)
5 to 17	(1420)
0 to 5	(1187)

% IoE: AHFF

ROI Average: 5.92%
NI Average: 3.01%

51 plus	(2)
39 to 51	(49)
27 to 39	(380)
17 to 27	(958)
5 to 17	(1420)
0 to 5	(1187)

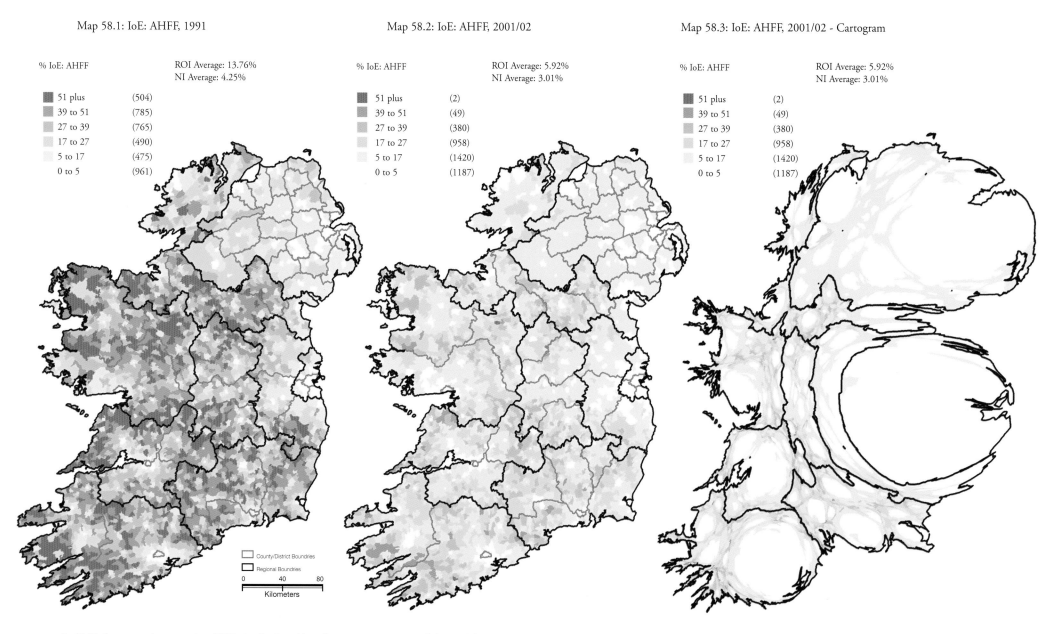

County/District Boundries
Regional Boundries

0   40   80
Kilometers

In 1991 there were just over 500 DEDs in the Republic where over 50 percent of the workforce was working in the sectors of agriculture, hunting, forestry and fishing (AHFF). Employment rates in the North were modest but still significant. By 2002, only 53 DEDs in the Republic had employment rates in AHFF above 39 percent. As the map and cartogram of change highlight, there was a sharp decline in employment in the agriculture, hunting, forestry and fishing sectors as a proportion of all employment over the decade, falling from 13.76 percent in 1991 to 5.92 percent in 2002. These declines were experienced particularly strongly in parts of Leinster, Connacht and the border counties. In the North although there was a small fall in the proportion of people working in these sectors (4.25% to 3.01%) the

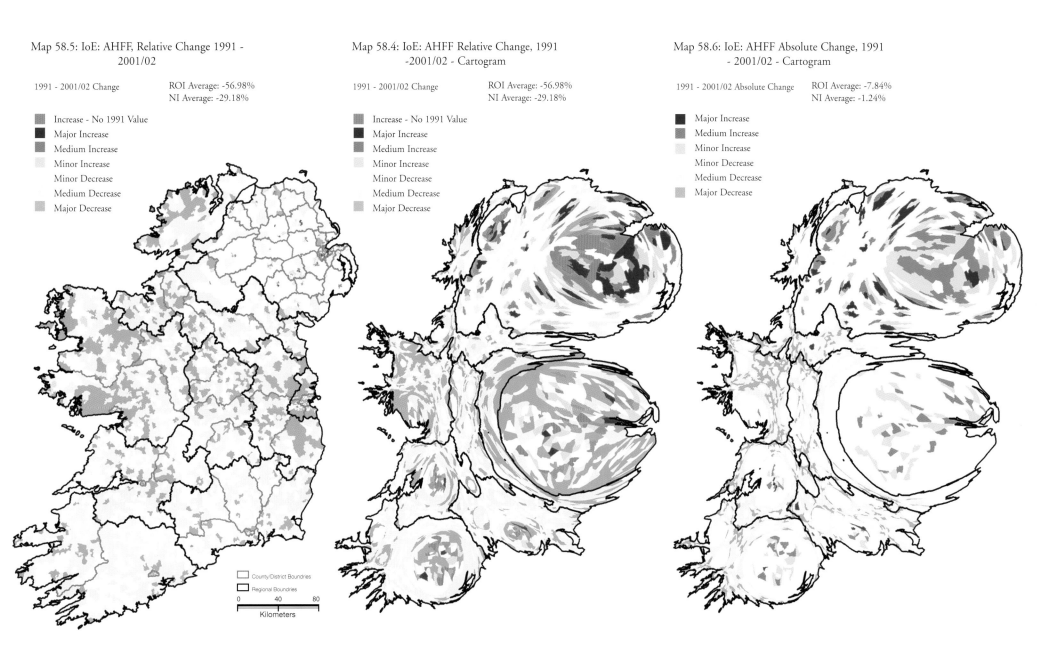

Map 58.5: IoE: AHFF, Relative Change 1991 - 2001/02

1991 - 2001/02 Change

ROI Average: -56.98%
NI Average: -29.18%

Increase - No 1991 Value
Major Increase
Medium Increase
Minor Increase
Minor Decrease
Medium Decrease
Major Decrease

County/District Boundries
Regional Boundries

0   40   80
Kilometers

Map 58.4: IoE: AHFF Relative Change, 1991 -2001/02 - Cartogram

1991 - 2001/02 Change

ROI Average: -56.98%
NI Average: -29.18%

Increase - No 1991 Value
Major Increase
Medium Increase
Minor Increase
Minor Decrease
Medium Decrease
Major Decrease

Map 58.6: IoE: AHFF Absolute Change, 1991 - 2001/02 - Cartogram

1991 - 2001/02 Absolute Change

ROI Average: -7.84%
NI Average: -1.24%

Major Increase
Medium Increase
Minor Increase
Minor Decrease
Medium Decrease
Major Decrease

sector was relatively stable as a small but significant part of the economy. Where there were increases in employment in these sectors they occurred predominately in the cities such as Dublin and in particular Belfast. Here, the proportional rate of employment is low (less than five percent) but modest gains have increased their relevance. These gains are likely to be from small enterprises most probably relating to small scale or intense farming, landscaping and gardening.

INDUSTRY OF EMPLOYMENT CLASSED AS MANUFACTURING INDUSTRIES

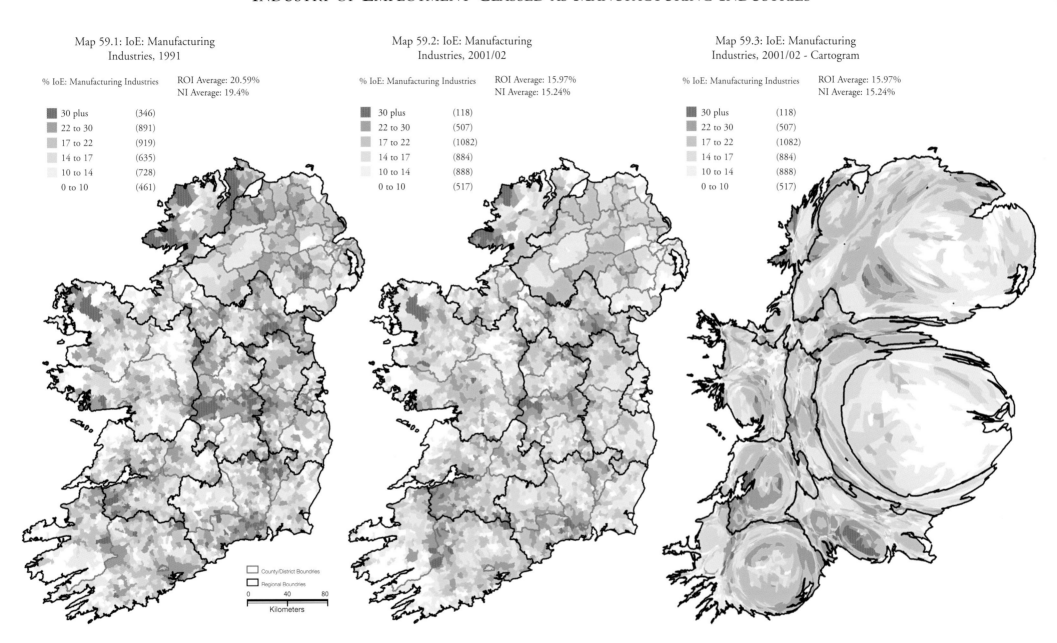

Map 59.1: IoE: Manufacturing
Industries, 1991

% IoE: Manufacturing Industries   ROI Average: 20.59%
NI Average: 19.4%

■	30 plus	(346)
■	22 to 30	(891)
■	17 to 22	(919)
■	14 to 17	(635)
■	10 to 14	(728)
□	0 to 10	(461)

Map 59.2: IoE: Manufacturing
Industries, 2001/02

% IoE: Manufacturing Industries   ROI Average: 15.97%
NI Average: 15.24%

■	30 plus	(118)
■	22 to 30	(507)
■	17 to 22	(1082)
■	14 to 17	(884)
■	10 to 14	(888)
□	0 to 10	(517)

Map 59.3: IoE: Manufacturing
Industries, 2001/02 - Cartogram

% IoE: Manufacturing Industries   ROI Average: 15.97%
NI Average: 15.24%

■	30 plus	(118)
■	22 to 30	(507)
■	17 to 22	(1082)
■	14 to 17	(884)
■	10 to 14	(888)
□	0 to 10	(517)

□ County/District Boundries
▭ Regional Boundries

0   40   80
Kilometers

In 1991, manufacturing constituted approximately 20 percent of the workforce in both the North (19.4%) and South (20.55%). As a proportion of the economy, manufacturing fell in absolute terms by 4.16% in the North and by 4.6% in the South over the following decade. Given that the workforce as a whole grew in the Republic by over a million people in the same period, manufacturing clearly expanded despite the relative drop vis-à-vis other sectors of the economy, notably construction and commerce. In other words, while manufacturing did decline in some areas, in many cases it grew, although other sectors of the economy grew at a greater rate. As a result, manufacturing has, in general, become less important to some local economies, especially in Northern Ireland, with the exception of some border areas. It remained,

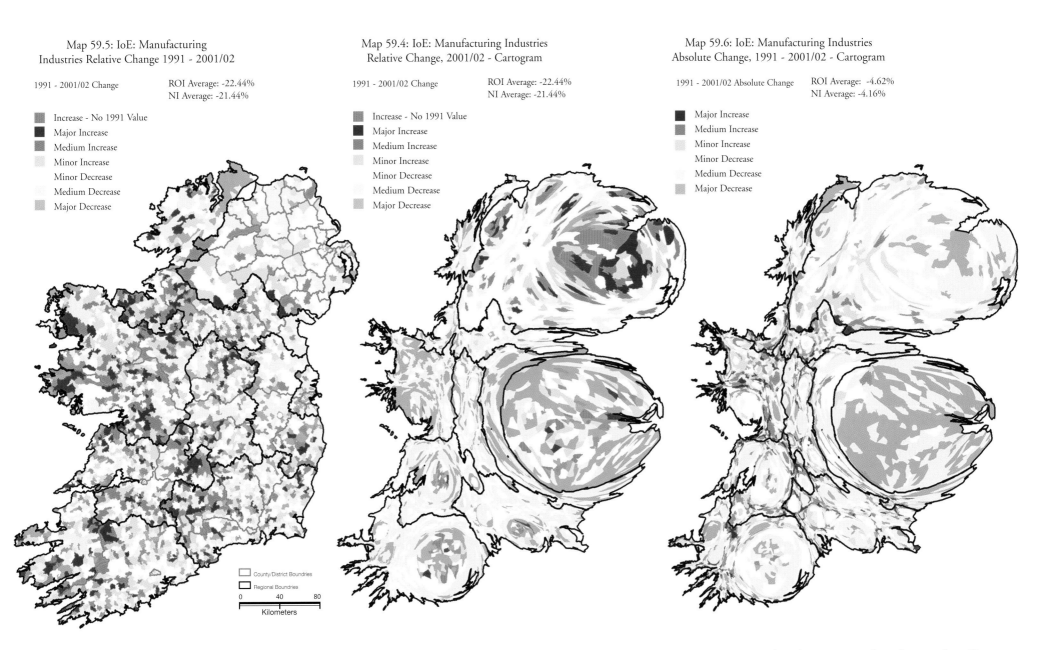

Map 59.5: IoE: Manufacturing
Industries Relative Change 1991 - 2001/02

1991 - 2001/02 Change

ROI Average: -22.44%
NI Average: -21.44%

Increase - No 1991 Value
Major Increase
Medium Increase
Minor Increase
Minor Decrease
Medium Decrease
Major Decrease

Map 59.4: IoE: Manufacturing Industries
Relative Change, 2001/02 - Cartogram

1991 - 2001/02 Change

ROI Average: -22.44%
NI Average: -21.44%

Increase - No 1991 Value
Major Increase
Medium Increase
Minor Increase
Minor Decrease
Medium Decrease
Major Decrease

Map 59.6: IoE: Manufacturing Industries
Absolute Change, 1991 - 2001/02 - Cartogram

1991 - 2001/02 Absolute Change

ROI Average: -4.62%
NI Average: -4.16%

Major Increase
Medium Increase
Minor Increase
Minor Decrease
Medium Decrease
Major Decrease

County/District Boundries
Regional Boundries

0   40   80
Kilometers

however, a key part of the economy in western Donegal, the central midlands, Limerick and Waterford, and has grown in importance in many rural areas given the reduction in agriculture, for example in Sligo, east Galway, North and South Tipperary.

INDUSTRY OF EMPLOYMENT CLASSED AS CONSTRUCTION INDUSTRIES

Map 60.1: IoE: Construction
Industries, 1991

% IoE: Construction Industries

ROI Average: 6.66%
NI Average: 7.29%

■	13 plus	(233)
■	9 to 13	(736)
■	7 to 9	(819)
■	6 to 7	(536)
□	4 to 6	(1027)
□	0 to 4	(629)

Map 60.2: IoE: Construction
Industries, 2001/02

% IoE: Construction Industries

ROI Average: 9.09%
NI Average: 8.99%

■	13 plus	(1209)
■	9 to 13	(1298)
■	7 to 9	(671)
■	6 to 7	(307)
□	4 to 6	(367)
□	0 to 4	(144)

Map 60.3: IoE: Construction
Industries, 2001/02 - Cartogram

% IoE: Construction Industries

ROI Average: 9.09%
NI Average: 8.99%

■	13 plus	(1209)
■	9 to 13	(1298)
■	7 to 9	(671)
■	6 to 7	(307)
□	4 to 6	(367)
□	0 to 4	(144)

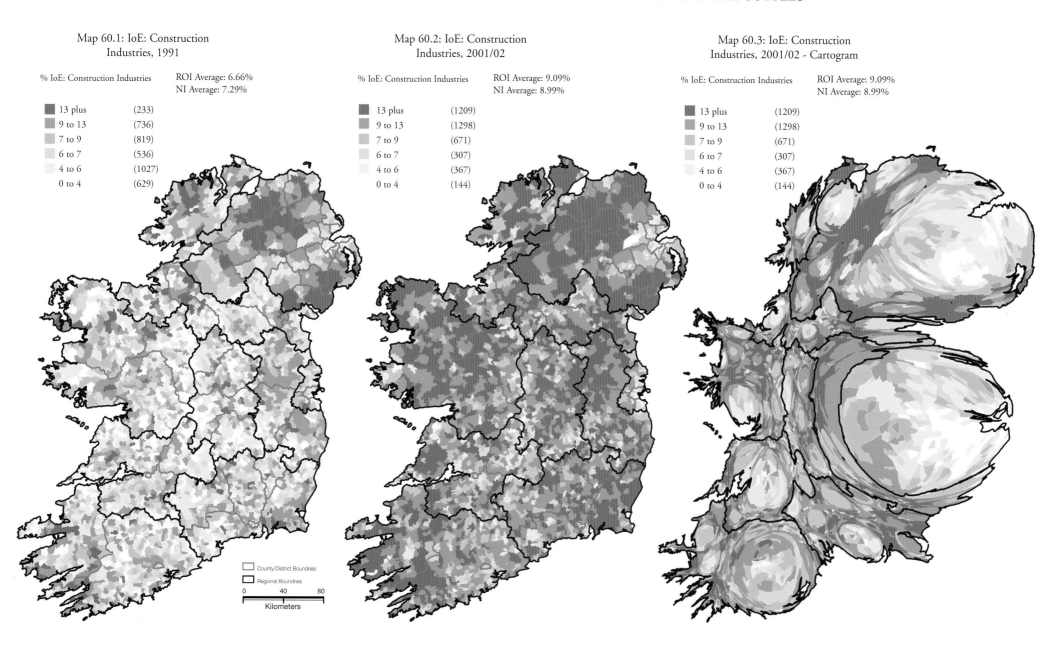

County/District Boundries
Regional Boundries

0   40   80
Kilometers

Construction grew in relative importance as a source of employment in nearly all parts of the island between 1991 and 2001/02, with the exception of central Dublin. While the growth in absolute terms has been relatively modest, rising from 6.66% of the workforce to 9.09% in the South and from 7.22% to 8.99% in the North, relative growth has been much more dramatic (36.49% in the South; 23.32% in the North). This growth has meant that the 233 areas that had more than 13% of its working population employed in the construction industry in 1991 had grown to over 1209 areas in 2002. This growth occurred across the island, especially in rural areas. In general it was only in the major towns where there was a highly diversified and competitive labour market that less than 4% of the population worked in construction.

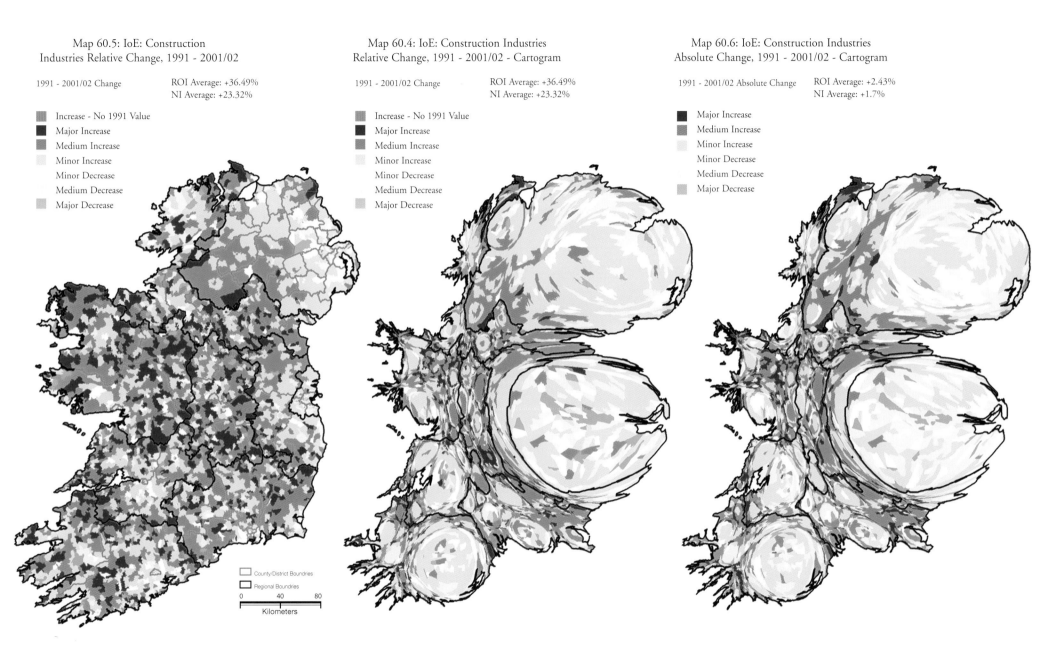

Map 60.5: IoE: Construction
Industries Relative Change, 1991 - 2001/02

1991 - 2001/02 Change

ROI Average: +36.49%
NI Average: +23.32%

Increase - No 1991 Value
Major Increase
Medium Increase
Minor Increase
Minor Decrease
Medium Decrease
Major Decrease

Map 60.4: IoE: Construction Industries
Relative Change, 1991 - 2001/02 - Cartogram

1991 - 2001/02 Change

ROI Average: +36.49%
NI Average: +23.32%

Increase - No 1991 Value
Major Increase
Medium Increase
Minor Increase
Minor Decrease
Medium Decrease
Major Decrease

Map 60.6: IoE: Construction Industries
Absolute Change, 1991 - 2001/02 - Cartogram

1991 - 2001/02 Absolute Change

ROI Average: +2.43%
NI Average: +1.7%

Major Increase
Medium Increase
Minor Increase
Minor Decrease
Medium Decrease
Major Decrease

County/District Boundries
Regional Boundries

0   40   80
Kilometers

INDUSTRY OF EMPLOYMENT CLASSED AS TRANSPORT, STORAGE & COMMUNICATIONS INDUSTRIES

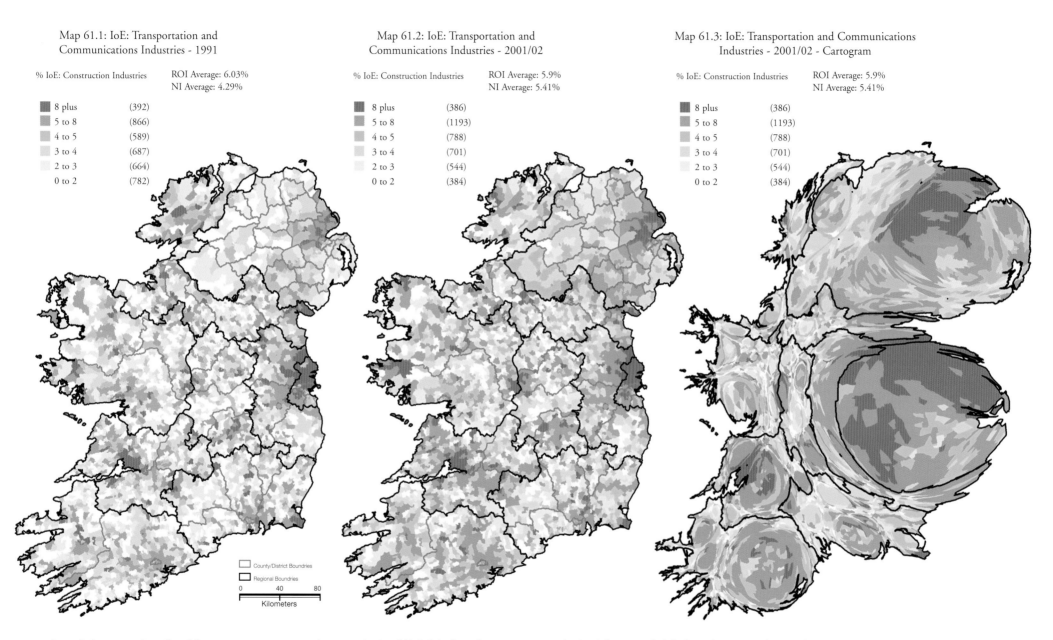

Map 61.1: IoE: Transportation and Communications Industries - 1991

% IoE: Construction Industries

ROI Average: 6.03%
NI Average: 4.29%

■	8 plus	(392)
■	5 to 8	(866)
■	4 to 5	(589)
░	3 to 4	(687)
░	2 to 3	(664)
░	0 to 2	(782)

Map 61.2: IoE: Transportation and Communications Industries - 2001/02

% IoE: Construction Industries

ROI Average: 5.9%
NI Average: 5.41%

■	8 plus	(386)
■	5 to 8	(1193)
■	4 to 5	(788)
░	3 to 4	(701)
░	2 to 3	(544)
░	0 to 2	(384)

Map 61.3: IoE: Transportation and Communications Industries - 2001/02 - Cartogram

% IoE: Construction Industries

ROI Average: 5.9%
NI Average: 5.41%

■	8 plus	(386)
■	5 to 8	(1193)
■	4 to 5	(788)
░	3 to 4	(701)
░	2 to 3	(544)
░	0 to 2	(384)

County/District Boundries
Regional Boundries

0   40   80
Kilometers

As a relative proportion of workforce, transport, storage and communication fell slightly from 6.03% to 5.9% in the South but grew slightly from 4.29% to 5.41% in the North between 1991 and 2001/02. As such, in general terms it was a sector of the economy that grew in line with overall economic growth. These sectors of the economy were highly concentrated in the principal cities in 1991 and over the decade grew in relative importance in the areas surrounding the cities and a few rural areas. Because of the low base rates, a small absolute increase or decrease in rates means high relative change giving the change map for Northern Ireland a more dramatic appearance than it really merits. The influence of the airports in North Dublin, Shannon and Aldergrove to the west of Belfast are clearly visible, each employing large numbers of people.

Map 61.4: IoE: Transportation and Communications
Industries, Relative Change 1991 - 2001/02

1991 - 2001/02 Change   ROI Average: -2.16%
                            NI Average: +26.11%

- Increase - No 1991 Value
- Major Increase
- Medium Increase
- Minor Increase
- Minor Decrease
- Medium Decrease
- Major Decrease

Map 61.5: IoE: Transportation and Communications
Industries, Relative Change 1991 - 2001/02 -

1991 - 2001/02 Change   ROI Average: -2.16%
                            NI Average: +26.11%

- Increase - No 1991 Value
- Major Increase
- Medium Increase
- Minor Increase
- Minor Decrease
- Medium Decrease
- Major Decrease

Map 61.6: IoE: Transportation and Communications
Industries Absolute Change 1991 - 2001/02 - Cartogram

1991 - 2001/02 Absolute Change   ROI Average: -0.13%
                                  NI Average: +1.12%

- Major Increase
- Medium Increase
- Minor Increase
- Minor Decrease
- Medium Decrease
- Major Decrease

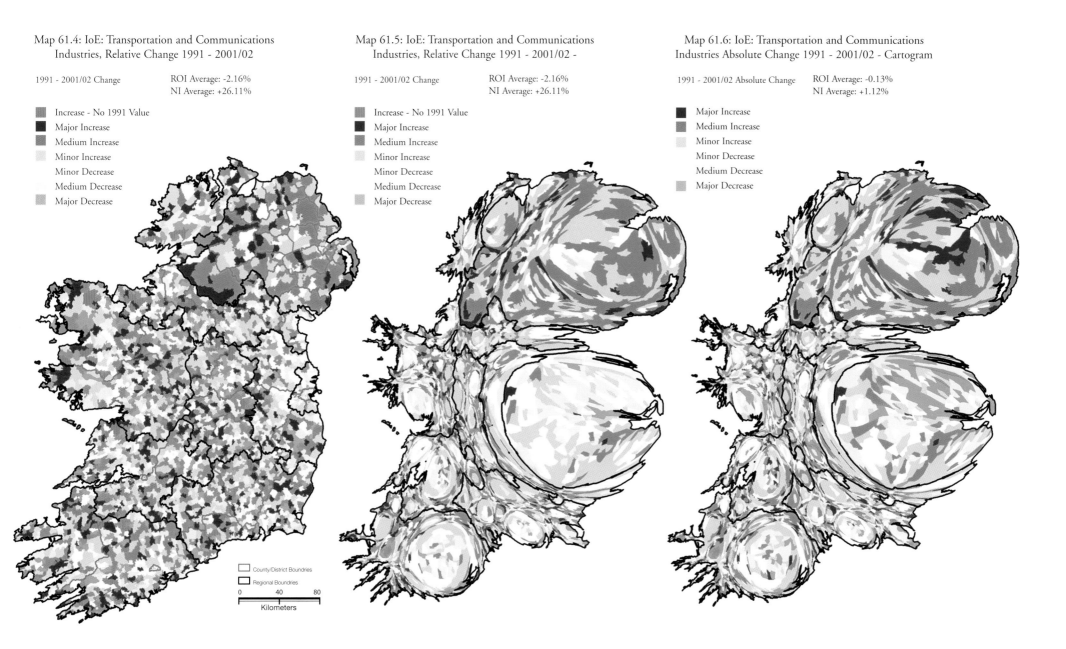

County/District Boundries
Regional Boundries

0   40   80
Kilometers

INDUSTRY OF EMPLOYMENT CLASSED AS COMMERCE

Map 62.1: IoE: Commerce, 1991

Map 62.2: IoE: Commerce, 2001/02

Map 62.3: IoE: Commerce, 2001/02 - Cartogram

% IoE: Commerce

ROI Average: 20.47%
NI Average: 7.09%

24 plus	(374)
18 to 24	(748)
13 to 18	(930)
9 to 13	(862)
6 to 9	(523)
0 to 6	(543)

% IoE: Commerce

ROI Average: 26.87%
NI Average: 27.51%

24 plus	(1279)
18 to 24	(1367)
13 to 18	(890)
9 to 13	(348)
6 to 9	(84)
0 to 6	(28)

% IoE: Commerce

ROI Average: 26.87%
NI Average: 27.51%

24 plus	(1279)
18 to 24	(1367)
13 to 18	(890)
9 to 13	(348)
6 to 9	(84)
0 to 6	(28)

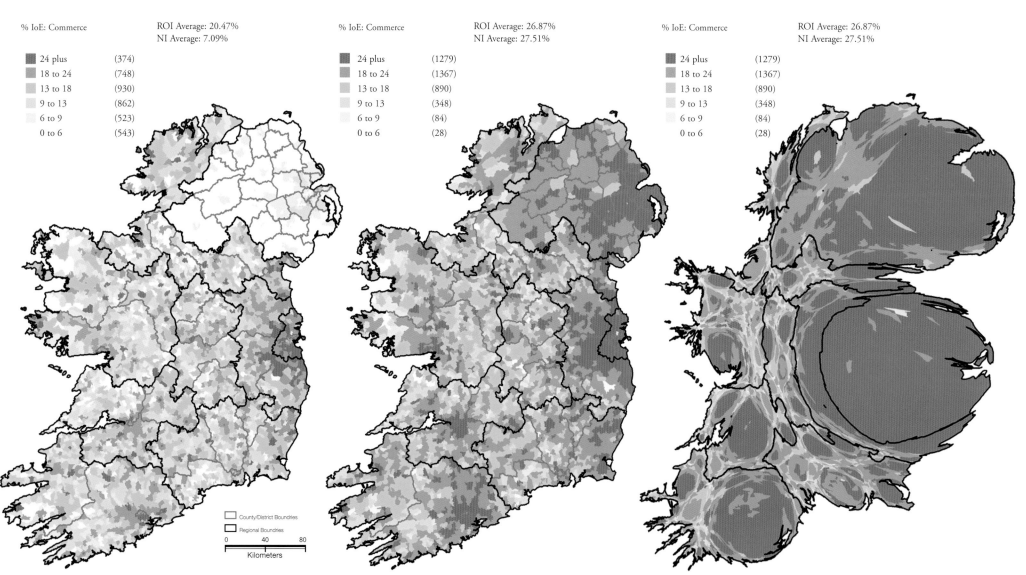

County/District Boundries
Regional Boundries

0   40   80
Kilometers

Commerce grew as a proportion of all employment in both the Republic of Ireland and Northern Ireland between 1991 and 2001/02. While the growth was relatively large for the South (31.27%), it was extremely high for the North (288.01%). This in part is due to a relative low base of employment in commerce in the North, but mainly due to a large expansion of work in sectors such as wholesale and retail trade, finance and banking, real estate, and general business activities. As a result, commerce grew in absolute terms by 20.42% in the North between 1991 and 2001, compared to 6.4% in the South. The lower figure in the South is also a reflection of the more strongly diversified economy in the Republic, where most sectors of the economy, with the exception of agriculture, grew in absolute terms maintaining relative employment proportions. Central Dublin is the exception, with the only concentrated growth rate to match that of the North, which is unsurprising given the expansion of business services in the city.

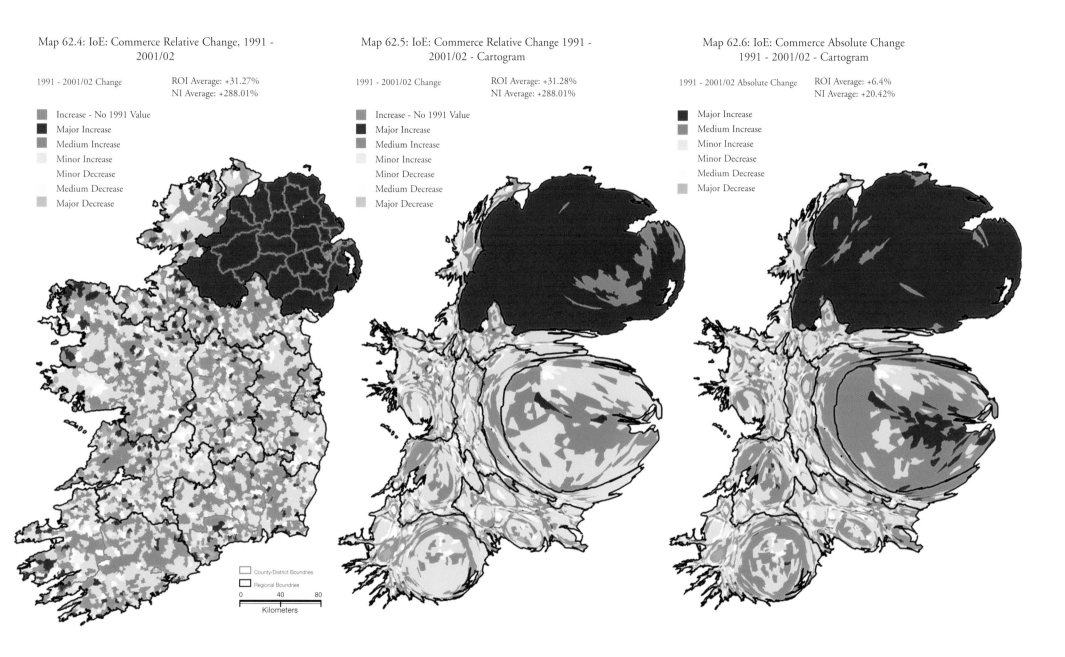

Map 62.4: IoE: Commerce Relative Change, 1991 - 2001/02

1991 - 2001/02 Change

ROI Average: +31.27%
NI Average: +288.01%

Increase - No 1991 Value
Major Increase
Medium Increase
Minor Increase
Minor Decrease
Medium Decrease
Major Decrease

County/District Boundries
Regional Boundries

0   40   80
Kilometers

Map 62.5: IoE: Commerce Relative Change 1991 - 2001/02 - Cartogram

1991 - 2001/02 Change

ROI Average: +31.28%
NI Average: +288.01%

Increase - No 1991 Value
Major Increase
Medium Increase
Minor Increase
Minor Decrease
Medium Decrease
Major Decrease

Map 62.6: IoE: Commerce Absolute Change 1991 - 2001/02 - Cartogram

1991 - 2001/02 Absolute Change

ROI Average: +6.4%
NI Average: +20.42%

Major Increase
Medium Increase
Minor Increase
Minor Decrease
Medium Decrease
Major Decrease

Chapter 6: Cross-Border Data Issues

Producing maps and cartograms of the whole island of Ireland is not as simple as one might think. For various technical and scientific reasons one cannot simply add the two main sets of data together and then output a map. There are two sets of issues – data interoperability and, what is termed in the scientific literature, the modifiable areal unit problem. In this chapter we discuss these issues and explain how we have sought to address them. In Appendix 1 we detail specific issues regarding certain variables.

DATA INTEROPERABILITY

Data interoperability concerns the extent to which datasets that have been sourced separately can be used in conjunction with each other. If two sets of data cannot be used together because they do not share common attributes, then they are said to have poor interoperability. In our case, poor data interoperability exists because, although the censuses in Northern Ireland and Ireland share a common legacy and appear to be quite similar, they are prepared largely independently of each other. As a result, while many of the questions asked are either directly the same or very nearly the same in wording, a substantial number of questions examine the same issue differently or there is no equivalent question (see Table 1 for examples).

Of the 1161 SAPS (Small Area Population Statistics) outputted from the 2002 census in Ireland, our analysis estimates that 32 percent of variables can be directly matched to the Northern Ireland census; 31 percent can be part-matched or reclassified so that they broadly match; and 37 percent have no equivalent.

This means that over two thirds of all census variables published in the South have no direct equivalents in Northern Ireland without manipulation. For those issues where similar but different questions are asked it is important to note that caution is necessary in comparing and interpreting the resultant answers across the two jurisdictions. This is because the question can be measuring highly related but subtly different phenomena or because the choices given to respondents do not match precisely. Accordingly, a reclassification of answers is sometimes needed in order to achieve a more meaningful correspondence.

Table 1: Comparing questions between North and South

RoI	NI	SAME
If your accomodation is rented how much does your household pay? - Answer in €'s and frequency	No question	No
No question	Over the last 12 months would you say your health has been Good/Fairly Good/ Not Good	No
What is the nature of the occupancy of your household's accomodation? • Owner occupied where loan or mortgage repayments are being made • Owner occupied where no loan or mortgage repayments are being made • Being purchased from a Local Authority under a Tenant Purchase Scheme • Rented from a Local Authority • Rented unfurnished other than from a Local Authority	Does your household own or rent the accommodation? • Owns outright • Owns with a mortgage or loan • Pays part rent and part mortgage (shared ownership) • Rents • Lives here rent free	Part

Similarly, the data being collected in the two jurisdictions might be recorded in different units (e.g., euros instead of sterling) or into different categories or be outputted into different classes. This effect is illustrated in Table 2 which shows the different categories into which people are classified with respect to social class/grade in Northern Ireland and Ireland. While the categories are broadly similar, there are some significant differences that make straight comparison problematic. For example, semi-skilled and unskilled are separate classes in Ireland but are classified together in Northern Ireland. Similarly Table 3 highlights how occupations classed into seven different categories in the broad classification (SAPS) for Ireland are all grouped into the same category in the broad classification for Northern Ireland (Elementary Occupation). The reverse can also happen: for example, in Northern Ireland a judge and a refuse worker are classed as Professional Occupation and Elementary Occupation respectively, but in Ireland both are classified in the SAPS data in an all-encompassing 'Managing, Administrative, Executive and Government Workers' class. In these cases full compatibility can only be achieved through the creation of common output classes for both parts of the island and the reclassification of data, but this takes time and careful thought to minimise any incompatability.

Table 2: Comparing Social Class/Social grade

RoI	NI
Professional Workers	
Managerial and Technical	AB. Higher and intermediate managerial / administrative / professional
Non-Manual	C1. Supervisory, clerical, junior managerial / administrative /professional
Skilled Labour	
Semi-skilled	C2. Skilled manual workers
Unskilled	D. Semi-skilled and unskilled manual workers
All Other gainfully occupied	E. On state benefit, unemployed, lowest grade workers

Table 3: Comparing the classification of occupations

RoI Census Code	Occupation	RoI Occupation Groups	NI Occupation Broad Groups
621	Waiters and waitresses	Servcices workers	Elementary Occupation
622	Bar Staff	Sales and Commerce Workers	Elementary Occupation
862	Packers, bottlers, canners, fillers, weighers, graders and sorters	Manufacturing workers	Elementary Occupation
900	Farm workers	Other agricultural and forestry workers and fishermen	Elementary Occupation
919	Labourers in engineering and other making/ Processing	Other workers (including not stated)	Elementary Occupation
930	Stevedores and dockers	Communication and transport workers	Elementary Occupation
933	Refuse and salvage collectors	Managing, administrative executives and government workers	Elementary Occupation

There are other data continuity issues in both jurisdictions. For example, in Ireland, for each census year between 1981 and 2002 the number of SAPS variables released has varied (from a low of 774 in 1981 to a high of 1750 in 1991) as some questions have been added to the census form and others discontinued. Clearly in these circumstances it is impossible to compare new or discontinued variables over time because no comparable data exist.

Moreover, because the census occurs every five years in the Republic and every ten in Northern Ireland we have not been able to create maps detailing the results of the 1996 and 2006 census in the Republic. Further, because the 2001 census was delayed in the Republic because of a feared Foot and Mouth outbreak, data were collected one year late in April 2002. This means that there is a slight temporal discrepancy between data from the two jurisdictions, hence the labeling 2001/02.

MODIFIABLE AREAL UNIT PROBLEM

These matters are compounded by another issue, that of spatial scale. The census data for Ireland and Northern Ireland have a different underlying 'output geography', varying quite significantly below the NUTS 3 level (which are counties in Ireland and five areas slightly bigger than counties in Northern Ireland). In Ireland, census variables are coded at Regional, County and District Electoral Division (DED) level (along with other more specialized units such as Gaeltacht areas). In the North they are coded at District, Ward,

Super Output Areas, and Output Areas (OA) - along with other areas such as Health and Social Service Boards, Education and Library Boards, and Parliamentary Constituencies. As illustrated by Table 4, the characteristics of these areas are quite different, with wards having populations on average significantly larger than DEDs, and OA populations significantly smaller. (comparable DEDs developed by NIRSA)

Table 4: Comparing output areas between North and South

Unit	Number	Av. Population	Av. Size (km²)
DED	3414	1062	20.4
OA	5022	337	2.8
Ward	582	2895	24

Because data in the two jurisdictions are reported at different spatial scales, a scalar modifiable area unit problem arises. In short, spatially referenced data can be aggregated into zones of varying sizes. The level of aggregation affects what patterns are revealed because the internal variances within a zone alter as more data are added. What that means is that the same data outputted at different spatial scales can show remarkably different patterns and statistical relationships with other data (see Fotheringham and Wong 1991). As we have discussed, in the case of comparing data between Northern Ireland and Ireland there is no common reporting unit.

As a result, the aggregation effects on internal variances are different between the two jurisdictions, making them statistically difficult to compare. The visual effect of this is displayed in Figure 1.

Here, the map on the left shows the population count for Cavan and Monaghan DEDs and Fermanagh OAs, and the map on the right shows the population count for Cavan and Monaghan DEDs and Fermanagh wards. In the first map, because DEDs have significantly larger populations than OAs the immediate inference one draws is that Fermanagh in Northern Ireland appears to have a uniformly lower population than either Cavan and Monaghan in Ireland. In the second case, wards, by and large, have a much greater population than DEDs and the converse inference is drawn whereby Fermanagh's population is uniformly higher than that of Cavan and Monaghan. In other words, the pattern that is displayed is not simply due to the population distribution, but is affected

significantly by the spatial scale of output. Addressing this problem in the absence of a common spatial data unit is a complex process and it is not easily resolved.

As well as there being issues concerning spatial scale, a problem exists with regards to spatial units and data continuity. While spatial boundaries are quite resilient in the Republic with no changes in DED boundaries between 1991 and 2002, due to confidentiality issues concerning the small number of people living within some areas, it was necessary to merge some DEDs and then to standardize these between 1991 and 2002 to produce comparable data.

Using some minor geo-computational techniques we have created an identical DED dataset of 3,414 individual units for both 1991 and 2002. In Northern Ireland, there have been significant changes to the spatial units for which data are outputted.

Figure 1: Comparing data outputted at different spatial scales

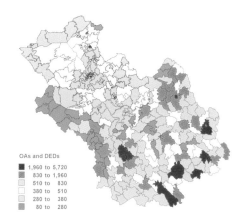

OAs and DEDs

■ 1,960 to 5,720
▨ 830 to 1,960
□ 510 to 830
□ 380 to 510
□ 280 to 380
▨ 80 to 280

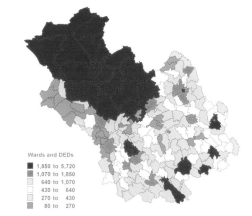

Wards and DEDs

■ 1,850 to 5,720
▨ 1,070 to 1,850
□ 640 to 1,070
□ 430 to 640
□ 270 to 430
▨ 80 to 270

Given the size discrepancy between OAs in Northern Ireland and DEDs in Ireland, and the fact that OA boundaries were new for 2001, we have chosen to create maps using wards for Northern Ireland and DEDs for Ireland. Examining change between 1991 and 2001/02 does not pose a major problem for Ireland as we have a comparable set of DED boundaries for both years. However, in order to accurately examine change in Northern Ireland we have re-assigned the 2001 ward population to the 1984 ward boundaries for the change maps as accurately as possible to make the Northern Ireland data comparable over time (Figure 2).

This procedure was undertaken by using the Northern Ireland Grid Square Product. This product assigns census returns to a range of 100m and 1km grid – squares across Northern Ireland. The product contains over 900 Census counts. However, steps have been taken to ensure confidentiality and a threshold has been put in place whereby data are not released for grid-squares with a population lower than 25 and households lower than 8. To allocate the 2001 population to the 1984 wards we have used a proportioning method based on the spatial distribution of grid squares within each ward. For every grid square we know the proportion of the total population (households etc) within the ward that lies within the grid square. For each demographic variable, we also know the total number of people in that category within a ward. We then allocate this number across the grid squares based on the proportion of the total population within each square (Figure 3). The 1984 ward boundaries can then be overlaid on the grid squares and it is then possible to do a simple point-in-polygon selection and aggregate the grid square values to the 1984 wards (Figure 4). The result is a matching set of wards (566) between 1991 and 2001 (Figure 5).

Figure 2: Re-assigning 2001 data to 1984 Wards – Source and Target boundaries

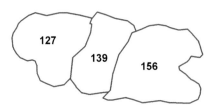

Source Data - 2001 Census population 65+

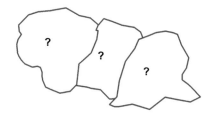

Target Data: 1984 Ward Boundaries

Figure 3: Step 1 - Overlay grid cells onto 2001 Wards and calculate percentage of population in each cell, Step 2 – Allocate 2001 65+ population into grid cells according to the proportion of total population in each cell.

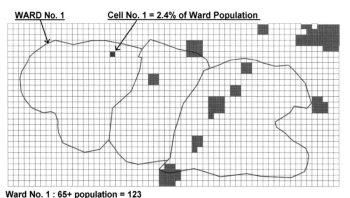

Ward No. 1 : 65+ population = 123
Cell Distribution = (123 / 100) * proportion of total population that each cell represents
Cell No. 1 contain approx 3 people aged 65+

Figure 4: Step 3 – Overlay 1984 Ward boundaries onto grid

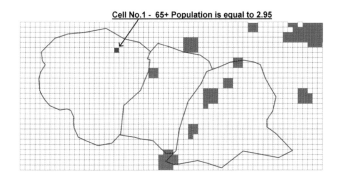

Cell No.1 - 65+ Population is equal to 2.95

Figure 5: Step 4 – Aggregate 65+ population figures from each cell to the target ward boundaries

Target Data: 1984 Ward Boundaries updated with 2001 Census data

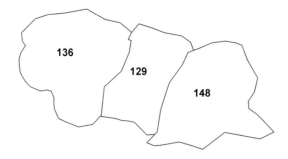

136

129

148

Chapter 7: Conclusion

The maps and cartograms in this atlas provide a fascinating insight into some of the social and economic changes that occurred across the Island between 1991 and 2001/02. They reveal that both Northern Ireland and Ireland have gone through a number of important changes with respect to population demography, housing, transport, and the economy – changes that have very important implications for future planning with respect to several key policy areas. Initial analysis from Census 2006 in Ireland show that these trends have, in general, continued, and it will be very interesting to once again compare Northern Ireland and Ireland after the 2011 census and to map the change from the 1991 base index created in this Atlas.

While the maps and cartograms are of interest and value, providing a useful set of data, it is fair to say that the Atlas could have been much broader in scope if the kinds of data interoperability issues discussed in the previous chapter could have been easily resolved. At present, it is simply impossible to produce all-island maps of some variables that would be of great value to policy makers and others. In a time when cross-border collaboration has increased substantially, it would be highly beneficial if initiatives could be conceived and planned based on sound evidence that can identify areas of most need, justify investment and reveal the benefits yielded by those living in different jurisdictions working together. The Atlas then provides a taste of what could be achieved when datasets are made interoperable.

The move towards the creation of such harmonious datasets is already underway, often driven at the supra-national scale of the European Union for example through the INSPIRE directive, though progress is often quite slow. Initiatives include:

1) data agencies talking to each other with regards to data definitions and spatial units to explore compatibility;

(2) the establishment of various international data standards and conventions;

(3) a drive towards national and transnational spatial data infrastructures that provide common frameworks and standards across borders and areas of concern (e.g., health, welfare, economy);

(4) the development of detailed metadatabases (data about data) that document what data are held by different agencies and their attributes; and

(5) the development of common data formats for recording and storing datasets so that they can be easily conjoined.

In the case of Ireland and Northern Ireland, these initiatives have largely been confined to the level of the nation state and only recently has there been any real concern to improve cross-border data interoperability. As a consequence, separate approaches to data generation have developed in Northern Ireland and Ireland leading to poor interoperability on a number of levels. These problems exist in relation to nearly all types of data, including those relating to health, economy and enterprise, transport, environment, housing, planning and development

In Chapter 6, in particular, we highlighted the various ways in which data for Northern Ireland and Ireland often lack interoperability and why such difficulties are important to address. While AIRO, ICLRD, and other related projects, are starting to tackle these issues, it is fair to say that substantial, long-term research and development is needed in order to achieve sustained progress. Such progress is needed on at least five fronts, namely:

(1) preparing interoperable data across several domains;

(2) addressing fundamental technical issues such as modifiable areal unit problems;

(3) providing new, more sophisticated tools of analysis that work on an all-island or cross-border basis;

(4) educating data users; and

(5) promoting inter-jurisdictional data analysis that will provide the kinds of evidence that will serve policy makers well.

The Atlas of the Island of Ireland is a step in the right direction, but there is a long way to go yet before evidence-informed analysis and policy formulation can be undertaken on a routine basis for the whole island. Our hope is that over time, those generating data will work with each other to address the issues we have highlighted, so that anybody with a little mapping know-how will be able to create their own maps of whatever variables they are interested in and undertake sophisticated spatial analyses. Initiatives such as the Small Area Project that seeks to create output areas in the South roughly equivalent to those in the North will greatly improve

interoperability and also enable much finer analysis of spatial patterns and processes.

Once in place, all-island data sets will be of immeasurable benefit to anyone interested in cross-border collaboration or issues on an all-island or regional basis, providing a ready means of analysing patterns of change and statis and to think through suitable public policy interventions. It is our belief that their creation should be given the highest priority by the government in Northern Ireland and Ireland to enable the highest quality, evidence informed decision making on issues of shared gain.

References

Fotheringham, A. S., and Wong, D.W.S. (1991).
The modifiable areal unit problem in multivariate statistical analysis.
Environment and Planning A 23: 1025-44.

Gastner, M.T. and Newman, M.E.J. (2004) Diffusion based method
for producing density equalising maps. Proc. Nati. Acad. Scai.
101, 7499 - 7504.
http://www.personal.umich.edu/~mejn/cart

Horner, A., Walsh, J.A. and Harrington, V.P. (1987)
Population in Ireland: A Census Atlas. Department of Geography,
University College Dublin.

Jenks, G. and Caspall, F. (1971) Error on Choroplethic Maps:
Definition, Measurement, Reduction. *Annals of the Association of
American Geographers* 61(2): 217-244.

Suchan, T. and Brewer, C. (2002) *Mapping Census 2000:
The Geography of US Diversity.* ESRI Press, Redlands.

Walsh, J. (Ed) (2007) *People and Place.*
NIRSA, NUI Maynooth.

Appendix

Given the issues outlined in Chapter 6 concerning data interoperability, here we detail how we have gone about creating workable all-island datasets.

Base population and students
In 1991 students in Northern Ireland were enumerated based on their home address whereas in 2001 students were enumerated based on their term time address (this is similar in the Republic of Ireland). Resulting from this, the 1991 base population for Northern Ireland was adjusted to allow for the re-distribution of students to their term time address. This adjusted population distribution was used to underpin the maps.

Map 6: Population Density: Person per km²
Population density was calculated based on the total population within each geographical area (ward/DED) divided by its size (in km²). The Republic of Ireland population is based on a de facto population, with persons enumerated where they spend census night. The Northern Ireland population is based on a de jure method, this enumerates persons based on their regular or legal residence.

Maps 10 to 19 – Age Bands, Demographic Vitality and Dependency
The Demographic Vitality Ratio was calculated based on the number of people aged 20-39 years old per the number of people aged 60+ within each ward/DED. The Dependency Rate was calculated based on the number of people aged 0-14 and 65+ as a proportion of the population aged between 16-64.

The Young Dependency Rate was calculated based on the number of people aged 0-14 as a proportion of the population aged between 16-64.

The Old Dependency Rate was calculated based on the number of people aged 65+ as a proportion of the population aged between 16-64.

Maps 21 to 23 – Marital Status and Married Fertility Rate
The population used for marital status in the Republic of Ireland is based on the population 15 years plus. The population used for marital status in the Northern Ireland is based on the population 16 years plus. Those categorised as ever-married persons in the Republic of Ireland census but at the time of enumeration were deserted, separated or divorced or whose marriages were annulled were included in the 'Single, Separated, Widowed and Divorced Persons' category.

Maps 24 to 27 – Religion and Ability to Speak Irish
The Central Statistics Office in the Republic of Ireland provides four religion categories through its small area statistics – (1) 'Catholic', (2) 'Other Stated Religion', (3) 'No Religion' and (4) 'Not Stated'. Statistical data for Northern Ireland is more detailed for wards and data is available for seven categories (8 in 2001) – (1) 'Catholic', (2) 'Presbyterian Church in Ireland', (3) 'Church of Ireland', (4) 'Methodist Church in Ireland', (5) 'Other Christian (including Christian related) and Other Philosophies', (6) 'No Religion' or (7) 'Religion not Stated'. Given the problems of overlap, only three aggregate categories could be mapped to show the distribution of religion and affiliations – (1) 'Roman Catholics', (2) 'Persons in Principle Protestant Denominations and other Religions' and (3) 'No Religion and None Stated'.

Persons 3+ are enumerated based on their ability to speak Irish. The mapped data for the Republic of Ireland relates to whether people can speak Irish or not regardless of frequency. The data for Northern Ireland relates to those who are classified as 'Speak but do not read or write Irish', 'Speak and read but do not write', 'Speak, read and write Irish'.

Maps 27 to 28 – Cars per Households
This data relates to the number of cars per households within the Republic of Ireland and Northern Ireland. The data for Northern Ireland in 2001 is based on the number of cars and vans per households.

Maps 29 to 34 – Distance Travelled to Work
These maps have been produced for 2001/02 only as data were not available for 1991. Data for both Northern Ireland and the Republic of Ireland represents the distance travelled to work for those aged 16-74 (NI) and those 15+ (RoI). The data used excludes those who work from home. An important difference in the census methodology for Northern Ireland and the Republic of Ireland here relates to the way distance has been coded. The Republic Of Ireland census asks people to write down the distance they travel to the nearest mile whereas the census in Northern Ireland calculates distance to work using the home postcode and the work postcode of the person completing the form. The data released via NISRA is incompatible with the Republic of Ireland as a result of the distance bands and distance units used. NISRA kindly reproduced their original tables to allow for a more comparable dataset to be used.

Maps 35 to 41 – Household Type and Tenure
Owner occupied in the Republic of Ireland in both 1991 and 2002 relates to those households who are (1) Owner occupied where no loan or mortgage repayments are being made, (2) Owner occupied where loan or mortgage repayments are being made, and (3) Being acquired from Local Authority under a purchase or vested cottage scheme, etc. Owner occupied in Northern Ireland in 1991 relates to those households who are (1) Owner occupied - owns outright and (2) Owner occupied - buying. In 2001 it relates to those households who are (1) Owner occupied – owns outright, (2) Owner occupied – Owns with a mortgage of loan and (3) Owner occupied – shared ownership.

Households whose tenure is classed as Local Authority/Social Rented and Others are aggregates of different social housing groups. The Republic of Ireland classification is based on, (1) Rented from a Local Authority and (2) Occupied free of rent (caretaker, company official etc) in both 1991 and 2002. The Northern Ireland classification for 1991 is based on, (1) Rented from a Local Authority, (2) Rented from a housing association or charitable trust, and (3) Other and not stated tenures. The 2001 Northern Ireland classification is based on, (1) Rented from Northern Ireland Housing Executive, (2) Rented from housing association, housing co-operative or charitable trust, and (3) rented from other.

Conventional Housing generally relates to detached, semi-detached and terraced housing.

Flats and Apartments relates to flats/apartments, converted or shared houses and commercial buildings in both the Republic of Ireland and Northern Ireland

Mobile or Temporary Housing relates to caravans or other temporary structures in both Northern Ireland and the Republic of Ireland.

Maps 42 to 56 – Labour Force
The data used in the mapping of labour refers to the population between 15/16 and 64 years of age. The 2002 SAPS data for the Republic of Ireland required extrapolation to represent the 15/16-64 age band as it was only made available for a 15+ population.

The Labour Force represents those 15/16-64 who are employed, unemployed, working on a Government Scheme and those looking for a first time employment.

The Non Labour Force represents those 15/16-64 who are students, retired, looking after the home/home duties and those unable to work.

Maps 57-61 – Industry of Employment

The AHFF classification is created by aggregating those who are employed in the agriculture, hunting, forestry and fishing sector. The classification for the Republic of Ireland in both 1991 and 2002 relates to those aged 15+ who are at work in an economic activity classed as Agriculture, forestry and fishing. The classification in Northern Ireland for 1991 is based on those aged 16+ (employees and self-employed) in (1) Agriculture and (2) Forestry and fishing. The 2001 classification for Northern Ireland relates to those 16-74 employed in (1) Agriculture, hunting and forestry, and (2) Fishing.

The MI classification is created by aggregating those who are employed within the Manufacturing Industries sector. The classification for the Republic of Ireland in both 1991 and 2002 relates to those aged 15+ who are at work in an economic activity classed as (1) Mining, quarrying and turf production, (2) Manufacturing industries, and (3) Electricity, gas and water supply. The classification in Northern Ireland for 1991 is based on those aged 16+ (employees and self-employed) in (1) Energy and water, (2) Mining, (3) Manufacturing metals etc., and (4) Other manufacturing. The 2001 classification for Northern Ireland relates to those 16-74 employed in, (1) Mining and quarrying, (2) Manufacturing, and (3) Electricity, gas and water supply.

The Cons classification is created by aggregating those who are employed in the construction sector. The classification for the Republic of Ireland in 1991 relates to those aged 15+ who are at work in an economic activity classed as building and construction, the 2002 economic activity is classed construction.

The classification in Northern Ireland for both 1991 (16+) and 2001 (16-74) is based on those at work in an economic activity classed as construction.

The TSC classification is created by aggregating those who are employed in the transport, storage and communications sector. The classification for the Republic of Ireland in both 1991 and 2002 relates to those aged 15+ who are at work in an economic activity classed as transport, services and communications. The classification in Northern Ireland for 1991 is based on those aged 16+ (employees and self-employed) in transport and communications. The 2001 classification for Northern Ireland relates to those 16-74 employed in transport, storage and communications.

The Commerce classification for Republic of Ireland in 1991 is commerce, insurance, finance and business services. The classification for 2002 is (1) Wholesale and Retail Trade, (2) Banking and financial services, and (3) Real estate, renting and business activities. The Commerce classification for Northern Ireland in 1991 is banking and finance, insurance, business services and leasing. The 2001 classification is (1) Wholesale and retail trade, repairs, (2) Financial intermediaries and (3) Real estate, renting and business activities.